SELF-CONSCIOUSNESS
AND
SOCIAL ANXIETY

A Series of Books in Psychology

EDITORS:

Jonathan Freedman
Gardner Lindzey
Richard F. Thompson

SELF-CONSCIOUSNESS AND SOCIAL ANXIETY

Arnold H. Buss
The University of Texas at Austin

W. H. FREEMAN AND COMPANY
San Francisco

Sponsoring Editor: W. Hayward Rogers
Project Editor: Nancy Flight
Copyeditor: Judy Madlener
Designer: Sharon H. Smith
Production Coordinator: Fran Mitchell
Illustration Coordinator: Cheryl Nufer
Artist: John Kordes, J & R Services
Compositor: Typesetting Services of California
Printer and Binder: The Maple-Vail Book Manufacturing Group

Library of Congress Cataloging in Publication Data

Buss, Arnold Herbert, 1924–
    Self-consciousness and social anxiety.

    (A Series of books in psychology)
    Bibliography: p.
    Includes indexes.
    1. Self-consciousness. 2. Anxiety. 3. Shame.
4. Bashfulness. I. Title.
BF575.S4 B87   152.4   79-20890
ISBN 0-7167-1158-3
ISBN 0-7167-1159-1 pbk.

Printed in the United States of America

1 2 3 4 5 6 7 8 9

CONTENTS

PREFACE

When you pay attention to yourself, you can examine what others can easily see: your body, clothes, gestures, manners, and other social behavior. Or you can focus on covert aspects of yourself that no one else observes: thoughts, feelings, moods, internal bodily sensations, and so on.

This book is about both kinds of self-consciousness. It presents my theory of self-consciousness and the relevant research, as well as the implications of the theory for future research and for a better understanding of self, personality, and social behavior. Other approaches to self-consciousness are discussed in relation to mine, and an attempt is made to put what we know about social anxiety in a single framework.

The emphasis is on scientific vigor. For centuries there has been speculation about the self and about consciousness. This prescientific, or nonscientific, tradition persists today. There are descriptions of the phenomenology of private events in both drug-induced and normal states.

There are suggestions for self-help through mystical and transcendental experiences. And there are philosophical treatises on the self and consciousness. This book, however, uses the scientific method of collecting facts and of testing hypotheses.

But how can we objectively study phenomena that are intrinsically subjective? How can we use science to measure hidden thoughts, feelings, and internal sensations? The same way we study images, dreams, and memory: indirectly. People have speculated about the meaning of dreams at least since the beginning of recorded history, but we have learned more about dreams in the last 25 years than in the previous 2000 years. And imagery is yielding its secrets under the scrutiny of scientific observers. One message of this book is that we should use the same scientific methods in studying self-consciousness that have been used in studying other cognitive processes.

The book is not about all aspects of the self. The self-concept is not mentioned, though there exists a comprehensive work by Ruth Wylie.[1] Self-esteem is mentioned, but it is not central to the major focus of the book; Stanley Coopersmith has written an interesting book on the subject,[2] and elsewhere I have theorized about how self-esteem develops.[3] Concerning consciousness, a phenomenon that seems to be uniquely human, there is a fascinating, speculative theory of its origin in human history by Julian Jaynes;[4] but this book does not discuss consciousness *per se*.

Although *Self-Consciousness and Social Anxiety* is aimed at the college student and the lay reader, its easy style and presentation of concepts should not preclude the interest of professionals in the field of psychology and re-

---

1. Wylie (1974)
2. Coopersmith (1967)
3. Buss (1979, Chapter 23)
4. Jaynes (1976)

lated disciplines. Jargon is avoided, and the occasional use of technical terms is accompanied by a brief explanation of their meaning. With only a few exceptions, the details of the methods of research or the statistical details of research findings are not discussed; these are, in any event, best read in primary sources, the journals. There are places, however, that require close attention to the text—especially Chapters 4 and 5, which deal with research on self-consciousness. I have tried to make the discussions of theory more accessible to the nonprofessional by furnishing everyday examples of abstract concepts and by including tables and figures that summarize theoretical concepts. Sometimes it is easier to see relationships when they are presented schematically instead of in the usual verbal sequence. Contrasts and similarities are often easier to remember when they are placed side by side for immediate comparison.

The exposition is relatively free of minor details, exceptions, and parenthetical remarks. These are placed in notes at the end of each chapter. Also contained in the notes are all references to books, journals, and unpublished works. The complete reference citations are listed alphabetically at the back of the book. A brief appendix contains statistical details of a self-report questionnaire on self-consciousness.

It is a pleasure to acknowledge my gratitude to those who have helped me in writing this book. In particular, I wish to express my gratitude to my former graduate students who are now teaching and contributing to our knowledge and understanding. Michael Scheier contributed to my theory of self-consciousness, collaborated with me, and originated his own research. Allan Fenigstein conducted the first experiment on public self-consciousness and also helped to develop the personality measure. Charles Carver and Gerald Turner have added considerably to our knowledge in this area and continue to do so. Karen Mathews helped me formulate several concepts of bodily self-awareness.

I am also grateful to my graduate students who will soon receive their doctorates and start on their professional careers. Stephen Briggs read the entire manuscript and helped me to sharpen many of my ideas. Both he and Jonathan Cheek have collaborated with me on research in this area. Lynn Miller and Richard Murphy have worked with me on the personality measure of bodily self-consciousness, and Lynn Miller has discussed with me many of the ideas presented here. To these students and the ones who went before them, I dedicate this book.

Robert Wicklund started it all with his theory and research on self-awareness, and Timothy Brock made some excellent suggestions about an earlier version of self-consciousness theory. My son, David Buss, has collaborated with me on self-consciousness research and conducted his own experiment; my daughter, Laura Buss, performed a highly original experiment on embarrassment; and my wife, Edith Buss, worked with Ira Iscoe and me on a developmental study of embarrassment.

Buck Rogers, my editor, has been encouraging and helpful throughout the preparation of this manuscript, and Jonathan Freedman made many crucial suggestions after reading the entire first draft. Much of the typing of earler drafts was done by Jean Roberts. The entire final draft was corrected and typed by Kitty Gary. I am grateful to all these people.

October 1979   Arnold H. Buss

SELF-CONSCIOUSNESS
AND
SOCIAL ANXIETY

INTRODUCTION

Although this book is about self-consciousness, not the self, we must nevertheless begin by making some crucial distinctions about the self. The first distinction is between an early, sensory self and an advanced, cognitive self. The second distinction is between private and public aspects of the self.

SENSORY VERSUS COGNITIVE SELF

You know that you have a self. What happens to you not only is more important than what happens to others but is also experienced differently. But we cannot accept our personal beliefs or feelings in this matter, or we would also have to accept such notions as "the mind's eye" that can see things real eyes cannot, as well as other fanciful ideas. We need more scientific grounds for inferring self than personal notions or speculations.

1

One set of facts that suggests a concept of self consists of *sensory* events. When you tickle the sole of your right foot, you receive *double stimulation,* that is, sensations from the fingers touching the foot and sensations from the foot being touched. Part of you is active, part passive. Such a combination of active and passive stimulation arises only in self-directed perception. Being stimulated by someone or something external induces entirely different sensory events; thus, tickling by another person produces a stronger itch than self-tickling. Clearly, self-induced sensory events are different from sensory events induced by others, and this distinction provides one basis for inferring a self.

Each of us is aware of *body boundaries:* where body ends and not-body begins. Events inside the body can easily be distinguished from events occurring outside it, a discrimination learned very early in life. This distinciton between "me" and "not me" is another basis for inferring a self.

You can obviously recognize yourself in a mirror. Such *mirror-image recognition* appears to be limited to humans and a few higher primates. When a chimpanzee has a red dot placed on its head and looks in a mirror, the chimpanzee tries to touch the dot on its face; it knows that the mirror image is of itself.[1] Monkeys are not capable of this mirror-image recognition; nor is there evidence that dogs, cats, or any lower animals recognize themselves.[2]

Human infants do not possess mirror-image recognition until late in the second year of life. In the 20–24 months range, one-half to two-thirds of infants recognize their own image.[3] Recognizing oneself via the head dot or by naming oneself when asked who is in the mirror are the last stages of a developmental progression that starts much earlier in life with simpler attainments.[4] In brief, mirror-image recognition is a human or near-human achievement that provides an unequivocal basis for inferring a self.

Double stimulation, body boundary, and self-recognition allow us to infer a self shared by humans and higher animals. Though only a few higher primates are capable of self-recognition, surely dogs and cats are aware of double stimulation and of body boundary. If the latter two are included as a basis for inferring self, most animals have a self. If only mirror-image recognition is accepted as a basis for inferring self, only humans and a few primates have a self. In any event, the self we are discussing is a *sensory self*. Adult humans share this sensory self with higher animals and human infants. But there is also an advanced self not found in infants or animals: the *cognitive self*.

Three kinds of behavior suggest a cognitive self. The first is *self-esteem*. As we criticize others, so we may criticize ourselves. As we praise others, so we may praise ourselves. As we love others, so we may love ourselves. When we evaluate others, evaluator and recipient are different persons. In self-esteem, evaluator and recipient are the same person. Thus, self-esteem is analogous to double stimulation in that the agent and the object are the same person. But double stimulation is sensory, whereas self-esteem is cognitive.

The second basis for inferring a cognitive self concerns *covertness*. We are aware of thoughts, feelings, images, memories, and ambitions that no one else knows about. We are also aware that we laugh, cry, converse, and aggress—all of which can be observed by others. And we are keenly aware of the distinction between these two classes of events: between inner and outer, between private feelings and public behavior, like knowing that you had a terrible dinner and thanking the hostess for a delicious meal. Private thoughts and images are difficult to study scientifically, but it can be done; witness the research on dreams, daytime imagery, and information processing. In brief, the presence of an "inner life" of thoughts, feelings, images, and so on (some of which are self-directed) provides another basis for inferring a cognitive self.

Finally, we also become aware of self by discovering that others view the world differently from the way we do. Infants do not know that others have a different perspective, but older children do. Girls discover this fact about boys, as do boys about girls; blacks discover this fact about whites,

TABLE 1.1

Primitive, sensory self versus advanced, cognitive self

	Sensory	Cognitive
Occurs in:	Higher animals	Older children,
	Human infants	Adults
Bases:	Double stimulation	Self-esteem
	Body boundary	Shared versus unshared feelings
	Mirror image self-recognition	Knowing others have different perspectives

and whites about blacks. The awareness of others' perspectives—part of the well-documented waning of self-centeredness that occurs throughout childhood—sharpens the distinction between oneself and others. If each of us has a particular perspective, my own perspective is one of the things that makes me unique. This accentuation of uniqueness surely heightens our sense of self.

Sensory and cognitive selves are contrasted in Table 1.1. The sensory self develops during infancy, but the cognitive self must await the more advanced cognitions and social awareness that develop later in childhood. Each of the three aspects of the sensory self may be regarded as developing into an analogous aspect of the cognitive self. Touching oneself (double stimulation) may be thought of as a primitive analogue of evaluating oneself (self-esteem). A body boundary might be a primitive form of the distinction between covert feelings and thoughts versus those feelings and thoughts expressed to others. And the recognition of oneself as appearing different from others (mirror-recognition) might be an early precursor of the later awareness of the distinction between one's own and others' perspectives.

Differentiating between sensory and cognitive selves may help to resolve a controversy about whether animals have a self. Gallup[1,2] and others have insisted that primates must have a self because they can recognize themselves in a mirror. Other psychologists, perhaps because they are implicitly thinking of the cognitive aspects of self, insist that the self is uniquely human. The argument may hinge on a failure to distinguish between a more primitive and a more advanced self. There are sufficient bases for inferring that higher animals and human infants have a sensory self, but only older human children and adults appear to have a cognitive self.

The sensory-cognitive distinction is also important for self-consciousness. Animals and human infants may be said to be self-conscious in the sense of double stimulation, body boundary, or mirror-recognition, but such awareness of self is so primitive or so tied to sensory events that it has nothing to do with the self-awareness that occurs once a cognitive self develops. This book is concerned with only advanced, cognitive self-awareness. Whenever the terms *self-awareness* and *self-consciousness* are used, they will refer only to the advanced form.

PRIVATE VERSUS PUBLIC SELF

Our keenest senses are directed toward the environment that surrounds us, and we spend most of our waking hours perceiving this environment. But when we do attend to ourselves, what do we observe? Though this question can be answered in several different ways, my answer is to classify the various components of the self into just two aspects: private and public.

The *private* aspects are so named simply because they can be observed only by the experiencing person. Only you can know directly a toothache, the taste of an apple, a fleeting image of a childhood memory, a momentary urge to kill, or a flicker of fear. This is not to deny that others may infer what your inner experience is, but obviously only you can experience it directly.

In contrast to the covertness of the private aspects of the self, the *public* aspects are entirely overt. Other people can easily notice your hair, posture, facial expression, gestures, manners, or the way you speak—in brief, the way you come across to others. And you can observe these same things, though only from your own egocentric perspective. Public self-awareness, then, consists of your attending to the same aspects of your appearance and social behavior that others might observe. It is a focus on yourself as a social object.

Concerning this separation between private and public aspects of the self, is the distinction merely a matter of common sense? The question arises because most people immediately recognize these two aspects of the self once the distinciton is made. However, no reference to these different aspects of the self is to be found in the literature. In 1972, when research in this area began, we were ignorant of the distinction, which in retrospect seems so obvious. And there are researchers who currently either ignore the private-public distinction or find it of little use.

This issue is of primary importance because the distinction between private self-awareness and public self-awareness is the foundation for all the theorizing in this book. If there were a crack in this foundation, it would shake the entire theoretical structure and weaken it. This is not to say that the self is always or inevitably differentiated into private and public aspects, but my theory of self-consciousness does not deal with an undifferentiated self. The theory applies only if the private aspects of the self can be distinguished from the public aspects. More of this later.[5]

PLAN OF THE BOOK

In this book, the private-public distinction is used to elaborate several theories and to organize certain knowledge about self-consciousness. There are two major sections and a final chapter.

The first major section deals with self-consciousness. There are two short chapters on a theory of self-consciousness, one dealing with private aspects and one dealing with public aspects. These chapters are deceptively brief and may require re-reading. The next two chapters review relevant research, that is, only studies that bear directly on the theory. For ease of exposition, they are divided into research on personality dispositions (Chapter 4) and research on transient states of self-awareness (Chapter 5). After this exposition of theory and relevant research, other approaches to self-consciousness are reviewed (Chapter 6). When appropriate, I compare the approaches of others with my own. The section closes with a discussion of general issues of self-consciousness: what we know and need to know; the limits of my theory; and the implications of the private–public distinction for body, self-esteem, morality, and identity.

The second major section of the book deals with social anxiety. Four kinds of social anxiety are specified, and a chapter is devoted to each one: embarrassment, shame, audience anxiety (stage-fright), and shyness. All these negative affects require the presence of at least one other person; hence the name *social anxiety*. It is assumed here that these four unpleasant reactions have something else in common: acute public self-awareness. True, each of the four reactions has its own particular inducers, experienced feelings, and consequences. But underlying all four social anxieties is an intense awareness of oneself as a social object. This section closes with a chapter that compares and contrasts the four varieties of social anxiety and presents an integrative theory.

The last chapter deals with development. What are the childhood origins of public and private self-consciousness and of the social anxieties? I can furnish only tentative answers to these questions. One kind of answer arises from our knowledge of the cognitive development of children. Another comes from previously unpublished research on the first appearance of embarrassment in children. Aside from this research, however, this chapter is more speculative than the rest of the book. Still, the speculations are empirically testable and so might lead to research that would help us to answer the questions posed above.

RANGE OF IDEAS

This book presents ideas that range from broad speculations to specific, directly testable hypotheses. Basically four kinds of ideas are introduced.

First, there are ideas that serve to organize a body of knowledge or to integrate a set of ideas. The distinction between an early, sensory self and a later, cognitive self is an example of such a schema. This distinction may clarify our thinking about the self and prevent mistakes in attributing a "self" to animals that is really different from the self we infer in mature humans. In addition, the schema attempts to link early childhood components of the self with later childhood components that involve advanced cognitions. Notice, however, that the idea contains no directly testable hypotheses.

The second kind of idea involves hypotheses so broad that they are not easily tested. These occur in several chapters but especially the last, on development. Thus, we assume that the development of a sense of oneself as a social object must await the decline of egocentricity and the development of social perspective-taking. Assuming that the presence of embarrassment is a marker variable that signals the presence of public self-consciousness, this hypothesis not only could be but was tested.

Third, there are more specific hypotheses, unconnected to any theory, that can easily be tested. These are essentially guesses that, if proved correct, add to our knowledge and understanding. For example, other things being equal, low sociable people tend to be shy (see Chapter 11). After separate, unconfounded measures of sociability and shyness were devised, the hypothesis was tested. The hunch was right, and the research revealed something more specific, that is, the extent of the relationship between sociability and shyness.

Such unconnected hypotheses, however, have no bearing on larger theories. But the fourth kind of ideas do. These are hypotheses that derive from a theory. My theory of private self-awareness, for instance, states that this transient state intensifies any emotion being experienced at the time. One hypothesis that follows directly from this theoretical assumption is that an angry person acts angrier when in a state of private self-awareness. If this specific hypothesis were disconfirmed in an experiment, the theory behind it would be weakened. If the hypothesis were confirmed, the theory would be strengthened.[6]

In brief, there are four kinds of theoretical notions scattered throughout this book. Some have implications for the theory that spawned them; some do not derive from a theory. Some are directly testable; some are not. Some are highly specific; some are integrative and speculative. No matter what your taste is in the kind of theorizing you prefer—and there are marked individual differences in such taste—remember that each kind of idea serves a purpose: immediate new knowledge, theory-testing, better understanding, or a novel perspective.

NOTES

1. Gallup (1977a)
2. Gallup (1977b)
3. Amsterdam (1972); Schulman and Kaplowitz (1977)
4. Bertenthal and Fischer (1978)
5. I discuss this issue, which involves the limits of my theory, in Chapter 7.
6. The theory is discussed in Chapter 2, and the test of this specific hypothesis is discussed in Chapter 5.

THE THEORY:
PRIVATE ASPECTS

Self-consciousness theory starts by specifying which aspects of the self are private, that is, the feelings, motives, and self-reflections mentioned in the last chapter. The theory then states the inferred psychological processes that presumably occur when attention is directed to the private aspects of oneself. These processes cause certain behavioral outcomes, observable consequences that can be used to test the theory. Next, the theory lists the conditions that lead to private self-awareness. Finally, there are individual differences in the extent to which people are aware of the private aspects of themselves, that is, there is a trait called *private self-consciousness.*

This chapter follows the sequence just mentioned. It starts with the domain of private self-awareness and follows with inferred processes and their behavioral consequences. Next are the inducers of private self-awareness and, finally, the trait of private self-consciousness.

THE DOMAIN

What are the various components of the private self? For convenience, I have classified them along a continuum that starts with specific bodily stimuli and ends with self-reflection.

There are particular bodily events that only the experiencing person can sense. Your scalp may itch, or your leg muscles may be sore from too much jogging. After a fast, your stomach may feel uncomfortably empty; after a feast, comfortably full. In the silence of a quiet room, you can hear your heart beat, your digestive system gurgle and rumble, and the air wheezing through your breathing passages. Unless a physician probes, no one but you is aware of these stimuli, and even a physician cannot sense itching or sore muscles.

There are also diffuse internal states that we experience only as vague, ill-defined stimuli. The states range from the tranquility of restful well-being to elation, depression, anger, romantic love, or lust. Some of these feeling states cannot be discerned by anyone else. If you feel at peace with the world or if you have a deep but unconsummated love for someone, such feelings will go undetected unless you reveal them. Feeling states that involve physiological arousal, however, can be detected. It is hard to conceal the facial expressions of fear or anger. But whether the underlying feelings are concealed or partially revealed, the experience of these feelings is entirely private. In fact, we communicate such feelings poorly and with great difficulty, relying on poets to provide the metaphor and imagery that connote but never denote the private experience.

One step away from the perception of internal states are the phenomena called *psychological motives*.[1] Achievement motivation, for example, consists of a drive to excel, break through obstacles, overcome resistance, and beat the opposition. In extreme form, it means settling for nothing less than being Number One. But such competitive striving involves no particular bodily stimuli in the sense that hunger does.

For present purposes, we will include anything that is ego-involving as a psychological motive. Strongly held attitudes favoring or opposing abortion have motivational properties. If you strongly oppose abortion, for instance, you may give money for the cause, support a constitutional amendment banning abortion, and react with fury against the opposition. Similarly, if you are an avid football fan, you will buy season tickets and vicariously share the ups and downs of your favorite team. What affects them to some extent affects you. You mourn losses and celebrate victories.

Why are motives such as achievement and fanatical team loyalty included as part of the domain of the private self, especially when their behavioral manifestations are so public? The public aspects of emotions—anger, fear, or sexual arousal—can also be observed, but emotions are part of the private self because they are experienced privately. Similarly, only the experiencing person knows what it is like from the inside to be competitive or to be extremely loyal to an athletic team. Thus, the crucial issue in deciding whether a psychological phenomenon is part of the private self is not whether it has observable components or consequences—if there were no observable consequences, we could never test any hypotheses about the private self—but whether there is a private, experiential component.[2]

The final category of the private self is self-reflection. Your fantasy may spin romantic daydreams of fulfillment, achievement, love, and the admiration of others. You may recall the events of your childhood or examine your own personality traits and tendencies. Perhaps you evaluate yourself and estimate some level of self-esteem. Or you may wonder about who you are and speculate about your present and future identity.

The four broad categories of the domain of the private self are listed in Table 2.1. Notice that the list starts with

TABLE 2.1

Domain of the private self

Category	Neutral	Examples affectively charged
Focal stimuli	Mild itch	Sore muscles
Diffuse internal states	Tranquility	Elation, anger, sexual arousal
Motives	—	Achievement motive, ego-involvement with a team
Self-reflection	About one's traits or past history	Self-esteem, romantic daydreams

specific bodily stimuli, moves to diffuse internal states, then to nonphysiological states of motivation, and finally to the purely cognitive acts of reflecting about oneself. Notice also that there are both neutral and affectively charged examples. This distinction is deliberately over-stated not only to aid the exposition but also to foreshadow an important theoretical issue. True, neutral phenomena shade imperceptibly into affect-laden phenomena, but the distinction is important for two reasons. First, the more intense psychological events of the private self are, by defini-tion, more easily and more keenly perceived. And second, affect-laden events often assume motivational prop-erties—they tend to impel action. Notice that there are no neutral motives. All motives are affectively charged—again, by definition.

INFERRED PROCESSES AND THEIR CONSEQUENCES

Intensification

Attention to the private aspects of oneself is assumed[3] to intensify the affective charge of bodily stimuli, moods, motives, fantasies, and self-esteem. The impact of such attention is to deepen melancholy, to heighten elation, to make pain more painful and pleasure more pleasurable, to augment hostility, to strengthen infatuation, and to boost high self-esteem and diminish low self-esteem. As these examples illustrate, private self-focused attention polarizes the affective component of any private event—positive aspects become more positive and negative aspects become more negative. Such polarization occurs, of course, only when the affective charge is bidirectional. When it is unidirectional as in anger, fear, and sexual arousal, private self-awareness only *elevates* the affective charge.

Such intensification has a clear impact on observable behavior when the internal event has a close link with behavior. Thus, self-directed attention should intensify anger. Because of the link between anger and aggression, intensification of anger should make subsequent aggression more likely, more severe, or both. Similarly, in a competitive situation, private self-awareness should enhance achievement motivation and therefore lead to better performance.

It bears repeating that only internal events that are affectively charged are intensified by private self-awareness. Neutral events are not amplified. Tranquility does not deepen, and neutral memory images of childhood are not intensified. If there is no amplification of neutral private events, how are they affected by private self-awareness?

Clarification

Private self-focus is assumed to make all private events, both affectively charged and neutral, clearer and more distinct. Such attention provides more precise knowledge about the gap in your gums where a tooth has been removed, your current tranquility, your memories of childhood, and your own personality traits. Private self-awareness lends clarity to your perception/cognition of your dry throat, anger, attitude toward abortion, present mood, and current level of self-esteem. In brief, private self-awareness serves to bring into sharper focus the neutral and affectively charged events that make up the domain of the private self.

Testing this hypothesized clarification effect is straightforward when the private events are neutral. Suppose, for instance, that subjects are given an inert drug (placebo) and told that it increases heart rate. Subjects who are privately self-aware should be more able to perceive their true heart rate and therefore be less affected by the placebo than would non-self-aware subjects. Or suppose that subjects are asked to report on their own personality traits. Privately self-aware subjects should provide a more veridical report than should non-self-aware subjects.

Testing the assumed clarification effect of private self-awareness is trickier when affect or motivation is involved. If we induce elation or depression, for instance, the mood should intensify, but how would we determine the subject's true mood? Where affects or motives are involved, we need some independent means of checking on the veridicality of the subject's report of internal events.

One way of testing the clarification effect is by means of an attitude change experiment. Begin by sampling subjects' attitudes toward abortion, selecting those who are ego-involved. Then reveal that their attitudes differ from those of their peers. This is a well-known method of inducing attitude change. Self-aware subjects should be more aware of their attitudes and therefore should change less than non-self-aware subjects.

Rationale

Self-consciousness theory assumes that two processes occur in private self-awareness: better knowledge of the domain and intensification of affect. Neither assumption requires any particular justification, merely testable deductions. Nevertheless, each assumption has a logical basis as an extrapolation from well-known psychological processes.

Attention is crucial for memorization. People who attend

to the stimuli around them remember these stimuli better than those who do not. On the north side of the base of the University of Texas Tower there is a Greek or Hebrew letter over each window of several floors. Though these letters are in plain sight, only a small percentage of the students who pass them every school day are aware of them. Facing the main square of the campus is a building that has the signs of the zodiac in blue and white over each of its huge windows, but, again, only a few students have ever noticed these mythological figures. When we are introduced to strangers, most of us forget the new names. The most important cause of this memory failure is inattention to the name as it is spoken. Those who attend carefully to introductions remember names better. Texas students who are more aware of their surroundings can report accurately the symbols inscribed on campus buildings. By extrapolation, those who are more aware of their inner events should know them better. If you are in a transient state of self-awareness, you should know more accurately and precisely your bodily reactions, emotions, motives, and fantasies. Such better self-knowledge is analogous to the better knowledge of external events that is the outcome of close attention to the everyday stimuli around us.

The logical basis of the intensification effect of private self-awareness involves even less extrapolation. As a simple example, if you look directly at a very bright light, its impact is more aversive than if you glance at it sidelong. A more important example concerns test anxiety. It is commonplace for students to gather before a crucial test to swap information and voice their concern. The more they talk about the difficulty of the exam, the more their fears grow. This incubation of anxiety occurs because the students are focusing on their fear and its cause. Such intensification, I suggest, is precisely what occurs in private self-awareness.

The last few paragraphs suggest that a focus on any stimulus should intensify its affective charge. This assumption is not mine alone. Abraham Tesser and colleagues have made a similar assumption from a different perspective. "When an individual is cut off from external information concerning some attitude object, his attitudes (i.e., affect/evaluation) toward that object will tend toward greater polarization given that he thinks about the attitude object."[4] This hypothesis has been verified in several different laboratory studies.[5] To cite just one: "Compared with subjects who were distracted from thinking about their partner, subjects who thought about a likable partner had a more positive attitude toward him and subjects who thought about a dislikable partner had a more negative attitude toward him."[6] These experiments involved neither private self-awareness nor self-consciousness, and therefore the findings cannot be viewed as confirming my theory. But the results closely parallel my intensification assumption and therefore help to provide a logical basis for it.

INDUCERS

Private self-awareness can be induced in several different ways, but the list is short. Self-attention can be self-produced. You may daydream about yourself when alone or when trapped in a group listening to a dull lecture. Or you might introspect and, for no particular reason, examine your moods, motives, identity, or even the fact of your existence.

Writing a diary can also turn attention toward the unshared aspects of oneself, depending on the topics on which one writes. If today's contents include a recital of the events of the day—the classes attended, the meals eaten, the people met, and the duties accomplished—then obviously attention is not directed toward one's private self. But it is a rare diarist who does not include private thoughts, fantasies, self-reflections, and speculations about his or her own past or future. So at least some of the time the diarist must be in a state of private self-awareness.

If diary-writing can induce private self-awareness, can this state also be produced by an interview or a self-report questionnaire? In my opinion, no. In an interview, you are communicating with another person and therefore attend both to your own speech and to the impact any self-revelations might have. Thus, most of your attention is directed outward, away from yourself. When you fill out a self-report questionnaire, you need to read the questions carefully and perhaps be careful of how you answer because others will read your replies. My guess, then, is that in both interviews and questionnaires, the distractions away from the self are sufficient to prevent any significant private self-awareness.[7]

Instructed meditation can also bring on private self-awareness. Certain kinds of meditation require that the meditator progress through certain mental states that seem identical to private self-awareness. Consider, for example, the state called mindfulness. "In mindfulness of mental states, the meditator focuses on each state as it comes to awareness. Whatever mood, mode of thought, or psychological state presents itself, he simply registers it as such."[8] But in this particular kind of meditation, mindfulness is merely the second stage that culminates in the penultimate stage of *nirvana* (consciousness stops having an object) and the ultimate stage of *nirodh* (total cessation of consciousness). Most varieties of meditation, in fact, have as their goal the abolition of awareness, especially self-awareness, which is regarded as egocentric and immature. Only certain varieties of meditation lead to private self-awareness, and of these, only certain stages in the meditational sequence.

The last inducer of private self-awareness is a mirror: not a large clothing mirror, but a small mirror of the size found on bathroom cabinets and used mainly for shaving or make-up. At first glance, this suggestion seems all wrong. Mirrors obviously reveal how we appear to others and therefore should induce public self-awareness. But consider the image of your head and shoulders that appears in such a mirror. You have seen this frontal view thousands of times. Barring some radical change in your face or hair, the mirror reveals nothing but your familiar visage. Any public self-awareness that once might have been induced by the mirror has long since habituated. A shaving/make-up mirror tells us virtually nothing about how others see us but only what we already know.

Yet, that image of the mirror is of your own face. As such, it directs your attention to yourself. In the absence of public self-awareness, long since waned, the only remaining self-focus is private self-awareness. When you gaze into a mirror, you should become aware of the private, unshared aspects of yourself, that is, the familiar litany of bodily processes, moods, emotions, motives, fantasies, and self-evaluations. You will then know yourself better, and any current affect will be intensified.

The logic of the argument, in brief, is that in older children and adults, the self-awareness elicited by a small mirror is private. If this hypothesis is correct, confronting a person with a small mirror should turn on the inferred processes of private self-awareness. It should increase the veridicality of self-perception and polarize affects.

THE TRAIT OF PRIVATE SELF-CONSCIOUSNESS

When private self-awareness is brought on by any of the inducers just discussed, the self-focus remains for a brief period and then wanes. There are so many stimuli around us to capture our attention that it cannot remain self-directed for very long. Thus, private self-awareness is a transient state.

In addition to this transient state, there is also the habit, tendency, or disposition to focus attention on the private aspects of the self. Some people, though they are probably rare, never self-reflect, fantasy about themselves, or examine their own feelings or motives. At the other extreme are people who meditate and reflect about their "inner self" regularly and often. Between these extremes are most of us, who occasionally turn inward toward the private aspects of the self.

At this point we must examine terminology. The distinction between the transient state and the disposition will be easier to bear in mind if separate terms are used for each. The transient state will be called *private self-awareness;* the disposition (trait) will be called *private self-consciousness.* This usage will also hold for the public aspects of the self: *public self-awareness* for the transient state and *public self-consciousness* for the disposition.[9]

Consider first people who have a strong disposition to attend to the inner, unshared aspects of themselves. Such private self-conscious people regularly inspect their bodily processes and moods, reflect about their motives and goals, and fantasy a lot about themselves. As a result of repeated self-reflection, they know themselves very well. If asked for a self-description, they should furnish a complete and, other things equal, a true account of their own personalities.[10]

The chronic self-attention of private self-conscious people also exaggerates the intensity of any pain, mood, emotion, or motive. They are more fearful when scared, happier when they succeed, more depressed when they fail, more enraged when they are angered, and more competitive when their achievement motive is engaged.

Consider now people who have only a weak disposition to attend to the inner, unshared aspects of themselves. They seldom examine themselves, reflect about motives, or fantasy about themselves. As a result, they know little about their own personalities, and their self-reports of personality, based largely on ignorance, are unlikely to be true. There is no exaggeration of affects or motives because of inattention to these inner aspects of the self.

Trait Versus Manipulation

Private self-awareness can be induced by a manipulation (small mirror, instruction to self-reflect, and so on), or such self-attention may occur naturally in private self-conscious people. Suppose we induced private self-awareness in various subjects. Would subjects high in private self-consciousness (Highs) be affected differently from those low in private self-consciousness (Lows)?

Given the theoretical perspective of this book, the possibility that a manipulation would increase private self-awareness in Lows but decrease it in Highs must be ruled out. There remain only three possibilities: main effects only, special susceptibility, and a ceiling effect.

If there were only main effects, Highs would start out being more privately self-aware than Lows. The manipulation would affect them equally, and they would both end up more aware but hold their relative positions (Highs more aware than Lows).

If Highs had a special susceptibility, the manipulation would have a much greater impact on them than on the Lows. The manipulation would widen the initial difference between Highs and Lows in private self-awareness.

A ceiling effect would mean that Highs are already so privately self-aware that an inducer could not drive them higher. The Lows of course can be affected by a manipulation. Thus a manipulation might cancel the initial difference in private self-awareness between Highs and Lows.

Research will most likely reveal that main effects occur most of the time.[11] It is hard to believe that Highs are so self-reflective that an inducer could not elevate their private self-awarensss (ceiling effect). And there comes to mind no reason why Highs should be especially susceptible to any manipulation when they can so easily turn their attention inward without any external influence. So we shall retain the simplest hypothesis of how the trait and any manipulation interact, that is to say, "main effects."

RECAPITULATION

The theory is now described in some detail, suggesting the domain of private self-awareness, inferred processes and their consequences, inducers, and the disposition of private self-consciousness. If this diversity has bred confusion, a summary of the theory, which is presented in Figure 2.1., is intended to clarify matters.

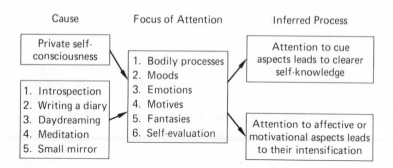

FIGURE 2.1

A Summary of Theory: Private Aspects

Private self-awareness, the transient state, may occur simply because of a strong, enduring tendency to focus on the unshared aspects of oneself. No specific condition or manipulation is necessary, only the trait of private self-consciousness. But there are several conditions or manipulations that can lead to private self-awareness. Introspection, diary-writing, daydreaming, meditation, and looking into a bathroom-sized mirror all produce private self-awareness.

Where does the spotlight of such self-attention fall? On any particular part of the unshared self that is salient at the time—bodily processes, moods, emotions, motives, fantasies, or self-evaluation. Private self-awareness furnishes a clearer picture of your present psychological status, and so you can offer a more detailed, truer picture of what you are at the moment. If you are high in the trait of private self-consciousness, you will have clearer, true knowledge of your usual, typical behavior and personality. Finally, private self-awareness intensifies or polarizes any affective or motivational component of behavior.

How can the theory be tested? The trait part of the theory can be tested by dividing people into those who are high and those who are low in private self-consciousness. The transient state part of the theory can be tested by using one of the manipulations (instructions to introspect or a small mirror) and then comparing its effects with those of a control condition. In either case, it is necessary to make one particular part of the private domain salient during the experiment. Suppose one wishes to test the effect of a mirror. One would induce a mood of mild elation or depression and test whether the presence of the mirror intensifies mood. Or one might anger subjects and test whether the mirror intensifies the anger or any associated aggression. In brief, to test the theory, researchers should specify in advance which part of the private domain is salient during the experiment.

NOTES

1. Motives such as hunger and thirst obviously have associated body stimuli (hunger pangs, dry throat). I have used the term *psychological motives* to mean only motives that involve no particular bodily reactions. Whether this distinction is accepted is not crucial for self-consciousness theory, for the distinction is merely a convenience used in describing the domain of the private self.

2. Concerning the motives, there is also a factual basis for including them as part of the private self. As we shall see in Chapter 4, awareness of one's own motives is an integral part of the trait of private self-consciousness, as measured by a self-report questionnaire.

3. Self-consciousness theory deals with assumptions, hypotheses, and predictions. It would become tiresome to repeat the words *assumed, hypothesized, presumably,* and so on. In the interest of a more readable style, therefore, in this and the next chapter, both on theory, I shall use the simple declarative, allowing the reader to fill in the above words where necessary.

4. Tesser and Conlee (1975), p. 262.

5. Sadler and Tesser (1975); Tesser and Dannheiser (1978); Clary, Tesser, and Downing (1978).

6. Tesser and Conlee (1975), p. 263. Tesser has his own explanation of these findings.

7. Self-report questionnaires are so widely used that this issue is of more than theoretical importance. Actually, there are some data that support my guess, as we shall see in Chapter 4.

8. Coleman (1977), p. 23. This book describes many different kinds of meditation, virtually all imported from the Orient; only a few are relevant to private self-awareness.

9. A source of confusion still remains in the title of this book and the name of the theory: self-consciousness. As a title of the book and the theory, *self-consciousness* is used in a non-technical sense to include both the transient state and the trait. Otherwise, self-*awareness* always refers to the temporary state, and self-*consciousness* always refers to the trait.

10. The other things that might not be equal are honesty and defensiveness. It is one thing to know oneself but another thing to reveal such information under the threat of punishment or ridicule. Thus, private self-conscious people should provide a veridical account of themselves unless there are good reasons not to do so.

11. The interaction of the trait with inducers of private self-awareness is of considerable interest, but it is not part of the basic theory of self-consciousness. There is nothing in the theory that would suggest one of the three possibilities over the other two, and perhaps all are true.

THE THEORY: PUBLIC ASPECTS

3

Ask people what they mean by *self-conscious,* and they refer to a feeling of being observed in the sense of being on stage. This usage is one of the dictionary meanings of the term: "Conscious of oneself, or prone to regard oneself as an object of observation by others; embarrassed or stagy because of failure to forget one's own self in society."[1]

This chapter follows a sequence slightly different from that of the last. Here the sequence will be (1) the domain of the public aspects of oneself; (2) inducers, inferred processes and their consequences; (3) dispositions; and (4) recapitulation. The chapter ends with a comparison between the private and public aspects of the self and a summary of the kinds of evidence needed to test the entire theory.

THE DOMAIN

The public aspects of oneself, by definition, include all the attributes that can be observed. The most obvious component is *appearance*. Like most societies, ours has minimal standards that govern how we present ourselves in public. We teach children to look at least presentable and perhaps even attractive to others. Virtually all adolescents know how important it is to have their hair arranged in the current style, their face unblemished, and their body trim. Those who consider themselves too tall or too short, too fat or too thin are usually acutely self-conscious on social occasions. Even worse, conditions like acne, scars, crossed eyes, a limp, or even early baldness can cause an uncomfortable feeling of being stared at and found wanting. Appearance also includes clothes (neat, in current fashion) and modesty (certain body parts appropriately covered).

The other major component of the public domain is *style*. We are taught to be aware that others are watching our posture ("Don't slouch; stand up straight") and coordination of movement ("Why are you so clumsy?"). We must speak up so that others can hear ("Don't mumble") but not so loud that nonlisteners are disturbed. We are supposed to use gestures when speaking but not excessively broad, stilted, or mechanical movements. It is easy to induce public self-awareness by mentioning that a person is "talking with his hands" and to suggest that he try to communicate with his hands in his pockets.

Style also involves the manner in which we deal with others in social situations. The issue may concern *manners* literally, for we are all taught "company manners." Consider how self-aware you are of your table manners when guests visit—how you eat soup, your politeness in asking for food, and your care not to appear gluttonous. Contrast these more formal manners with your more easy going ones when eating alone or with close family.

Style also involves the *expressive* component in role playing. We are generally more relaxed and informal with old friends, and more stiff and formal with strangers and new acquaintances. When we feel conspicuous (because of scrutiny) or unsure (because of novelty), we tend to become more inhibited and put on a social mask. In other words, when we become acutely aware of ourselves as social objects, we tread cautiously, inhibiting individuality and playing our social roles close to the norms expected of us.

Part of public self-awareness is assuming the role of the other and regarding oneself as another might. Of course, the perspective is different, and no one can fully escape the subjectivity of self-observation. But the publicly self-focused person is attending to the same things about himself or herself that any observer might scrutinize: the externals of appearance and behavior that are open to inspection. This is the meaning of the phrase "aware of oneself as a social object," that is to say, to focus on the overt aspects of oneself that can be perceived by others.

There is an implied social reference to public self-focus, this reference being the perceptions and reactions of others. When people are publicly self-focused, they are concerned about how their appearance and behavior are interpreted by onlookers. It follows that, other things equal, publicly self-focused people tend to be sensitive to the reactions of others in social situations. But self-aware people attend mainly to themselves, not to others. When people unexpectedly find themselves the center of attention—for example, when they appear late at a social event and everyone stops talking and gazes at them—they might be painfully aware of themselves as social objects. Their attention is self-directed, not other-directed.

The distinction being made is between a *direct* focus on one's public self and an *implied* attention to others. With exceptions to be noted, no one is publicly self-focused unless there are others to observe them. When being observed, however, the publicly self-focused people attend to their own appearance and behavior, not to those of the observers. They may implicitly take the perspective of others and see themselves through others' eyes, but when doing so, they are still attending primarily to their own appearance and behavior.

In brief, public self-focus consists of attending to one's own appearance and overt behavior. These are precisely the same things that others can attend to, and therefore a person may sometimes attempt to take the perspective of another. But taking another's perspective is not a necessary condition for public self-awareness.[2] The knowledge that one is exposed or being observed is enough to induce self-awareness.

INDUCERS

The most frequent inducers of public self-awareness are the actions of others. The stare of another person is often enough to make you concerned about yourself as a social object. Are your clothes on correctly? Do they have gaps, tears, or smudges? Is something missing? Do two items clash? Or perhaps your voice is too loud or your gestures too flamboyant.

Public self-awareness

Stares are especially effective when they come from strangers or mere acquaintances. Public self-awareness rarely occurs when you are with close friends, family, or lovers.

The most potent cause of public self-attention is a group of people. We are most conspicuous, most open to close scrutiny, when standing in front of an audience, either lecturing or performing on stage. People unaccustomed to speaking in public may become so intensely self-aware that the feeling spills over into acute social anxiety. No one should be surprised that fear of public speaking is the most frequent fear reported by adults.

Close public scrutiny, being stared at by another person or closely observed by an audience, is but the high end of a dimension of social attention. At the other end is an absence of attention—being ignored when at least some attention is normally expected. If I knew you and walked past without saying a word, you would probably feel rejected. If several of us at a party or similar social occasion simply shunned you, you would be as much aware of your-

self as a social object as if you were the focus of all eyes.
And you would probably feel humiliated and embarrassed,
that is, socially anxious.

To be sure, not all social attention is unpleasant. Between being totally ignored and being closely observed is a
large middle ground of moderate, pleasant social attention.
In the give and take of everyday social contacts, each of
us is looked at and listened to, but the scrutiny of others
is ordinarily neither intense nor prolonged. And as highly
social animals, we are pleased by moderate attention
from others. At either extreme, being ignored or being
the center of attention, we usually develop acute public
self-awareness and a rather unpleasant intensity of social
anxiety.

These assumptions are diagrammed in Figure 3.1. Virtually everyone is upset by being shunned and, as a consequence, becomes publicly self-aware. Shy people are
slightly pleased by moderate attention but may become

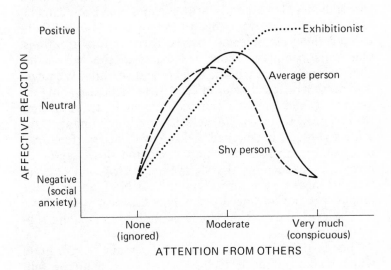

FIGURE 3.1
The Dimension of Social Attention (Hypothetical)

upset and self-aware at normal levels of attention from others.[3] Average people—by this I mean most of us—are pleased to have others look at us and respond to us. When such attention increases until we are conspicuous, however, we start becoming sharply aware of ourselves as social objects. Close scrutiny by others can easily cause social anxiety, that is, sufficient public self-awareness to be uncomfortable and distressing to us.

A small minority of people are not upset by close inspection. Exhibitionists thrive on it. They welcome almost any kind of attention. If many people are watching and are intent in their vigilance, so much the better. Moderate attention may not be enough for them, and they are especially sensitive to being ignored. But exhibitionists are the exception, not the rule. Being observed by strangers or mere acquaintances makes most of us at least a little uncomfortable.

Public self-awareness can also be induced by recording devices which are, in effect, mechanical replacements for a live audience, for example, still camera, television camera, and tape recorder. Announce to friends that you are about to take their picture and observe their various reactions. One will complain about her hair, another about his clothes, and a third will make faces and act silly. Whatever the idiosyncratic behavior of each, those who are being examined by the lens of a camera are acutely aware of how they appear to others. A television camera induces the same self-focus, heightened perhaps by a stronger feeling of being on stage.[4] And the microphone and slowly spinning reels of a tape recorder sharply remind most people of eventual listeners to the tape recording. In brief, some of the products of our advanced technology can neatly substitute for the eyes and ears of people as inducers of public self-awareness.

The instruments just mentioned produce recordings, which make up the last class of inducers of public self-awareness, feedback from devices. A photo reveals how you appear to others, a videotape or movie shows not only your appearance but also your gait, gestures, and facial expressions over time. Voice recordings reveal something we could not discover without technology, the sound of one's own voice as it is heard by others. When you listen to your own voice naturally, your perception is altered by the conduction of vibrations from the throat through the bones of the head. This bone conduction makes your voice sound different to you than it does to everyone else. So when you hear your voice on a tape recording, you hear what others hear, that is, you receive feedback about one aspect of your social self, your voice.

Finally, a three-piece, full-length mirror offers profile and partial back views of your face and body that ordinarily only others can see. Again, you are confronted with an aspect of your social self about which you can possess only vague information. As in the other instances of feedback, your reaction will usually be greater public self-awareness.

INFERRED PROCESSES AND THEIR CONSEQUENCES

The process assumed to occur in public self-awareness depends on the conditions that produce it. As we just saw, there are two sets of inducing conditions: (1) being observed by people or being recorded by machines and (2) receiving perceptual feed-back from either recordings or a three-sided mirror.

Being observed

Most people become at least a little uncomfortable when they are watched by others. The observers may be a small group or a more formal audience. Or the inspection may be done by a mechanical device such as a camera or tape recorder, which records the observations for later scrutiny. When others stare or when a camera is pointed at them, most people become acutely aware of themselves as social objects. Men straighten their ties, women their dresses;

they stand up straighter and are more careful of where they place their hands. A camera may elicit uncertainty about whether to smile or look serious. A tape recorder usually causes concern about the pitch and timbre of one's voice, as well as the syntax and content of speech. An audience may bring on feelings of being exposed and vulnerable. The vigilance of others tends to make us feel clumsy, unworthy, incompetent, and perhaps even psychologically naked ("They can see right through me"). Why? Could it be that much of the social training by parents and other socialization agents consists mainly of corrections and negative comments? As children, we were told not to slouch or mumble, to wash our hands, watch our manners, and not swear, and to be more polite, more concerned for others' feelings, and in general realize that we were presenting ourselves in a bad light to others. It is a rare parent or schoolteacher who accentuates the positive in shaping the social behavior of children. Parents and teachers tend to emphasize incorrect social behavior and the effect of children's bad behavior on others. This predominantly negative conditioning establishes a firm bond between scrutiny by others and having done something that is socially wrong. Put another way, most of us implicitly believe that if we are being watched closely, there must be something wrong with our appearance or style of behavior. In brief, for most people, being observed leads to discomfort that varies from mild squirming to intense social anxiety.

Perceptual feedback

Each of us suffers from an egocentricity of perspective—we cannot see ourselves as others do. The image we see in a mirror is only a small sample of what others see, but missing are our two profiles and backsides. Our voices do not sound the same to others because they lack the bone conduction that changes the quality of what we hear. The major way to overcome this egocentricity of self-perception is by means of visual and auditory devices that present us as we are to other people. A full-length, three-piece mirror can show us not only the front but both profiles and a little of the back. A photo can display our bodies from any perspective. Even better is a sound movie or videotape, which can show us how we look, move, and sound from the perspective of other people.

Feedback from such devices induces public self-awareness. We become aware of our appearance, voice, or movements from the perspective of others. We literally become aware of our social selves. The visual or auditory perception that confronts us is almost always different from the image of ourselves. Reactions such as "Do I look like that?" and "Is my voice so high?" are common. Most of us do not realize how fat or thin we are. We did not know that we slouched; that our hair style looked peculiar; that we looked so bald, so gray, so lined; that we were duckfooted or pigeon-toed, bowlegged or knockkneed. We are surprised to discover that our voice is too loud or soft, raspy, and nasal; that our accent is so pronounced and we slur certain words. And so on, through a list of self-attributes that we either did not know about or merely ignored.

Suddenly a mirror, tape recording, or photograph presents a true picture of the way others perceive our appearance and style. The true picture that confronts us is almost always worse than we had imagined. Most of us are not grandiose about our looks or style, but our enduring image of these attributes is more positive than that provided by feedback devices. This negative discrepancy between immediate perception and enduring image should cause a temporary drop in self-esteem. Though at first we are surprised and displeased at how we really look or sound, we slowly habituate and reclaim our lost self-esteem.

The effect of hearing a tape recording of one's own voice has been documented.[5] Laboratory subjects reported that they listened especially to the nasality, rasp, tone, and rhythm of their voices. A minority found their voices pleasant, but most found their voices surprisingly unpleasant. They were initially disturbed and evaluated themselves negatively, but they eventually accepted the reality of their voices and felt less upset.

In brief, the two classes of inducers lead to different processes and outcomes. Being observed leads to at least mild discomfort and a concern about one's own appearance and style. The discomfort is relatively mild when the "observer" is a machine, such as a camera or tape recorder. But when the observers are other people, the discomfort is usually more intense, shading into acute social anxiety, and accompanied by an inhibition of social behavior. Nonsocial feedback from movies, tape recordings, and mirrors leads to a more specific public self-awareness, a focus on one or a few aspects of the observable self. The immediate percept is usually worse than the more optimistic and vague memory image. This negative discrepancy leads to temporary uneasiness and self-doubt about one's own worth.

PUBLIC SELF-CONSCIOUSNESS

A reminder about usage of terms may be in order. The transient state is called public *self-awareness;* the trait or disposition to be publicly self-aware is called public *self-consciousness.*

Public self-conscious people tend to focus on themselves as social objects. Is your hair neat? Are your clothes in disarray? Are your manners correct? Is your behavior appropriate? In asking such implicit questions, public self-conscious people are vaguely aware that their own style or appearance is not equal to social expectations or their own mental image of themselves. But there are exceptions— exhibitionists who revel in the attention they receive for their appearance, grace, coordination, or style. Vigilant about these external aspects of self, they approve of what their inspection reveals, and their self-approval often is matched by approval and applause from others. But such people constitute only a small minority of those extremely high in public self-consciousness. Most of those high in public self-consciousness are concerned about themselves as social objects. It is not so much a low opinion of their own style and appearance as it is uncertainty. They need assurance from others, feedback about the impression they are making. And their self-observations are repeatedly checked against a standard of social expectations or a stereotyped self-image. For many of those high in public self-consciousness, the concern about the external self spills over into anxiety, in this instance, social anxiety.

Social anxiety must be added as a third disposition, one linked to public self-consciousness. Many people who are high in public self-consciousness react to what they observe about their social selves with fear and acute discomfort. The discomfort reveals itself directly in embarrassment (blushing) or stage fright (agitation and shaking in front of the audience), or indirectly in shyness (avoidance of social responses where they are normal and appropriate). It follows that there is at least a moderate relationship between social anxiety and public self-consciousness. Those who are socially anxious should be high in public self-consciousness. However, not everyone who is high in public self-consciousness is necessarily socially anxious. Some may be exhibitionists; others may merely be conscious of themselves as social objects without reacting negatively to this information.

Trait versus inducers

The trait of public self-consciousness and the inducers of public self-awareness are closely linked. Suppose two people, one high and one low in public self-consciousness, meet for the first time. There are the usual greetings. Each person quietly observes the other, but each receives only a small amount of social attention. Presumably, the person high in public self-consciousness becomes publicly self-aware, but the person low in public self-consciousness does not. The general rule is: Highs react more strongly to inducers of public self-awareness than to Lows.

This rule is another way of defining public self-consciousness. With an exception to be noted, public self-awareness

does not occur unless it is turned on by a manipulation
(being observed or nonsocial feedback). In the absence of
an inducer, neither Highs or Lows are aware of themselves as social objects. It is in their reaction to inducers
that Highs and Lows differ. Highs tend to react strongly,
becoming very upset or losing self-esteem. Lows tend to
react weakly. In the face of potent inducers, they do not
become very upset or lose much self-esteem.

The exception to these statements involves fantasy.
Knowing that you are to meet a famous person or speak to
a high-status audience, you might imagine the situation. If
your imagery were sufficiently vivid, it might make you
temporarily and weakly aware of yourself as a social object.
Presumably, such vicarious public self-consciousness would
occur only among Highs, never among Lows. Notice that
there are no inducers, but public self-awareness does occur. This is the only exception. Otherwise, public self-
awareness occurs only when people are observed or exposed to nonsocial feedback.

RECAPITULATION

The public part of self-consciousness theory is summarized
in Figure 3.2. Notice that the diagram includes only the
most likely inferred processes. Public self-awareness need
not lead to social anxiety or diminished self-esteem.
Awareness of oneself as a social object furnishes information about one's public self, information that can be used to
make a good impression and to charm others. Good hostes-
ses and successful politicians are keenly aware of themselves as social objects yet suffer neither low self-esteem
nor social anxiety. But such people are the exception, not
the rule. For most of us, acute public self-awareness tends
to be an uncomfortable state, often accompanied by social
anxiety, lowered self-esteem, or attempts to escape the
situation.

The first major cause of public self-awareness, virtually
by definition, is being observed by other people or by

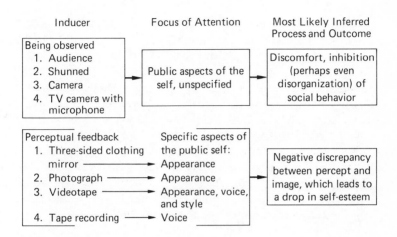

FIGURE 3.2
Summary of the Theory: Public Aspects

technological devices. At the other end of the dimension of social attention, being shunned also causes an acute public self-focus, though such rejection is rare. Being observed usually causes attention to your appearance and style of behaving. Such attention usually leads to at least mild social anxiety and inhibition of social responsivity and liveliness. If you are playing a role, public self-awareness should cause you to conform more to the usual role requirements. If standards of performance or morality are relevant, you should struggle harder to meet such standards not only because you fear punishment, but also because you do not want to be seen as deficient in ability or morality.

The other major cause of public self-awareness is nonsocial feedback from mirrors, photos, and recordings that reveal how you look or sound to others. In contrast to being observed, such perceptual feedback is specific and detailed. You are confronted with a precise perception, usually less attractive and more detailed than the vague image you have been carrying with you. This negative discrepancy leads to a drop in self-esteem.

You may have noticed that public self-consciousness is

missing from Figure 3.2. This is an intended omission. Public self-awareness presumably does not occur unless there are conditions (being observed or perceptual feedback) that induce it.[6] Then what is the role of public self-consciousness? Those high in public self-consciousness (Highs) are assumed to be more responsive to manipulations that induce a public self-focus. Lows are less responsive to such manipulations and so reach lower levels of public self-awareness. In the absence of a manipulation, both Highs and Lows are unaware of themselves as social objects. When they are observed or receive feedback, however, Lows become somewhat aware and Highs become extremly aware of themselves as social objects.

TESTING THE THEORY

Self-consciousness theory has been described in this chapter and the previous one. Several issues remain, however, which need to be discussed before research relevant to the theory is described.

Private versus public

Can private and public self-awareness occur simultaneously? Over any brief time span, both can be present, and attention would presumably fluctuate from one to the other. But one will predominate over the other, depending on the intensity of the inducers and the strength of the two traits. For the purpose of testing the theory, however, the major focus will be treated as if it were the only focus. Thus, when a person is privately self-aware, public self-awareness presumably plays so minor a role that it can be ignored. Similarly, when a person is publicly self-aware, any private self-awareness would be considered trivial and safe to ignore.

   This simplifying assumption, considering only the major focus of self-attention, is necessary for rigorous theory-testing. Without the assumption, results opposed to the theory could be explained after the fact in terms of the minor focus. If, for example, introspection failed to cause polarization of affect, the failure might be attributed to the interfering presence of public self-awareness. If we consider only the dominant focus, however, the theory would not be protected by such excuses. In brief, though private and public self-awareness may occur within the same brief time span, only the dominant focus will be used to make theoretical predictions. Of course, it is the researcher's responsibility to use experimental control to ensure that either private or public self-awareness is dominant and that the alternative state is minor.

What determines the major focus? When you are alone and imagine having stage fright while performing in front of an audience, is your self-awareness private or public? One answer is that the self-awareness is private because no one else is around, and you are engaging in the private process of fantasy. On the other hand, the content of your fantasy concerns the social aspects of yourself, and so your state must be public self-awareness. Which determines the kind of self-awareness, the process or the content? The answer comes directly from the theory. Private and public self-awareness are aspects of the self, defined by their domains, that is, events available to the experiencing person alone versus personal attributes observable by others. Thus it is content that determines whether a state is private or public. You might be in the middle of a noisy party and still drift into a daydream about yourself; here you would be privately self-aware. And if you were concerned whether your dinner partner later that day would find you attractive, you would be publicly self-aware. Though not actually being observed, you imagine what would happen in the company of another and, through imagery, induce public self-awareness in yourself. But the important point to be made here is that whatever the mental process, it is the content or domain that determines whether the state is private or public self-awareness.

Needed evidence

If self-consciousness theory were not supported by at least some evidence, this book would not have been written. As a prelude to the next two chapters, which present research relevant to the theory, we may ask which kinds of evidence are needed.

We need evidence that there are two separate dispositions or traits, one for private and one for public self-consciousness, as well as a trait of social anxiety. We need research demonstrating that, for each trait, Highs behave differently from Lows when the appropriate aspects of the self are engaged.

We also need to discover whether the inducers listed for each kind of self-awareness do indeed elicit the appropriate self-focus. An empirical basis for the assumed role of a shaving-sized mirror is especially important. And a crucial issue concerns whether the inferred processes are correct, especially those involving private self-awareness because, unlike the effects of public self-awareness, they are hard to observe in everyday life.

Finally, we need evidence of how the traits and inducers interact. Such evidence is especially important for public self-awareness, which is assumed not to occur unless it is initiated by some form of manipulation.

NOTES

1. *Webster's New International Dictionary.* Unabridged. Springfield, Mass.: Merriam, 1960, second edition, p. 2270.
2. This statement refers to any particular situation. If you are being scrutinized by several other people, you do not necessarily view yourself through their eyes. But the ability to take another's perspective of oneself is essential for the development of public self-awareness, as we shall see in Chapter 13.

3. The social behavior of shy people will be discussed in Chapter 12.
4. An exception occurs when a television camera scans the audience in a studio or sports event. Most spectators wave and act as exhibitionists. But they are part of the crowd, and many are trying to signal any friends who might be watching the telecast. If a single member of the audience were isolated and had to remain on camera, he or she would probably be intensely self-aware.
5. Holzman and Rousey (1966)
6. The exception is vicarious public self-awareness produced by imagery.

CHAPTER

4

RELEVANT RESEARCH:
DISPOSITIONS

The research relevant to the theory of self-consciousness falls naturally into two categories: manipulations and dispositions. Researchers have induced private and public self-awareness by using small mirrors, audiences, television cameras, and instructions; these studies will be reviewed in Chapter 5. This chapter reviews research on private and public self-consciousness. A necessary first step was constructing a questionnaire that would identify people with varying degrees of private and public self-consciousness. Once these traits could be measured, research could test the impact of these traits on behavior.

THE QUESTIONNAIRE

In the early 1970s, several students and I constructed a questionnaire on self-consciousness.[1] We started by asking ourselves and our colleagues about the content of self-consciousness and came up with seven basic areas:

1. Preoccupation with past, present, or future behavior.
2. Recognition of one's own positive and negative attributes.
3. Sensitivity to inner feelings.
4. Introspective behavior.
5. A tendency to visualize oneself.
6. Awareness of one's own appearance and style of presentation.
7. Concern over the appraisal of others.

We made up 38 items that tapped into these areas of self-consciousness and administered them to more than 200 college students. Each item was to be answered on a scale from *extremely uncharacteristic* (0) to *extremely characteristic* (4) of the person answering the item. An examination of the students' responses showed that some items were ambiguous, some were answered the same way by almost everyone, and some were misleading. Accordingly, some items were changed, others were discarded, and still others were added. Using factor analysis,[2] we trimmed the number of items to 23, which were divided into three factors or scales. Then the questionnaire was administered to over 2000 students in samples of a few hundred each. The factor analyses of successive samples consistently yielded the same three factors. The details of the final factor analysis on the last sample of students are presented in Appendix 1.

The first factor, containing 10 items, was easily identifiable as *private self-consciousness:*

I reflect about myself a lot.

I'm generally attentive to my inner feelings.

I'm always trying to figure myself out.

I'm constantly examining my motives.

I'm alert to changes in my mood.

I tend to scrutinize myself.

Generally, I'm aware of myself.

I'm aware of the way my mind works when I work through a problem.

I'm often the subject of my own fantasies.

I sometimes have the feeling that I'm off somewhere watching myself.

A person who endorses these items is one who introspects, examines moods and motives, is aware of mental processes, spins fantasies, and in general is self-reflective.

The second factor, containing 7 items, was appropriately labeled *public self-consciousness:*

I'm concerned about what other people think of me.

I usually worry about making a good impression.

I'm concerned about the way I present myself.

I'm self-conscious about the way I look.

I'm usually aware of my appearance.

One of the last things I do before leaving my house is look in the mirror.

I'm concerned about my style of doing things.

People who endorse these items are concerned about their appearance, style of behavior, and in general about the impression they make on others.

The third factor, containing 6 items, was not so easy to name, but the closest approximation was *social anxiety:*

It takes me time to get over my shyness in new situations.

I get embarrassed easily.

Large groups make me nervous.

I find it hard to talk to strangers.

I feel anxious when I speak in front of a group.

I have trouble working when someone is watching me.

The picture here is of a person who is shy, easily embarrassed, and anxious in the presence of others. There is one common denominator underlying all this anxiety: the presence of others—in other words, social anxiety.

To discover the relationships among these scales, we correlated each with the other two in several samples of subjects. The correlations varied from one sample to the next, as correlations inevitably do, but within a reasonable range. The Private and Social Anxiety scales were essentially unrelated, the average correlation being near zero. But the Public scale showed a moderate correlation, about .30, with the Private scale and the Social Anxiety scale.

My interpretation of these correlations stays fairly close to the data. People may be aligned on a dimension that starts with excessive attention to oneself and ends with virtually no attention to oneself. To some extent, those who attend to themselves are above average in both public and private self-consciousness; those who do not attend to themselves are below average in both. Such a dimension would account for the moderate relationship between the Private and Public scales. Notice, however, that the relationship is moderate, which means that the private aspects of the self are discernibly different from the public aspects. Concerning the relationship between the Public and Social Anxiety scales, many people, though not all, who are high in public self-consciousness are likely to become upset and nervous in the presence of casual acquaintances and strangers. Those who are low in public self-consciousness are less likely to become upset in social contexts. Put another way, virtually everyone who is high in social anxiety should be high in public self-consciousness, but perhaps only a bare majority of those high in public self-consciousness should be high in social anxiety. The remainder would be aware of themselves as social objects but not nervous about it. (Understanding social anxiety requires an examination of its various components and the research that has been conducted on each of them. These issues will be discussed in the next section of the book.)

The Private and Public scales have been used to identify people who are high and low in each of these two traits. Before we discuss laboratory research on such subjects, two studies should be mentioned briefly. In one study, college students were asked to make up a list of adjectives that described themselves.[3] Private self-conscious subjects used the adjectives warm, reflective, and complicated. Public self-conscious subjects tended to describe themselves as emotional, worrying, and nervous. Though both the questionnaire and the adjective-listing were self-reports, none of the terms listed by the subjects was mentioned in the questionnaire, with the exception of reflective. Why private self-conscious people should see themselves as warm is not clear, but their seeing themselves as complicated is certainly no surprise. Nor is it surprising that public self-conscious students saw themselves as nervous, given the correlation between public self-consciousness and social anxiety.

In a study of almost 1400 college students, the Self-Consciousness Questionnaire was correlated with other self-report measures of personality.[4] Table 4.1 lists the most important findings. The finding that neither self-consciousness scale correlates with a Social Desirability scale means that no one expects social disapproval for admitting or denying paying attention to oneself. Imagery correlates moderately with the Private scale but not with the Public scale. Thoughtfulness has a solid correlation with the Private scale but a weak correlation with the Pub-

TABLE 4.1

*Correlations among the two self-consciousness
scales and other questionnaires*

	Private SC	Public SC
Social desirability	Near zero	Near zero
Imagery	.30	Near zero
Thoughtfulness	.48	.22
Sociability	−.13	.16

From Turner et al., 1978.

lic scale. And Sociability is only weakly correlated with both self-consciousness scales, but notice that the correlations are opposite in sign. Sociability correlates negatively with the Private Scale and positively with the Public scale—facts that have been corroborated in my own recent unpublished research.

In order to construct a meaningful pattern from these data, they have been combined with the previous study on lists of self-descriptive adjectives. Private self-conscious people tend to introspect, use fantasy, and have a relatively weak need to be with others; and they consider themselves warm and complicated. Public self-conscious people may or may not introspect or use fantasy but have a stronger need to be with others; and they see themselves as emotional and worrying (presumably about themselves as social objects).

RESEARCH ON PRIVATE
SELF-CONSCIOUSNESS

Self-consciousness theory specifies two different inferred processes, depending on the presence of affective or motivational components. In their absence, private self-consciousness leads to clearer knowledge about internal cues. In their presence, self-consciousness intensifies them. For clarity of exposition, the research on cues is separated from that on affects and motives.

Cues

The more you know your own mind, the more resistant you are to attempts of others to persuade you otherwise. The better you know your immediate reaction to something, the harder it is for others to fool you about that reaction. Private self-conscious people are supposed to know themselves better, so it follows that they should be harder to fool and more resistant to being coerced.

In one study, subjects drank a peppermint-flavored drink and rated how strong the flavor was.[5] Then a second drink was presented, and half the subjects were told that it was stronger than the first drink. Subjects high in private self-consciousness (Highs) gave almost the same intensity ratings to this second drink, but the Lows rated it as much more intense. The rest of the subjects were told that the second drink was weaker. Again, the Highs hardly changed their ratings at all, but the Lows rated the second drink as much weaker. Thus the Highs were not susceptible to suggestions about their taste reactions, but the Lows were.

Suppose that you mildly supported a political candidate who was running for a local office. If I agreed with your position but also insisted that he was the only rational choice and that you really had no option but to agree with me, you might change your mind. Why? Because my assertions would in effect threaten your freedom to choose the alternative position, and you might react negatively to my reducing your freedom to choose. High private self-conscious people know themselves better and have a strong sense of who they are; therefore they should react strongly to having their freedom of choice restricted. Low private self-conscious people, being relatively unaware of the private aspects of themselves, are less aware of their options and so they care less about restrictions on their choices.

College men were divided into those high and those low in private self-consciousness and were asked about their degree of favorableness toward a fictitious candidate for a political office. After being told that he was the only rational choice and that they really had no option but to agree with this notion, they again rated the candidate. This time the attitudes of the Highs were much less favorable, but the attitudes of the Lows remained essentially unchanged. When other subjects were put through the same procedure without any coercion, neither Highs nor Lows changed their attitudes the second time.

These two experiments demonstrate that high private self-conscious people seem to know precisely what is going on "inside." They cannot be fooled by suggestions that a drink is either more or less intense in flavor when the drink is really unchanged. And they react negatively when coercion is used to try to change their attitudes because, being more aware of themselves, they are more sensitive to threats to personal freedom. Evidently, Highs really know just who they are. Lows, on the other hand, do not know what they are really like "inside" and so can easily be fooled about the taste of drinks and do not react negatively to coercion.

People who have been scrutinizing themselves, trying to figure themselves out, and examining their motives (these are some of the items on the Private Self-Consciousness Scale) should know themselves better and therefore offer more complete descriptions of themselves than people who have not maintained the same degree of self-attention. When college students were asked to list self-descriptive adjectives, those high in private self-consciousness wrote down more self-descriptive traits than did the Lows.[6]

Finally, if private self-conscious people know themselves better, their self-reports should be more accurate.[7] The best way to tell if someone's self-report is true is to check it against objective evidence. This is precisely what was done in a study that compared self-reports of aggressiveness with objectively measured aggression.[8] First, college men and

women filled out the Self-Consciousness Questionnaire.
Then they filled out a self-report of aggressiveness, which
contained items of this kind: "Once in a while I cannot
control my urge to harm others," "I get into fights about as
often as the next person," "I sometimes spread gossip about
people I don't like," "I can remember being so angry that I
picked up the nearest thing and broke it," "I often feel like
a powder keg ready to explode," and "I can't help getting
into arguments when people disagree with me."[9] Several
weeks later they were brought individually into a laboratory and given the opportunity to deliver painful electric
shocks to another person in a situation known to measure
the intensity of aggression.[10] Thus there were two measures: a self-report of aggressiveness and an intensity-of-
shock measure of aggression. The correlation between
these two measures was .34 for the entire sample of subjects. This moderate correlation is typical of the relationships found between self-reports and objective measures of
personality. Separating the sample into those high and
those low in private self-consciousness, however, yielded
different results. For the Lows the correlation was .09; not
very different from zero. For the Highs the correlation was
.66, which is unusually strong for the relationship between
a self-report and objectively-measured behavior. What do
these correlations mean? Evidently, the Lows know so little about themselves that their self-reports of aggressiveness are unrelated to their aggressive behavior. Evidently,
the Highs know themselves well enough to produce a
strong relationship between their self-report of aggressiveness and their aggressive behavior. These results raise the
possibility that self-reports may be of little value for some
people (Lows) but of great value for others (Highs); more on
this later.

Affect and motivation

As we view the world around us, seeing sights both lovely
and ugly, we react with pleasure or revulsion. According to

self-consciousness theory, such affective reactions should be more intense in high private self-conscious people. They should react with more pleasure to beautiful scenes and more revulsion to ugly scenes. Private self-conscious people also should become more fearful when they are frightened, depressed when they are made sad, more sympathetic when they are exposed to objects of sympathy.

Several studies bear on the intensification hypothesis. In one study, college men were shown slides of beautiful nude women and slides of atrocities such as a pile of dead human beings or the body of a person just executed.[11] The students rated these slides on a scale ranging from *extremely unpleasant* to *extremely pleasant.* Subjects high in private self-consciousness rated the atrocity slides as being more unpleasant and the slides of nude women as being more pleasant than did the Lows. Put another way, the High's affective reactions were more extreme than those of the Lows.

In a follow-up study, positive and negative moods were experimentally induced.[11] In the Elation condition, subjects read statements that became more and more positive, from "I feel lighthearted" to "I feel like bursting with laughter." In the Depression condition, subjects read statements that became more and more negative, from "I feel rather sluggish now" to "Everything feels utterly futile and empty." Obviously, merely reading such statements will not produce extreme mood states, but in previous research they did lead to states of mild elation or depression. After reading one or the other set of statements, the subjects reflected about them for a few minutes and then completed a self-report questionnaire on their present mood. After reading the positive statements, subjects high in private self-consciousness reported being more elated than the Lows; after reading the negative statements, Highs reported being more depressed than the Lows. In brief, in both this and the previous experiment, the Highs' affective reactions were more polarized than the Lows'.

We sympathize with handicapped people. As an affect,

sympathy should be greater in private self-conscious people. As a test of this hypothesis, college students listened to one of two interviews.[12] One interview was with a normal man, the other with a man labeled handicapped. Then the subjects rated this man on bipolar scales, such as *unintelligent–intelligent* and *lazy–hardworking*. These individual ratings were summed to yield a total *attractiveness* rating. Subjects high in private self-consciousness differed little from the Lows in their ratings of the normal man. But the Highs rated the handicapped man as more attractive than did the Lows. Notice that in the absence of affect (normal man) private self-consciousness had no effect, but when affect was present (sympathy for the handicapped man), the Highs reacted more intensely than the Lows.

Suppose we confront a person with a conflict between two motives: desire to help versus fear of harm. If fear of harm is minimized, most people would help, but if fear of harm is intensified, helping behavior would decrease sharply. Private self-conscious people should be more extreme in each instance. In comparison with Lows, Highs should help more when fear is low and help less when fear is high.

To test this polarization hypothesis, college men and women were told that electric shock was often used in surgery to cauterize blood vessels and that the present research on reactions to electric shock would have implications for medical therapy.[13] They were to receive electric shock on the forearm. Subjects were told that the forthcoming shock was as mild as "someone's squeezing your arm with his hand," or they were told that the shock would be intense and would feel like receiving a hypodermic injection. They were reminded of the benefits of the research and then given the choice of continuing or not.

When fear was low (mild shock), about three-quarters of those low in private self-consciousness and all of the Highs volunteered to continue. When fear was high (intense shock), the percentage of Lows volunteering remained about the same, but only about half the Highs volunteered. A question about distress at the prospect of receiving electric shock yielded consistent findings. When the shock was to be mild, neither group was distressed; when the shock was to be intense, the Lows were no more distressed, but the Highs were. As in previous research, private self-conscious subjects reacted more intensely when affect was induced—in this instance, fear. And their motive to help was stronger, as reflected in the 100% rate of volunteering when they were not threatened.

The last study concerns anger and aggression. Suppose we insult someone and allow him to aggress. Self-consciousness theory predicts that high private self-conscious people would become angrier and aggress more than Lows. As a test of this hypothesis, a confederate insulted subjects and the subjects gave the confederate electric shock as part of the aggression machine procedure.[14] Subjects high in private self-consciousness gave more intense shock and later rated themselves as angrier than did the Lows.

In summary, private self-consciousness has been shown to intensify elation, depression, sympathy, helping behavior, fear, anger, and angry aggression. These findings strengthen the *affect-motivation* part of the theory of private self-consciousness. And in the immediately preceding section, we saw that private self-consciousness led to greater resistance to suggestion about taste, greater resistance to pressure, more self-descriptive adjectives, and substantially greater veridicality of self-report of aggressiveness. These findings strengthen the *cue aspects* of private self-consciousness theory.

In all the research cited so far, private self-consciousness has had an impact: Highs reacted more intensely and paid more attention to internal cues than did Lows. What about public self-consciousness? In each instance, public self-consciousness was examined and found to have no impact on the behaviors being investigated. Those high in public self-consciousness did not differ from the Lows in accuracy of self-report, awareness of the unshared aspects of self, or in intensity of affects or motives. In brief, when private self-consciousness was a determinant of behavior, public self-consciousness was not.

PUBLIC SELF-CONSCIOUSNESS

Public self-conscious people should be particularly susceptible to what happens in social situations, especially where there is scrutiny, confrontation, or shunning. In an experiment on shunning, each female subject waited in a room with two other women (ostensible subjects but, in reality, experimental accomplices).[15] Though all were supposedly strangers, the accomplices stayed away from the subject and spoke only to each other. They barely responded if the subject spoke and were uninterested in her; there was no hostility, only a lack of interest. These acts occurred in the experimental group. In the control group, the accomplices were moderately friendly and responsive.

Then the subjects were separated and told that in the experiment proper each had the choice of participating in a three-person group with the same two others or a new pair. The data for this affiliation measure are shown in Table 4.2. Most Control subjects chose to affiliate with the original pair, and public self-consciousness did not affect this choice. In the experimental group there was much less affiliation. Of those low in public self-consciousness, half affiliated and half did not; only 3 out of 20 Highs chose to affiliate. Thus shunning had a moderate impact on the Lows and a strong impact on the Highs.

The replies of the rejected subjects to two other questions are of some interest. The Highs liked the other pair less than did the Lows, but the Highs felt more personal responsibility for the way the others behaved than did the Lows. In brief, the public self-conscious subjects who had been shunned responded by liking the shunners less, choosing not to affiliate with them, but blaming themselves more for what happened.

TABLE 4.2

*Number of subjects who chose to affiliate or
not with the original pair*

Public self-consciousness	Affiliate/not affiliate	
	Control	Experimental
Low	14/6	10/10
High	15/5	3/17

From Fenigstein, 1979.

In this experiment, private self-consciousness had no impact on the subjects' behavior. In the remaining research on
public self-consciousness, private self-consciousness was
varied independently, and both dispositions had an impact.

It is well known that attitudes are not always expressed
in behavior. And the attitudes we verbalize in social contexts may be different from those we hold in private.
Michael Scheier studied attitude–behavior consistency in
relation to both kinds of self-consciousness, using the following rationale.[16] People high in public self-consciousness
should be inconsistent in public contexts because of their
concern about others' opinion of them. People high in private self-consciousness should be consistent because they
really know their own attitudes. People high in both private and public self-consciousness would be so affected by
others' opinions that the effect of private self-consciousness
would be nullified, and they would therefore be inconsistent. People low in private self-consciousness would not
know themselves well enough to be consistent, whether
they were high or low in public self-consciousness. The
only people expected to be consistent are those high in
private (and therefore veridical) and low in public self-
consciousness (and therefore unaffected by the social
context).

Scheier pretested subjects to discover their attitudes to-

ward the use of physical punishment as a learning technique. In filling out the nine-item scale of attitudes toward
punishment, the subjects were, in a sense, making their attitudes public. But filling out a questionnaire that is tabu-
lated by a researcher and never revealed to anyone else is so
little public that in practice it may be considered private.[17]
Months later they were brought to the laboratory in groups
of two to four subjects. Each was asked to write an essay on
the use of physical punishment as a childrearing technique,
after which they would discuss their views with each
other. The essays were scored for attitude toward punishment, and these scores were correlated with the attitudes
that the subjects espoused on the pretesting several months
earlier. There were four groups of subjects, split into high
or low on private/public: high/high, high/low, low/high, and
low/low. For three of these groups the correlations were
nearly zero. Only the high private/low public group had a
significant correlation, .64. Thus Scheier's line of reasoning
was on target: only high private self-conscious subjects
know themselves sufficiently well to be consistent, and
only low public self-conscious subjects express their true
attitudes without worrying about how others view them.

One more fact completed the pattern that emerged from
Scheier's experiment. When they wrote the essays, the subjects expected to discuss their attitudes toward punishment
with the other subjects. In these essays, the attitudes of the
high public self-conscious subjects were less extreme than
those of low public self-conscious subjects. Scheier concluded, "Thus, the mere anticipation of discussing one's attitude with another was enough to cause high public self-
conscious persons to adopt a more moderate position."

In this experiment, people expected to interact with others. When people actually do mingle, public self-consciousness should be an equally potent influence. In another study,
three-person groups, each composed of two accomplices
and a real subject, discussed a crucial decision to be made
if the country was threatened with a nuclear attack: if the
fallout shelter holds four people and twelve people want

shelter, which four should be allowed in?[18] The real subject was told to be as assertive and dominant as possible, and his or her behavior was later rated for dominance by the two accomplices.

Prior to the discussion, subjects wrote stories about an imaginary situation: a professor divides his class into groups of six people who are to arrive at a joint decision. They were to write about how they would behave if they were as assertive and dominant as possible. These stories were later scored for dominance.

The correlation between dominance (story) and dominance (actual discussion) was .50 for the entire sample. When subjects were divided on the basis of self-consciousness, public and private had opposite effects. The correlations were: high private, .67; low private, .33; and high public, .30; low public, .71.

These results differ somewhat from Scheier's research on attitudes. In his research, only the combination of high private and low public self-consciousness yielded a significant correlation. In the research on dominance, both high private and low public self-consciousness yielded significant correlations. The experiments differed in two ways. First, in the dominance experiment, instructions emphasized dominance in both the story-telling and the group discussion. This attention to the behavior being rated served to elevate the overall correlation between story-dominance and discussion-dominance to .50, in contrast to the usual test-behavior correlation of about .30. This attention to dominance also diminished the impact of private self-consciousness. The instructions focused so strongly on dominance that less private self-consciousness was required; even low private self-conscious subjects had a story-versus-discussion correlation of .33. Being high in private self-consciousness still had an impact, and the Highs' correlation was .67.

Second, the group discussion about a fallout shelter made public self-consciousness more important. Even though they were instructed to be dominant, subjects had to express this tendency in relation to two other people. The subjects' awareness of themselves as social objects would surely affect their assertiveness. This additional social awareness evidently reduced the correlation of those high in public self-consciousness to .30. In contrast, the Lows' correlations was .71, which reflected their unconcern for the opinion of others; this lack of concern allowed them to be as dominant as they had written about in the stories.

In brief, the dominance experiment had two features that would diminish the impact of private self-consciousness and enhance the impact of public self-consciousness. First subjects were instructed to be dominant, which would make knowledge of oneself (high private self-consciousness) less important. Second, subjects had to discuss a decision with two other people; this interaction surely made them aware of themselves as social objects, enhancing the impact of public self-consciousness.

If this interpretation is correct, it follows that if subjects were instructed to act in ways already familiar and well-known to them, the impact of private self-consciousness would be further diminished. It also follows that if subjects did not interact but knew they were being observed, public self-consciousness would be a potent influence on their behavior. In an experiment on anger, subjects told a story about how angry they might become.[19] Later, in the laboratory, they were to express maximal anger by shouting, throwing objects, and so on. Though all of the subjects expressed anger alone, they knew that they were being observed behind a one-way mirror. When their story anger was correlated with their laboratory anger, private self-consciousness was found to have little impact, but public self-consciousness had a strong impact.

To reveal trends in the data, I have compared the results of three experiments in Table 4.3. Comparison of the columns of correlations is especially revealing. For high private self-conscious subjects, the correlations are uniformly high: knowing oneself increases the accuracy of self-report or strengthens the relationship between stories and behav-

TABLE 4.3

Correlations between self-report or stories and laboratory behavior in relation to private and public self-consciousness

Behavior: procedure	Self-consciousness			
	Private		Public	
	High	Low	High	Low
Anger: no instructions, no interaction, no observation[20]	.66	.09	.38	.31
Dominance: instructions, interaction[21]	.67	.33	.30	.71
Anger: instructions, no interaction, observation[22]	.66	.52	.28	.74

ior. For low private self-conscious subjects, the pattern is different. When subjects are not instructed how to act, the correlation is nearly zero (.09). Instructions raise the correlation to .33 for dominance and .52 for anger. When subjects are told what to do, they need not know themselves well; so even low private self-conscious subjects have at least a modest story-behavior relationship. And it is only mild speculation to suggest that all of us know how to express anger better and more precisely than dominance, which may account for the higher correlation for anger.

Concerning the correlations for high public self-conscious subjects, they are low to moderate in all three experiments. Why are they not near zero? When the sample of subjects is divided into high and low public self-conscious subjects, subjects high in private self-consciousness are distributed in both groups. As a consequence, the high public self-conscious group contains a fair number of subjects who are high in private self-consciousness. Presumably, these subjects, who know themselves well, elevate the correlation for the high public self-conscious group to its modest level (ranging from .28 to .38).

Finally, consider the correlations for low public self-conscious subjects. In the absence of instructions, interaction, or observation, this correlation (.31) was modest. That there was any relationship at all is due to the presence of high private self-conscious subjects randomly assigned to this group. But when subjects were instructed and either interacted or were observed, the correlations were in the seventies. Why? I suggest that instructions elevated the story–behavior relationship, but this stronger relationship could be revealed only in subjects who were unconcerned about themselves as social objects when they interacted with others or were observed.

In sum, when people are instructed how to behave and are observed by others, private self-consciousness diminishes in importance, and public self-consciousness increases in importance. But explicit instructions for behavior are uncommon in everyday life, and, in any event, we are interested primarily in behavior in the absence of specific instructions. Without instructions, self-report-behavior consistency is high only in people high in private self-consciousness. This fact is a plus for the private part of self-consciousness theory, which predicted such consistency on the assumption that high private self-conscious people know themselves better.

In everyday life, much of our behavior is social, some asocial. In the absence of social interaction or observation by others, public self-consciousness is not an important personality disposition. But in social contexts, only people low in public self-consciousness are free to express their true attitudes and behavioral dispositions. This fact is a plus for the public part of self-consciousness theory.

These findings are of some practical interest. We now know that we can trust the self-reports of people high in private self-consciousness, but not those low in private self-consciousness. And in social contexts, public self-consciousness is important: we can trust the Lows to express their true feelings but not the Highs. Put another way, private and public self-consciousness appear to be important moderator variables that affect the consistency between behavior and self-reports or attitudes.

Notice also that the two kinds of self-consciousness act

in opposite directions: consistency is linked with high private self-consciousness and with low public self-consciousness. This opposition demonstrates the importance of separating the two kinds of self-consciousness. This point was driven home in an experiment completed as this book went to press. It was a conformity experiment, in which individual subjects were pressured by being confronted with the apparently unanimous opposing choice of other "subjects."[23] Each subject listened to clicks delivered through earphones; the response on each trial was to announce how many clicks had occurred. Each subject responded after the other three had responded. Unbeknown to the subjects, they were fed preprogrammed information on each trial: the group had unanimously made either the correct or the incorrect response. When the group's choice was incorrect, the subject had to decide whether to go along with the group or to stick to her guns. A moderately strong negative correlation was found between private self-consciousness and conformity—that is, subjects higher in private self-consciousness tended more to resist the group pressure and stick to their own perceptions. On the other hand, there was a moderate positive correlation between public self-consciousness and conformity—that is, subjects higher in public self-consciousness had a slight tendency to yield to group pressure. These findings are in line with the research just mentioned, which revealed the opposition between public and private self-consciousness. The results also make sense. Private self-conscious people, knowing themselves, trust their own perceptions and therefore cannot easily be coerced or pressured by others. Public self-conscious people, being concerned with the way others regard them, are susceptible to pressure to conform.

Finally, the research just discussed adds to the growing body of evidence demonstrating how different the two self-consciousness traits are, despite their moderate positive correlation. People who reflect about their psychological "insides" are very different from people who are concerned about themselves as social objects.

NOTES

1. Fenigstein, Scheier, and Buss (1975)

2. Factor analysis is a statistical tool used to interpret relationships among many measures or items when all the measures
   or items are correlated with one another. Important as it is in
   the construction of the Self-Consciousness Questionnaire—or
   any test, for that matter—it is too complex to be discussed
   here. This is why I have relegated the table of factor loadings
   to the Appendix.

3. Turner (1977). I have selected only those adjective significantly related to self-consciousness for both the men and
   women in the study.

4. Turner, Scheier, Carver, and Ickes (1978)

5. Gibbons, Scheier, Carver, and Hormuth (1979)

6. Turner (1977). This is the same study on self-descriptive traits
   that was cited earlier.

7. This prediction assumes that other things—honesty, desire
   for social approval, subjectivity, and so on—are equal. Since
   these things are not equal, the self-reports of Highs will not
   be entirely accurate.

8. Scheier, Buss, and Buss (1978)

9. These are sample items from the aggressiveness factor, num-
   bering 43 items, of the Buss-Durkee Hostility Scale (1957)

10. The apparatus-procedure is called the *aggression machine*
    (Buss, 1961). Subjects are told that they will be experimenters
    in a study of learning. Whenever the learner—actually an ex-
    perimental accomplice—makes a mistake, he is to receive an
    electric shock (actually, he receives none). The intensity of
    electric shock delivered has proved, in the past two decades,
    to be a useful measure of physical aggression.

11. Scheier and Carver (1977)

12. Scheier, Carver, Schulz, Glass, Wishnick, and Katz (1978)

13. Scheier, Carver, and Gibbons (in press)

14. Scheier (1976)

15. Fenigstein (1979)

16. Scheier (1978)

17. If a subject does not declare somewhere what his attitude is, we can never discover it. Thus for research purposes, filling out a questionnaire on attitudes is as near to private as we can get.

18. Turner (1978)

19. Turner and Peterson (1977)

20. Scheier, Buss, and Buss (1978)

21. Turner (1978)

22. Turner and Peterson (1977)

23. Froming and Carver (1979)

RELEVANT RESEARCH: CHAPTER
TRANSIENT STATES 5

The research on transient states involves more complex issues than the research on dispositions. When an experimenter selects subjects who are high in private self-consciousness, we know that they frequently turn their attention inward to the unshared aspects of themselves because they say so. But if an experimenter induces private self-awareness with a small mirror, we cannot be entirely sure that the subjects are in a temporary state of private self-awareness. Concerning a small mirror, other theorists see no difference between it and a television camera as inducers of self-awareness,[1] whereas I specify private self-awareness for a mirror and public self-awareness for a television camera. In brief, the interpretation of results in this chapter is more controversial than in the last chapter.

PRIVATE SELF-AWARENESS

Cues

According to the self-consciousness theory, the state of private self-awareness is defined as paying attention specifically to the unshared aspects of oneself. Such attention results in clearer self-knowledge of your present status: body, thoughts, fantasies, and memories. The narrowing of attention to only the private aspects of yourself should produce a more accurate perception of what you are experiencing right now, as well as a true account of any memories you attempt to recover.

It follows that private self-awareness should weaken the effect of false suggestions about one's own body. When "little pink pills" and powders are given with the strong suggestion that they work, they are often effective even though their chemical components are inert. These substances are called *placebos,* from the Latin "I shall please." In one study, college women were given an inert powder, called Cavanol, and told that it would cause "a slight increase in heart rate, sweatiness in the palms of your hands, and a tightness in your chest."[2] Half the women sat in front of a small mirror; the other half, not.

The control subjects (no mirror) reported the presence of some of the symptoms that had been suggested. Subjects made privately self-aware (mirror) resisted the suggestions of the experimenter:

> The responses of the self-aware subjects indicated that they did not simply report the internal state that they had been led to expect. In contrast, they reported experiencing less arousal during the period when the drug was supposed to be active, less arousal from the drug itself, and fewer symptoms ascribed to the drug than did the less self-aware subjects.[3]

The section on cues in Chapter 4 described an experiment on attempted coercion. According to the evidence, high private self-conscious people are less susceptible to coercion when their freedom of choice is restricted. In a similar study, such pressure was applied to subjects in the presence or absence of a mirror.[4] In comparison with the control group (no mirror), the self-aware group (mirror) reported a greater intent of the other person to coerce, and they resisted the pressure more. Why? Presumably, because private self-awareness leads to such clear self-knowledge that coercion is more readily recognized and pressure to change is more easily resisted.

How closely does the behavior of people follow their beliefs? College students, on the basis of a questionnaire, were separated into two groups.[5] One group opposed electric shock in experiments and was unwilling to use it; the other group condoned electric shock and was willing to use it. All subjects were given the opportunity to use electric shock as part of the aggression machine procedure.[6] In the absence of a mirror (half the subjects), those who condoned the use of electric shock gave no more intense shock than those who opposed its use. This surprising absence of a difference may be due to particular beliefs studied in the experiment. Most people do not have strong and deeply felt beliefs about the use of electric shock in experimentation. If we selected a more intense belief—about abortion, for instance—behavior might follow belief. In any event, in the absence of a mirror, there was no difference between opposers and condoners. In the presence of a mirror—the remaining half of the subjects—condoners shocked more intensely than opposers. Evidently, it required private self-awareness, induced by a mirror, for subjects to focus sufficiently on the relevant belief, so that this belief would affect their behavior.

I suggest that only private self-awareness would bring about the required focus on the relevant belief. Public self-awareness would not cause the appropriate self-focus and might even distract attention from the relevant self-focus. This theorizing leads to a straightforward prediction: whereas a mirror would cause subjects to behave in accord with their beliefs, as in the punishment experiment, a television camera would not. A television camera should induce public self-awareness, which I assume would not lead to better, clearer knowledge of the relevant belief.

The difference between a television camera and a mirror might be especially important for behaviors that are strongly socialized—reactions to pornographic pictures and literature, for instance. A television camera would probably cause subjects to behave as they thought they were supposed to behave, whereas a mirror would probably cause them to allow their true reactions to surface. Unfortunately, in the research relevant to this issue, only a mirror was used.[7] In one experiment college men were pretested to discover their attitudes toward pornography. A month later they were brought to the laboratory, shown pictures of nude women, and asked to rate how excited these pictures caused them to be. In the absence of a mirror, the correlation between attitude toward pornography and excitement was −.21; in the presence of a mirror, .60. A followup experiment pretested women for sex guilt. At a later session, they read erotic passages from a novel. In the absence of a mirror, there was no relationship between sex guilt and the subjects' report of how arousing, enjoyable, and well-written the erotic passages were. But when a mirror was present, the correlation was −.71: the stronger the sex guilt, the less enjoyable were the passages.

These two experiments are in line with the earlier research on attitudes toward aggression. Every experiment showed that in the absence of a mirror there was virtually no relationship between a previously expressed position and current behavior; when a mirror was present, this relationship was strong. Thus, in the research just described, the more positive was men's attitude toward pornography, the more exciting were nude pictures, and the stronger was women's sex guilt, the less enjoyable and arousing was erotic literature. If in fact the mirror induces only private self-awareness, these high correlations may be interpreted as having been caused by private self-awareness.

The punishment and pornography experiments induced private self-awareness while the subjects behaved but not while they filled out the questionnaire about their beliefs. A subsequent experiment reversed this procedure. This time a mirror was used to induce private self-awareness during the self-report, but not while the subjects behaved.[8] College men filled out a sociability questionnaire with a mirror present. A few days later they were brought to the laboratory, and each waited for a few minutes with another "subject," who was a female experimental accomplice. The number of words the subject spoke was counted, and the experimental accomplice rated him for sociability. The word count and rating were combined to form a single index of sociability. When the self-report was filled out in front of a mirror, the correlation between self-reported and observed sociability was .55; in the absence of a mirror, the correlation was .03. When the experiment was repeated, the correlations were: with mirror, .73; without mirror, .28.

These results are difficult to understand, especially the low correlations that occurred in the absence of a mirror during self-report. Do college men know so little about their own sociability that their self-report is uncorrelated with their own behavior (a near-zero correlation in the first sample)? Such ignorance is especially hard to understand when some of the self-report questions were so specific: "I can usually communicate well with members of the opposite sex," "I usually take the initiative in making new friends," and "I usually have difficulty in starting conversations with strangers." These are precisely the behaviors that were observed in the laboratory only a few days later. Regarded in this light, the low correlations in the absence of the mirror are puzzling.[9]

Whatever the resolution of these puzzling data, a mirror's presence during self-report evidently does enhance accuracy of self-report. The effect is probably caused by private self-awareness; public self-awareness has no impact. I predict that if subjects filled out the sociability questionnaire in the presence of a television camera, the camera would have no impact—that is, it would not increase accuracy of self-report.

In summary, private self-awareness evidently causes people to (1) resist false suggestions about bodily symptoms, (2) recognize coercion and resist it, and (3) bring their beliefs to bear on their behavior. These facts are consistent with the hypothesis that private self-awareness enhances self-knowledge of both ongoing personal events and residuals of the past.

Affect and motivation

Private self-awareness should intensify anger, thereby causing a higher level of aggressive behavior. College men were harassed, annoyed, badgered, insulted, and otherwise angered by a male experimental confederate.[10] The subjects were then allowed to punish this confederate in the context of the aggression machine procedure. For half the subjects, a small mirror was placed in front of the apparatus so that they could see themselves; for the other half, there was no mirror. The presence of a mirror caused the angered subjects to deliver higher intensities of electric shock. Thus, as predicted, private self-awareness elevated anger level, thereby intensifying aggression.

The mirror was also used in two studies reported in Chapter 4.[11] In the first experiment, college men looked at pictures of nude women and rated them for attractiveness. Private self-awareness was expected to intensify the pleasant affect, and it did. Compared to a no-mirror condition, the presence of a mirror caused subjects to rate the pictures as more attractive. In the second experiment, college students read statements known to induce mild elation or mild depression. Subjects in the mirror condition reported a more positive mood in response to elation statements or a more negative mood in relation to depression statements than did control subjects (no mirror). Thus private self-awareness polarizes mood.

If you are given positive information about yourself, you

would react with pleasant affect; negative information would probably result in unpleasant affect. Both kinds of affect should be intensified by private self-awareness. College women were interviewed in either the presence or the absence of a small mirror.

> After asking the subject for some preliminary background information, the interviewer reviewed the "findings" on the relation of birth order to 11 different personality characteristics including warmth, assertiveness, independence, achievement, and intelligence. For half the subjects, firstborns were credited with the favorable aspects of these traits, and the later-borns were given the unfavorable end. For the remaining subjects, this was reversed.[12]

Compared with the control condition, the mirror caused the positive evaluations (after receiving the favorable "findings") to be more positive, and the negative evaluations to be more negative. Again, private self-awareness polarized affective response.

In the last experiment to use a mirror, the subjects were college students who feared snakes.[13] These snake phobic students put on gloves and were asked to walk toward a caged snake and, if possible, to touch or pick up the snake. Most of them did not get as far as the cage. In the presence of a mirror, fearful subjects stopped farther away from the snake than did fearful control subjects (no mirror). Private self-awareness evidently intensifies anxiety.

Only one experiment did not use a mirror to induce private self-awareness. College students were told to count from 1 to 12, and at 8 a loud annoying noise was delivered.[14] Their reaction was assessed by the nonspecific galvanic skin response, a measure of emotional arousal. One group of subjects was instructed to concentrate on feelings and reactions; another group was told to concentrate on the experiment and the stimuli; and a control group was told nothing. The group told to concentrate on feelings and reactions had the highest nonspecific arousal. Thus private self-awareness—attention to one's own bodily reactions—intensified emotional arousal.

In summary, private self-awareness manipulations (1) intensified angry aggression, (2) enhanced the pleasant affect
caused by attractive pictures, (3) heightened mild elation
and deepened mild depression, (4) amplified fear of a snake,
and (5) caused a more severe emotional arousal to an unpleasant stimulus. These facts are consistent with the
hypothesis that private self-awareness intensifies motives
and polarizes affect.

Small mirror

Self-consciousness theory assumes that a small mirror induces private self-awareness (the rationale is stated in
Chapter 2). In the research just reviewed, a small mirror did
lead to the two effects expected of a private self-awareness
manipulation: (1) better knowledge of oneself (dispositions,
beliefs, and bodily reactions) and (2) intensification of affect
and motivation (anger, mood, fear, and discomfort).

In addition, the effects of a mirror parallel those of private self-consciousness (see Table 5.1). As this table reveals, the mirror manipulation and the disposition of private self-consciousness cause the same or highly similar
changes in behavior. Both elevate the accuracy of self-
report, both increase resistance to coercion (reactance),
both intensify angry aggression and the pleasantness of pictures, and both polarize mood. (No details of all these
studies are provided here because they have already been
discussed in this chapter and the last one). There exists no
research in which the disposition of public self-consciousness has yielded effects similar to those of a mirror.

The evidence summarized in Table 5.1 provides two sets
of facts. First, the mirror does indeed produce the effects
predicted for a private self-awareness manipulation. Second, effects of the mirror closely parallel or match those of
private self-consciousness but not those of public self-
consciousness. Hence the conclusion that a small mirror
induces private self-awareness.

TABLE 5.1

Parallel effects of mirror and private self-consciousness

	Mirror (Private self-awareness)	Private Self-consciousness
Self-report versus behavior	Punishment more consistent with beliefs	High correlation between aggressiveness and aggression
	High correlation between self-reported and behavioral sociability	High correlation for personality measure of dominance versus behavioral measure of dominance
Reaction to coercion	Resistance to persuasion	Resistance to persuasion
Affect and motivation	Intensification of angry aggression	Intensification of angry aggression
	Polarization of mood	Polarization of mood
	Pleasantness of pictures enhanced	Pleasantness of pictures enhanced

PUBLIC SELF-AWARENESS

In laboratory experimentation, two sets of manipulations have been used to induce public self-awareness. The first set includes placing a subject in a strange situation to induce shyness, providing an audience that causes audience anxiety, and placing the subject in an embarrassing situation. (This research will be discussed in the chapters on social anxiety.) The second set includes observers, shunning, a video image of the subject, and a tape recording of the subject's voice; this research is relevant here.

Shunning

When a person is ignored, the lack of social attention is expected to cause as much public self-awareness as would excessive social attention. In an experiment mentioned in

Chapter 4, college women were shunned. The details of the shunning manipulation are worth repeating because such research is rare:

> Upon entering the room, the subject was subtly directed toward one end of a rectangular table which had one side against the wall and a chair at each end. About one minute later, the first confederate arrived and was given the same introduction as the subject. The experimenter brought another chair into the experimental room, placed it halfway between the two ends of the table, and then left. The first confederate took this seat and remained quiet. If the subject attempted to initiate a conversation, the confederate made as brief and neutral a response as possible.
>
> Approximately 30 seconds later, the second confederate arrived and was told that one more subject was expected. After she took the remaining chair opposite the subject and the experimenter had left, both confederates remained quiet for about 20 seconds (to establish the lack of any acquaintance between them). The second confederate then began a casual conversation with the first confederate, who was reticent at first, but slowly became more talkative.
>
> During the conversation, both confederates directed their comments only toward each other and ignored the subject. If the subject tried to speak, the older confederate made a brief, unenthusiastic remark such as "I see." Eye contact with the subject was minimal. The impression created by the confederates was not dislike or hostility, but simply disinterest.[15]

In a control group the subject received attention and acceptance from the confederates, and she entered into the conversation. All subjects were asked whether they wanted to remain with the other two women or change to a new set of partners. In the control group, 29 of 40 subjects wanted to remain; in the shunned group, only 13 of 40 subjects wanted to remain. The shunned subjects liked their three-person group less than did control subjects. In addition to these data, there were interesting comments at the end of the experiment when the subjects were told about the nature of the experiment. On being debriefed, control subjects said merely that the experiment was interesting, but many of the shunned subjects were relieved because they had believed that something about themselves must have caused the others to ignore them.

In a similar experiment, ignored women were found to converse less and also to give themselves and their accomplices poorer evaluations than did control subjects.[16] Both experiments used women as subjects. Do men react to shunning in the same way? Yes, in an earlier study, college men wished to affiliate less with someone who had shunned them than did men who were not shunned.[17] These are the only studies on shunning. They provide an experimental analogue that closely parallels a situation we have all experienced: being ignored by two or three people at a dinner, a party, or some other social gathering. Our affective reactions may vary from mild to intense or from anxious to hostile. But whatever the affect, in the face of obviously insufficient social attention, we experience acute public self-awareness.

Observation and feedback

Self-consciousness theory predicts that hearing your own voice on tape should lower your self-esteem. One group of college women filled out a self-esteem questionnaire while listening to their own voice; another group listened to another woman's voice.[18] Those who heard their own voice reported lower self-esteem.

Seeing your image on a television screen should also diminish self-esteem. College women filled out a self-esteem questionnaire while in one of three conditions: sitting in front of (1) their own television image on a monitor, (2) a test pattern, or (3) a Western television program.[19] Self-esteem was lowest when the subjects saw their own faces. There were several attempts to duplicate these findings with a small mirror, but all failed.[20]

Before we discuss the remaining research on public self-awareness, a brief theoretical note is appropriate. In a group of men, if a traditionally masculine man is challenged by another man, the machismo aspect of masculinity demands that he be stalwart and courageous. And, when others are watching, both men and women are expected not to cheat or lie and to be helpful to others. These examples illustrate social standards and expectations. When observed, we are more likely to go along with group norms, to behave courteously, to be honest, and in general to fulfill role expectations. These comments are not novel, for the knowledge is commonplace. What, then, is the contribution of self-consciousness theory? The theory specifies that the above behaviors occur only when we are made aware of ourselves as social objects. The theory also specifies the two major conditions that lead to public self-awareness: (1) being observed by others or by technological substitutes for an audience, and (2) feedback from records, videotapes, and large three-sided clothing mirrors. I must add that being observed should lead to greater conformity to group expectations and social standards than receiving perceptual feedback. This theoretical note should make clear the relevance of the remaining research to self-consciousness theory.

When you are being observed, you are more likely to present yourself as a reasonable person, not given to undue stubborness. College students, given a visual task, were led to believe that two other "subjects" consistently disagreed with their perceptions.[21] During the task, some subjects saw their live image on a television monitor; the straight-ahead video picture of their own faces offered little perceptual feedback, but it did mean that they were being closely monitored. Compared with control subjects, those who saw their television images conformed more to the estimates of the other two "subjects." Contrast this conformity in public self-awareness (television monitor) to the resistance to coercion that occurs in private self-awareness (mirror).

In a complex experiment, auditory and visual feedback were combined; subjects heard their own voices and saw their own video pictures.[22] After performing a task, they could use either a private standard or a social standard as a basis of rewarding themselves. Compared with a control group, the public self-awareness group (1) rewarded themselves less and felt less satisfied with their performance when they surpassed their own standard but not the social standard, and (2) rewarded themselves more and felt more satisfied when they surpassed the social standard but not their own standard. The authors concluded: "Thus when attention to standards was held uniformly high for all participants, self-aware subjects relied more upon the social than personal standard when the two were discrepant." Why should attention to themselves cause people to focus on a social standard rather than a personal one? Because the attention was to the public aspects of self: how you are seen or heard by others. This attention to yourself as a social object should direct you to social standards rather than your own. On the other hand, if private self-awareness were induced by a small mirror, self-consciousness theory predicts that you would use your personal standards rather than social standards.

When others are watching, we tend to play our social roles more completely. One aspect of the masculine role is the ability to "take it." It follows that being observed should increase men's tolerance for pain. College men were administered painful electric shock under one of two conditions: (1) they were alone, or (2) they were being observed by others behind a one-way screen.[23] The ratings of pain were lower when they were observed than when they were alone. Thus public self-awareness makes men tolerate pain better. Would women react the same way? It is doubtful; they are not concerned with maintaining a tough-guy image. What would a mirror do? As an inducer of private self-awareness, a mirror should induce less tolerance for pain because it would intensify the negative affect.

CONCLUSIONS

The research reviewed in this chapter and the last one provides support for self-consciousness theory. Here is a short list of the positive findings:

1. Factor analysis yields two separate dispositions, one for private and one for public self-consciousness.

2. Individual differences in each disposition affect behavior in important ways and, though the two dispositions are correlated, the effect of each on behavior is different.

3. In the presence of affect or ongoing motivation, private self-awareness and private self-consciousness have an intensification or polarization effect.

4. In the absence of affect, private self-awareness and private self-consciousness—through better self-knowledge—enhance the accuracy or veridicality of behavior and strengthen resistance to coercion.

5. Public self-awareness increases conformity, and feedback-induced public self-awareness lowers self-esteem.

6. Public self-consciousness enhances susceptibility to public self-awareness manipulations,[24] and in social contexts it decreases the consistency or veridicality of behavior.

Though these facts offer considerable empirical support for self-consciousness theory, several cautions must be added. First, when a theory is first proposed, the early findings are usually strongly confirmatory. Subsequent research usually unearths some negative findings and mixed results, partly because theories inevitably have flaws and partly because research stretches theories beyond their reasonable limits. More will be said about the limits of self-consciousness theory in Chapter 6.

This chapter includes no research that does not bear directly on the theory. For example, in an experiment on cheating, the researchers used both a mirror and the subject's tape-recorded voice, a double manipulation that combines private self-awareness with public self-awareness.[25] This experiment is not relevant to self-consciousness theory, which maintains that the two kinds of self-awareness produce different effects. Cheating, however, is part of a larger issue: behavior in relation to standards, especially moral standards. Research on standards has been omitted because it so clearly demonstrates the difference between my approach to self-awareness and that of other psychologists. These other approaches—both complementary and opposing—will be discussed in the next chapter.

Notes

1. The major alternative theory, the self-awareness theory of Robert Wicklund, will be discussed in Chapter 6.
2. Gibbons, Scheier, Carver, and Hormuth (1978)
3. Gibbons, Scheier, Carver, and Hormuth (1978)
4. Carver (1977)
5. Carver (1975)
6. Buss (1961). This procedure was described in Chapter 4.
7. Gibbons (1978). This paper reports three separate experiments, but I shall describe only the first two. The third experiment was almost the same as the second one, and it yielded essentially the same findings; therefore, I omitted it from the text.
8. Pryor, Gibbons, Wicklund, Fazio, and Hood (1977)
9. The mystery deepens when we consider that there should have been a fair proportion of high private self-consciousness subjects in these samples. Private self-consciousness people know themselves quite well. The correlations between their self-reports and their behavior are uniformly high, as we saw in Chapter 4.

   There is a separate issue concerning why a self-report questionnaire does not induce private self-awareness. After all, subjects are being asked to answer questions about themselves. The fact is that self-reports do not turn on self-awareness. As to why they do not, I shall try to answer this question in the context of similar theoretical issues in Chapter 7.

10. Scheier (1976). This paper includes not only the present experiment on private self-awareness, but also the one on private self-consciousness reported in Chapter 4.

11. Scheier and Carver (1977).

12. Fenigstein (1979, p. 82)

13. Carver, Blaney, and Scheier (1979)

14. Epstein, Rosenthal, and Szphiler (1978)

15. Fenigstein (1979, p. 78)

16. Geller, Goodstein, Silver, and Steinberg (1974)

17. Metee, Fisher, and Taylor (1971)

18. Ickes, Wicklund, and Ferris (1973)

19. Ferris and Wicklund, reported in Wicklund (1975)

20. The failure to find that a small mirror systematically affects self-esteem may be one reason why the research, conducted at the University of Texas, was never published. Most journals are reluctant to publish negative findings.

21. Duval (1976)

22. Diener and Srull (1979)

23. Kleck, Vaughn, Cartwright-Smith, Vaughn, Colby, and Lanzetta (1976)

24. This fact refers to Fenigstein's (1979) research, in which he showed that high public self-conscious women reacted stronger to shunning than did lows.

25. Diener and Wallbom (1976)

OTHER APPROACHES 6

So far only my theory of self-consciousness has been discussed. But there are other approaches.[1] Since the turn of the century, sociologists have been interested in the social aspects of the self, a topic related to public self-consciousness. And within the last decade or so, several psychologists have theorized about the impact of attention directed toward oneself.

Of particular interest are speculations made almost 50 years ago by the psychiatrist Carl Jung.[2] His concept of *introversion* bears a vague resemblance to my concept of private self-consciousness. The introvert turns to the inner world of ideas, thoughts, and feelings. Introverts should be especially comfortable in the realms of philosophy, mathematics, and music composition. They like to plan, scheme, and imagine. They are likely to be aware of the private aspects of themselves. But Jung's concept and mine are demonstrably different. Introversion is a generalized tendency to focus attention inward and engage in mental

activities. Private self-consciousness is a more specific tendency to reflect only about oneself—not about all thoughts,
ideas, and feelings but only those that center on oneself.
Using your imagination to devise a short play is an example of introversion; daydreaming about yourself as a hero is
an example of private self-awareness. The crucial difference
is whether only the self is the focus of attention: in private
self-awareness, yes; in introversion, not necessarily.

Jung's concept of introversion is related to private self-
consciousness. The other approaches to be discussed here
either relate to public self-consciousness or deal with attention to an undifferentiated self. These approaches fall into
two distinct classes. The theories of sociologists take the
perspective of society and seek to explain how individuals
fit into the aggregates and institutions that make up society. The theories of psychologists take the perspective of a
single behaving individual and seek to discover the cognitive and affective processes that occur when attention is
directed toward oneself.

SOCIOLOGICAL PERSPECTIVES

The term *perspectives* is used here because sociologists
have offered theoretical propositions that are not especially
testable. They make no predictions and suggest no empirical checks on their theoretical statements. In fairness, it
must be said that their goal was not a precise, testable
theory. These sociological approaches are valuable in offering us perspectives we might otherwise overlook. They
suggest ways of regarding self-consciousness that might
eventually lead to testable hypotheses.

Looking-glass self

It all started with Cooley's idea that we develop a self on
the basis of the appraisals of others.[3] We use the reactions
of others as we might use a mirror: to determine what each

of us is like. This concept has been labeled *the looking-glass self.*

Cooley's idea was elaborated by Mead, who reasoned that awareness of self derives from taking the perspective of others. It does not derive merely from being in a social group, but rather from back-and-forth interaction with others. The individual develops a self by assuming a new perspective: "He becomes a self in so far as he can take the attitude of another and act toward himself as others act. It is the social process of influencing others in a social act and then taking the attitude of others aroused by the stimulus, and then reacting to this response, which constitutes a self."[4]

This emphasis on the social aspects of the self is similar to the way I approach public self-consciousness, but there are several differences. Cooley and Mead neglect the actions of socializing agents in the development of a social self, whereas I emphasize socialization (see Chapter 13). They view the self solely in social terms, whereas I also include a private component. Finally, they specify no individual differences, whereas I do.

Institution versus impulse

Sociologists tend to define the self in social terms: anchored in roles, status, and institutions. Turner suggests that this perspective is too narrow, that for some people the self is anchored in impulse: "To varying degrees, people accept as evidence of their real selves either feelings and actions with an *institutional* focus or ones they identify as strictly impulse."[5] He divides people into two groups, institutionals and impulsives, on the basis of their dominant orientation.

The goal of institutionals is to adhere to standards, to match their behavior to what is expected of them; a hypocrite is someone who asserts standards but fails to live up to them. The goal of impulsives is to do what they want to do, to match behavior to impulse; hypocrites adhere to standards when they would rather not.

For an institutional, the self is revealed by performance under pressure: honesty despite temptation, courage under fire. Such pressure requires full control of oneself, and self-control is an important standard for an institutional. For an impulsive, the true self is discovered only when he acts spontaneously, without planning or self-control; only when self-control is impaired by fatigue, or drugs, or a retreat from the demands of everyday life; only then can he reflect and discover his true self. Impulsives admire actors who always play themselves; institutionals admire actors who submerge their personalities to the particular role they are playing.

Finally, institutionals make commitments and so are oriented toward future goals and achievements. Impulsives want to be themselves in the here and now, without being stuck with future commitments.

These various distinctions between institutionals and impulsives are summarized in Table 6.1. Turner suggests that the past several decades have witnessed a shift away from an institutional emphasis and toward an impulsive emphasis. Perhaps. Of greater relevance to this book is the relationship between the institutional-impulsive dichotomy and the private–public dichotomy. Institutionals would try to conform to public standards, but they would also try to meet private standards and aspirations. An institutional would not only experience shame (public) but also guilt (private). Thus, with respect to self-consciousness, institutionals would not be especially private or public.

To the extent that impulsives are self-conscious at all, it would be private. If they reflect and attempt to discover "the true self," they are obviously focusing on the private aspects of themselves. But many impulsives do not reflect; they merely do whatever they feel like doing. This subgroup of impulsives is so preoccupied with "doing your own thing" that they do not have the time or inclination to introspect. Thus some impulsives should be high in private self-consciousness, some low; but none of them should be high in public self-consciousness. In brief, the

TABLE 6.1

Institutionals versus impulsives

	Institutionals	Impulsives
Goal	Match behavior to standards	Match behavior to impulse
Hypocrisy	Fail to live up to standards	Adhere to standards when you don't want to
Self is revealed	By achievement, when in full control	By reflection and discovery when control is lost
Time perspective	Future	Present

From Turner, 1976

institutional–impulsive dichotomy is distinct from the dichotomy between private and public self-consciousness.

Self-presentation

Erving Goffman comes close to stating his basic assumption in the title of his first book, *The Presentation of Self in Everyday Life*.[6] He assumes that in our dealing with others we are something like actors in a stage play: by our dress, gestures, and speech we present ourselves in particular roles that mesh with one another and keep the play moving forward. Presumably, we must discover how others interpret our behavior as well as find a correct interpretation of their behavior. We are continually checking the symbolic meaning of our acts against our self-images in order to know precisely how to present ourselves to others. Perhaps the best example of his overall approach is the concept of *demeanor:*

> that element of the individual's ceremonial behavior typically conveyed through deportment, dress, and bearing, which serves to express to those in his immediate presence that he is a person of certain desirable or undesirable qualities. The well-demeaned individual possesses the attributes popularly associated with 'character training' or 'socialization,' those being implanted when a neophyte of any kind is housebroken.[7]

As a sociologist, Goffman focuses mainly on the societal roles each of us plays and on how we maintain a smooth continuity of social give-and-take. Less concerned about individuals, he asks: "What minimal model of the actor is needed if we are to wind him up, stick him in amongst his fellows, and have an orderly traffic of behavior emerge?"[8] His answer is that we need to be concerned mainly about the desire to present ourselves in a manner consistent with the current role we are playing, with the current "face" we have put on. Failure of appropriate self-presentation usually causes embarrassment. Goffman's emphasis is not on the individual, but on individuals as actors in a play, the play being social interaction.

When do we become especially aware of ourselves as social objects? Goffman offers several examples: (1) when
others are scrutinizing us closely—for example, when a
woman walks past a group of construction workers; or (2)
when we are trying to maintain composure in the face of an
upsetting occasion—for instance, when sitting next to a
drunk on a bus or when having to take one's clothes off to
be examined by a physician. In brief, Goffman suggests that
we are all actors who look to others for cues, present ourselves in a variety of roles, and maintain proper demeanor;
failing in any of these things, we become acutely aware of
ourselves as social objects or even become embarrassed.[9]

PSYCHOLOGICAL APPROACHES

In contrast to sociologists, psychologists have emphasized
the inferred cognitive processes that presumably occur
when attention is self-directed. Of the four approaches to
be discussed, two lean toward the public aspects of the self,
and two lean toward the private aspects.

Self-monitoring

Goffman's concept of self-presentation assumes that we fill
the various roles of everyday life in a manner similar to the
way stage actors do. There may be variations among individuals in the extent to which they are aware of and regu-
late social affects and/or behavior. Emphasizing the processes underlying self-presentation, Mark Snyder developed
a self-report scale of self-monitoring. His description of
those who score high on the scale is also a definition of the
concept:

> The prototypic *high self-monitoring individual* is one who,
> out of concern for the situational and interpersonal appro-
> priateness of his or her social behavior, is particularly sensi-
> tive to the expression and self-presentation of relevant
> others in social situations and uses these cues for monitor-

ing (that is, regulating and controlling) his or her own verbal and nonverbal self-presentation.[10]

Using the Self-Monitoring scale, Snyder and others have discovered that high self-monitors attend more to social cues, read these cues better, are better at acting out roles, are seen by others as having better control of emotional expression, seem to be more aware of themselves and others as social objects, try to present themselves in ways they deem appropriate, and assume that others are likely to do the same.[11]

Snyder and others have compared his scale with a wide variety of self-report personality questionnaires and found that virtually none of them correlated with the Self-Monitoring scale. On the basis of these findings and the research mentioned earlier, Snyder concluded: "It has become increasingly clear that self-monitoring exists as a unique psychological construct that can be measured reliably and validly only by the Self-Monitoring scale."[12]

Though Snyder has never explicitly stated that his scale measures only a single component (self-monitoring), he has implicitly assumed so in the above conclusion and other writings. Is self-monitoring a unitary concept, or does it consist of several components? Translated into research terms, this question becomes: does a single factor underlie the Self-Monitoring scale, or are there several factors?

To answer this question, two colleagues and I administered the scale to a total of 1115 college women and men.[13] We computed correlations among all 25 items and then factor analyzed the correlation matrix. The women's and men's data yielded similar factors, so we combined their data. We found three factors,[14] which included 19 of the 25 items on the scale.

The Acting factor is shown in Table 6.2. Notice that four of the five items mention acting, entertaining, or spontaneous public speaking. The fifth item concerns the ability to lie, which obviously involves acting. Notice also that item 4 is reversed—that is, when answered as false or not

TABLE 6.2

Acting factor of the Self-Monitoring scale

1. I would probably make a good actor.
2. I have considered being an entertainer.
3. I can make improptu speeches even on topics about which I have almost no information.
4. I have never been good at games like charades or improvisational acting.
5. I can look anyone in the eye and tell a lie with a straight face (if for a right end).

applicable, it is scored in the direction of self-monitoring. There is another reversed item in the third ("Other-Directed") factor, and the entire "Extraversion" factor consists of reversed items.

The second factor, "Extraversion," is shown in Table 6.3. The reason for the quotation marks is that two items are never found on extraversion questionnaires. Nevertheless, these two items—"I am not particularly good at making other people like me" and "I have trouble changing my behavior to suit different people and different situations"— may well be associated with extraversion in the sense that

TABLE 6.3

"Extraversion" factor of the Self-Monitoring scale

1. I feel a bit awkward in company and do not show up quite as well as I should.
2. I am not particularly good at making other people like me.
3. In a group of people I am rarely the center of attention.
4. At a party I let others keep the jokes and stories going.
5. I have never been good at games like charades or improvisational acting.
6. I have trouble changing my behavior to suit different people and different situations.

extraverts tend to make people like them[15] and find it relatively easy to become noisy or quiet, depending on who is
present. In brief, *extraversion* seems to be a reasonable
label for these six items.

The third factor, "Other-Directed," is shown in Table
6.4. These items are a mixture of two tendencies: a minor
tendency to seek social cues from others and a major tendency to present oneself in a way that is expected or will be
liked. The only thing that appears to connect these dispa-
rate items is that one's orientation is toward others, hence
the term *other-directed.*

These three factors are relatively independent of one
another. Acting correlates moderately (.32) with Extraversion, but only weakly (.19) with Other-Directed. Extraversion and Other-Directed are essentially uncorrelated. These
low to moderate correlations suggest that it is a mistake to
combine these factors into a single score. Put another way,
the Self-Monitoring scale has three distinct components.

To discover more about these components, we correlated
the factors with a brief self-esteem questionnaire and with

TABLE 6.4

"Other-directed" factor of the Self-Monitoring scale

1. In different situations and with different people, I often act like very different persons.
2. When I am uncertain how to act in social situations, I look to the behavior of others for cues.
3. Even if I am not enjoying myself, I often pretend to be having a good time.
4. I'm not always the person I appear to be.
5. I guess I put on a show to impress or entertain people.
6. At parties and social gatherings, I do not attempt to do or say things that others will like.
7. I may deceive people by being friendly when I really dislike them.
8. I laugh more when I watch a comedy with others than when alone.
9. In order to get along and be liked, I tend to be what people expect me to be rather than anything else.

sociability and shyness scales that will be presented in
Chapter 11.[16] These correlations, together with those for
the full Self-Monitoring scale, are shown in Table 6.5. As a
start, let us examine the rows of this table. Sociability correlates modestly with the full scale, barely with Acting,
higher with Extraversion, and not at all with Other-
Directed. Shyness does not correlate with the full Self-
Monitoring scale. The reason is not hard to find: a negative
correlation for Extraversion cancels a positive correlation
for Other-Directed. Self-esteem correlates negatively with
Self-Monitoring. This is a surprise, for Snyder's description
of the high self-monitor implied the presence of at least
average self-esteem. Self-esteem also correlates negatively
for Other-Directed but positively for Extraversion.

Now let us examine the columns of Table 6.5. The
Self-Monitoring scale correlates positively with Sociability
and negatively with Self-esteem. None of the three factors
of the scale show the same pattern of relationships. The
three correlations for Acting are modest and reveal only a
slight tendency for those who score high to be sociable and
not shy. The correlations for Extraversion, on the contrary,
are moderate to strong. Extraverts, as defined by the six
questions on this factor, tend to be sociable, not shy, and
high in self-esteem. Finally, Other-Directed reveals an entirely different pattern of relationships: none for Sociabil-

TABLE 6.5

*Relationships between self-monitoring and three personality
variables for 1020 subjects*

	Full scale of SM	Acting	Factors Extraversion	Other-directed
Sociability	.20	.13	.36	.03
Shyness	−.10	−.23	−.56	.29
Self-esteem	−.17	0	.38	−.42

ity, a moderate one for Shyness, and a strong relationship with Self-esteem. Other-Directed people tend to be shy and low in self-esteem.

This detailed examination of the factors underlying the Self-Monitoring scale has revealed several facts that help us to interpret the concept of self-monitoring. The scale itself is a mixture of three distinct factors plus six items that do not appear on any factor. Snyder has found that actors score higher on the Self-Monitoring scale.[17] This difference, however, can be explained solely by the five items on the Acting factor. Would an actor deny the statements listed in Table 6.2? Would actors score higher on the remainder of the items on the Self-Monitoring scale? Probably not.

Concerning Extraversion, Snyder has suggested that, "Early in the course of becoming acquainted with another individual, high self-monitoring individuals adopt an active, initiatory, and directive approach to social interaction."[18] This description is close to that of an extravert, but notice that Extraversion is only one of three factors on the Self-Monitoring scale, comprising only six items.

Finally, consider the Other-Directed factor, which comes closest to Snyder's phrase "particularly vigilant and attentive to social comparison information that could guide their expressive self-presentation."[19] People who score high on this factor tend to be shy and low in self-esteem, so perhaps the reason they are seeking cues about how to behave with others is that they are insecure.

The problem posed by the presence of these three factors is that there are different ways to achieve a high score on the Self-Monitoring scale. One person might score high on Acting and Other-Directed, another on Acting and Extraversion, and a third on Extraversion and Other-Directed. The same score might represent quite different items being endorsed. As a result, the subjects labeled self-monitors in one study might be different from those labeled self-monitors in another study.

In one experiment, subjects were asked to act as though they were elated or depressed. Later they watched a videotape of people expressing emotion.[20] Self-monitors, by definition, are expected to simulate emotions easily and to perceive even subtle cues when others are behaving; in previous research they had displayed these tendencies. In this experiment, however, they did not. There was no relationship between self-monitoring and the ability to perceive the cues of emotional expressiveness. Concerning the sending of emotional cues to others, the experimenter concluded:

> Even though the SM scale contained items concerned with acting, impression management, and deception skills, individuals scoring high on the SM were not significantly more successful as senders than individuals scoring low on the SM.[21]

This quotation reflects the concern any researcher would have: why do the self-monitors not act the way they are supposed to? One reason may be the scale itself. Those selected in this experiment as high in self-monitoring may have endorsed items mainly from the Extraversion factor and the remaining group that did not appear in the three factors, but few of the items from the Acting and Other-Directed factors. Given that the Self-Monitoring scale is not homogeneous, we must expect the make-up of the high self-monitoring group to vary from one study to the next. In this light, discrepant results are not surprising.

In conclusion, there is no obvious way of squaring Snyder's concept of self-monitoring with the fact that his scale measures three different personality traits. The presence of an "Extraversion" factor also means that the Self-Monitoring scale is not unique, for extraversion has been represented on personality questionnaires for decades.

Critical as these comments are, they should not detract from the concept of self-monitoring or from the research done using the scale. The concept and the scale have been interesting and informative. There is a serious problem, however, in interpreting the results of research with the Self-Monitoring scale. This problem can be solved by using factor scores rather than the entire scale. Thus, researchers could define high self-monitors as those who scored high on all three factors. If this solution is not satisfactory, there is a more radical one: scrap the present scale and construct a Self-Monitoring questionnaire that meets the psychometric standards we require for all self-report personality measures.

Being observed

The concept of self-monitoring emphasizes how awareness of oneself as a social object can be used for self-presentation; this is the positive side of public self-awareness. The negative side of public self-awareness is seen in social anxiety, and it is this darker side that Michael Argyle emphasizes: "*Self-consciousness* is the extent to which a person is shy, easily embarrassed, and anxious when watched by other people."[22] He also comes close to the way I view public self-awareness: "Self-consciousness also has a purely cognitive component—the extent to which a person focuses his attention on how (he thinks) others see him, rather than on how he sees them."[23]

Viewed in this perspective, self-consciousness is the feeling of being observed. Are you the observer or the observed? Subjects were asked this question in several different social contexts.[24] Interviewees feel more observed than observing, which is only natural. Women feel more observed than men, and both genders feel more observed when with elders. There was also a laboratory situation in which the experimenter's accomplice looked more or looked less at subjects, but such differences in being looked at did not affect the subjects' feeling of being observed. Subjects who looked less at the accomplice, however, felt more observed.

Argyle suggests that there are individual differences in the degree to which people feel observed. Such individual differences are essentially what is measured by the Public

Self-Consciousness scale.[25] It follows that subjects who score high on the Public Self-Consciousness scale would report feeling more observed both when in the laboratory in a two-person situation and when asked about hypothetical two-person situations.

Clearly, Argyle's approach to self-consciousness is similar to my approach to public self-consciousness (he does not consider private self-consciousness). He includes social anxiety as part of self-consciousness, but I do not. I assume that, other things being equal, socially anxious people are likely to be high in public self-consciousness. Those high in public self-consciousness, however, are not necessarily socially anxious. They may use knowledge about themselves as social objects for the purpose of self-presentation—as in self-monitoring.

Self-schemata

How do we think about ourselves and organize the various memories that bear directly on the self? Markus answers this question with the concept of *self-schemata*, which are cognitions about the self, *"derived from past experience, that organize and guide the processing of self-related information contained in the individual's social experiences."*[26] As organized memories, self-schemata have two main properties.[27] First, they are generalizations about one's own behavior, especially enduring traits and attributes. Second, these schemata determine how future information about oneself is attended to, stored, and weighed on a scale of importance; as such, self-schemata tend to move the person to deny contradictory evidence and to push for consistency.

People who have self-schemata should find it easy to attend to and remember self-related information, predict their own future behavior, and resist evidence that conflicts with any self-schema. To test these predictions, Markus had college students rate themselves for independence or dependence on scales that ranged from 1 to 11.

Those who rated themselves at the high end of the scale were called *Independents;* those at the low end, *Dependents.* Both groups were assumed to have self-schemata about independence-dependence. Subjects who rated themselves in the middle (from 5 to 7) of the 11-point scale were assumed to have no self-schema. Thus Markus identified those who were extremely independent or extremely dependent as having a self-schema. She then demonstrated that these extreme subjects provided different self-descriptions and different predictions of future behavior from subjects in the middle of the scale.

If this description has been adequate, the flaw in Markus' study may be apparent: being extreme on a personality dimension (in this instance, independence–dependence) cannot be used to identify the presence of a self-schema. At the very least, such a definition confounds self-schema with extremeness: we do not know whether subjects behave the way they do because they have a self-schema or because they are extreme.

Whatever the confounds in Markus' research, her concept of self-schemata still might be valuable. It is a reasonable guess that people high in private self-consciousness tend to have many self-schemata simply because they think about themselves so often. If this assumption were true, it would offer a way out of the confound mentioned above. High private self-conscious people, having self-schemata, would be expected to attend to and remember self-related information better and to give it greater importance. If this prediction turns out to be correct, it will link private self-consciousness with self-schemata: one, the tendency to think about oneself; the other, the cognitive structure of such thoughts that results from prolonged attention to the private aspects of oneself.

Theory of self-focused attention

In 1972 Shelly Duval and Robert Wicklund published a book called *A Theory of Objective Self-Awareness.* The theory and research in this book have been a stimulant for many psychologists, including me. The term *objective* caused confusion and was later dropped. Now the theory is called *self-focused attention* or *self-awareness*. The theory was revised in 1975 and restated in 1979 by Wicklund. In light of these revisions by Wicklund and because of possible confusion between my theory (self-consciousness) and their theory (self-awareness), we shall refer to the other theory as Wicklund's theory.[28]

Wicklund's theory starts out by assuming that attention can be directed toward or away from the self. This assumption must be made by any theory involving the self. If attention were not at times self-directed, there would be nothing to explain, no need for a theory.

The major part of the theory can be summarized briefly. Self-focused attention causes an immediate self-appraisal. This self-evaluation reveals a discrepancy between one's current condition or behavior and one's standards or goals. The dominant response to this discrepancy is escape: leaving the immediate situation or directing attention elsewhere. If such escape is not possible, one tries to reduce the discrepancy, almost always by changing one's behavior.

This summary seems to be a correct statement of the theory, but to be doubly sure, following are appropriate quotations from Wicklund's latest theoretical statements:

> The initial reaction to objective self-awareness is postulated to be self-evaluation.[29]

> The core of the original idea has to do with "within-self discrepancies." A discrepancy consists of two points: on the one hand is the person's current condition, attainment, or status; on the other hand is a goal, rule or more generally, an "end point" for behavior. Everyone carries around such discrepancies, not always being aware of them.[30]

> Self-awareness, particularly when focused upon a sizeable discrepancy, will produce a desire to avoid the conditions that lead to continued self-focus.[30]

> If there is no escape from self-focusing stimuli, discrepancy reduction will then follow.[31]

> Without the possibility of avoidance, the primary route to reduction of the discomfort is to cope directly with the salient discrepancy.[30]

> Discrepancy reduction means an effort to bring the present condition of oneself into line with an aspiration or ideal—an "end point" for behavior. More generally, it means the attempt to make different parts of the self consistent with one another.[30]

> It is a reasonable assumption that all naturally occurring discrepancies are negative.[32]

The last quotation is important. Wicklund admits that positive discrepancies are possible; occasionally our behavior exceeds our standards or goals. But, as the quotation suggests, such positive discrepancies are rare. The theory can deal only with negative discrepancies, because only negative ones are aversive. When you exceed your goals, the discrepancy is not painful, and you would not avoid thinking about it. But behavior that falls below your goals or standards establishes an uncomfortable discrepancy.

Research. Wicklund's theory has spawned many experiments and has been used to explain a large body of data.[33] This section will cover only a few experiments, each being an example of a different kind of research.

In the self-esteem experiments mentioned in the last chapter, women who heard their own voice or saw their own image on a television monitor reported lower self-esteem than control subjects.[34,35] These findings fit Wicklund's theory. Self-awareness, induced by a voice recording or a television image, causes a discrepancy between what you are and your ideal; as a result, your self-esteem diminishes.

In another experiment reported in the last chapter, subjects' use of shock matched their attitudes towards shock only when they used electric shock in the presence of a mirror.[36] Again Wicklund's explanation is reasonable. The subjects' attitudes toward the use of electric shock can be construed as a standard or a rule. If their behavior (actual use of electric shock) deviated from their attitudes, this discrepancy would become acute only if they were made self-aware. Such self-awareness would cause them to reduce the discrepancy—in this case, by matching their behavior to their already-declared standard.

The last chapter discussed my alternative interpretation of these two experiments. There is no obvious reason for preferring my interpretation over Wicklund's, so how do the two theories differ? They differ in the predictions each would make if the self-awareness manipulations were altered. In my theory, a small mirror induces only private self-awareness. If a television camera were substituted in the electric shock experiment just mentioned, the public self-awareness would, I predict, cause all subjects to lower their shock levels.

In the self-esteem research, only public self-awareness manipulations (voice recording, television monitor) were used. If a private manipulation (a small mirror) were used, there should be no effect on self-esteem.[37] In both instances, electric shock and self-esteem, the substitute manipulations would make no difference to Wicklund. He does not distinguish between private and public manipulations; he mentions only self-awareness manipulations. Therefore, he would predict the same results regardless of how self-awareness was induced.

Now consider an experiment not previously mentioned.[38] Using the aggression machine procedure described in the last chapter, two colleagues and I studied the effect of self-awareness on aggression. Male subjects were given the opportunity to shock female "victims" in one of three conditions: in front of a small mirror, while being watched by a small audience, or in a control condition with neither a mirror nor an audience. Compared with a control condition, both the mirror and the audience caused a significant reduction in aggression.

For Wicklund, the explanation is clear-cut. When men aggress women, there is a standard: minimal aggression against women, a principle that all boys learn while growing up. Both a mirror and an audience induce self-awareness, which itself causes self-evaluation. In this self-evaluation, each subject compares his behavior with the appropriate standard. He then adjusts his behavior to meet the standard; in this instance, he reduces the level of aggression. Wicklund never uses an audience to induce self-awareness for reasons of his own,[39] but he uses the explanation stated above.

My explanation makes the same assumption about standards. In fact, in devising the experiment, my colleagues and I deliberately used male aggressors and female victims because of prior knowledge that this particular aggressor–victim combination inhibits aggression. It is assumed, however, that there are two kinds of standards: private and public. The mirror presumably induces private self-awareness and therefore a focus on the male subjects' personal principles about aggression against women. The audience presumably induces public self-awareness and therefore a focus on the standards of public behavior: how the subject should behave when others are watching. In this instance both the private and the public standards coincide, and both a mirror and an audience reduce the intensity of aggression.

Comparing Wicklund's explanation with mine, we discover that his is more parsimonious: he uses the same explanation for the effects of both mirror and audience, whereas I suggest two different explanations.[40] Why should anyone prefer mine to his? There are two reasons.

First, regardless of self-consciousness theory, there are good reasons for distinguishing between private scruples and public standards as determinants of behavior. The public standard for men aggressing against women is constant, and no normal man will aggress intensely against a woman when he is being observed. When he is not observed, however, his behavior will depend on whether he privately adheres to the principle that one does not hurt women. There is sufficient incidence of wife-beating in this country to suggest that some men, at least, have not had the usual socialization. They beat their wives in the privacy of their homes, not in public places. This example suggests that it is worthwhile to keep the private and public determinants of behavior separate, even though it is less parsimonious to do so in explaining the results of this particular experiment.[41]

Second, because standards, goals, rules, and end-points are not an intrinsic part of my theory but merely another determinant of behavior to be considered, behavior that involves no particular standards can be explained.[42] Consider the same aggression machine procedure but this time with men aggressing against men.[43] We know from previous research[44] that there are virtually no inhibitions on men aggressing against men. The "victims" (in reality, experimental accomplices) angered the male subjects, who were then allowed to aggress against their victims. One group aggressed in front of a mirror; the other had no mirror. Notice that though self-awareness was induced in the mirror condition, there was no appropriate standard, goal, or end-point. Wicklund therefore can make no prediction other than that of no difference between groups. On the other hand, my theory offers a direct prediction: private self-awareness induced by a mirror should intensify the affect of anger and thereby amplify the subject's aggression. As predicted, angered subjects in the mirror condition aggressed more.

When there is no clear standard, goal, rule, or end-point, how can there be a discrepancy? And if there is no discrepancy, how can Wicklund's theory apply? Concerning the anger-aggression experiment just mentioned, Wicklund's theory seems not to apply. And there may be others in this category, including several experiments mentioned in the last chapter.

In the elation-depression study, the presence of a mirror polarized these affects, elevating elation and deepening depression.[45] Where was the standard or end-point? What was the rule or goal that would be discrepant with the actual elation or depression? In the placebo experiment, a mirror caused subjects to resist suggestions that an inert drug would cause bodily changes.[46] What was the standard or rule here? If it was the suggested changes, self-awareness (induced by the mirror) should have resulted in more bodily symptoms reported, not fewer—less resistance to suggestions, not more. Examination of the placebo and the elation–depression research fails to reveal a standard or any other basis for inferring the negative discrepancy required by Wicklund's theory. The lesson is clear: in attempting to use Wicklund's theory, researchers must specify not only the behavior or current status of the subject but also the rule, goal, standard, or end-point required for a discrepancy to exist.[47]

Comparison of two theories. Wicklund's theory can be compressed into three assumptions:

1. Self-awareness causes self-evaluation.
2. This evaluation reveals a negative discrepancy between behavior and goals or standards.
3. To achieve self-consistency, behavior is altered to reduce the discrepancy.

These assumptions bear some similarity to part of the public aspect of my theory. Concerning perceptual feedback from three-sided clothing mirrors, photographs, videotapes, and tape recordings, one assumes that such information is compared to an inferred memory image. This comparison usually results in a negative discrepancy: we usually look or sound worse than our memory image of ourselves. Thus when perceptual feedback is used to induce self-awareness (in my view, public self-awareness), Wicklund's theory and mine make the same predictions.

But when public self-awareness is induced by an audience, camera, or microphone, the two theories differ. Wicklund specifies a negative discrepancy, whereas I predict inhibition and perhaps even the discomfort of embarrassment, shyness, or audience anxiety.

When self-awareness is induced by a small mirror or by

introspection, I insist that it is specifically private self-awareness, and here the two theories diverge even more. No self-evaluation or negative discrepancy is assumed. Instead, it is assumed that cue aspects are known better and affective-motivational aspects are intensified. As we saw earlier, however, the two theories may make similar predictions: when there are clear standards present. Thus when there are rules of morality or standards of performance, both theories predict that the behavior of self-aware subjects will adhere closer to the standard. But I distinguish between public standards and private standards—for instance, between not wanting to be observed cheating and not cheating even when you are alone.

In summary, my theory differs from Wicklund's in these ways:

1. Distinctions are made between private and public self-awareness, and the manipulations that induce each state are specified.

2. Except for the public self-awareness induced by perceptual feedback, no negative discrepancies between behavior and some standard (standards are not part of the theory) are assumed.

3. That people are strongly motivated to be self-consistent is not assumed.

4. It is assumed that there is a disposition to match each transient state: the traits of private and public self-consciousness.

Finally, let me correct any false impressions. Each theory has its own sphere of application; in some areas they overlap. Whatever the differences between the two theories, Wicklund's has been valuable in opening up a vital area of research. Nothing said here can detract from this achievement.

NOTES

1. The relevant theoretical views concern self-consciousness. Philosophers and others have speculated about the self for thousands of years. Consciousness has also been a popular topic. But we are concerned with mainly the hyphenated version of these two concepts: self-consciousness, rather than the self or consciousness alone.

2. Jung (1933)

3. Cooley (1902)

4. Mead (1934, p. 171)

5. Turner (1976, p. 990)

6. Goffman (1956)

7. Goffman (1967, p. 77)

8. Goffman (1967, p. 3)

9. Goffman's approach to embarrassment will be discussed in Chapter 8.

10. Snyder (in press, a)

11. Snyder (in press, a and b). These two chapters review the out-pouring of research with the Self-Monitoring scale, only a small part of which is mentioned here.

12. Snyder (in press, b)

13. Briggs, Cheek, and Buss (in press). We had subjects rate each item on a scale of 1 (extremely uncharacteristic) to 5 (extremely characteristic). This procedure yields reliable correlations among items, whereas Synder's true–false procedure does not.

14. The details of the factor analysis, including the factor loadings and other statistical matters can be found in Briggs, Cheek, and Buss (in press).

15. In fact, extraverts are liked better than introverts, and this preference is stated by both extraverts and introverts (Hendrick and Brown, 1971).

16. A typical self-esteem item on this scale is: "I am basically worthwhile." The sociability scale dealt only with the tendency to be with others. A typical item is: "I like to be with

others." The shyness scale concerned only feelings of tension and awkwardness in a social context. A typical item is: "I feel inhibited in social situations."

17. Snyder (1974)

18. Snyder (in press, b)

19. Snyder (in press, a)

20. Cunningham (1977)

21. Cunningham (1977, p. 580)

22. Argyle (1965, p. 360)

23. Argyle (1965, pp. 360–361)

24. Argyle and Williams (1969)

25. Fenigstein, Scheier, and Buss (1975). Refer to Chapter 4 for an account of the Public Self-Consciousness scale.

26. Markus (1977, p. 64)

27. Most readers may already know that *schemata* is the plural of *schema,* and that a schema is a scheme or concept or a grouping principle.

28. The references for the three works are: Duval and Wicklund (1972), Wicklund (1975), and Wicklund (in press). My use of the term *Wicklund's theory,* though justified by his revisions and continued association with the theory, in no way weakens the contributions of Shelly Duval. If my attempt to avoid confusion has in some small way denied him credit, I apologize.

29. Wicklund (1975, p. 238)

30. Wicklund (in press)

31. Wicklund (1975, p. 273)

32. Wicklund (1975, p. 238)

33. For reviews of research, see the 1972 book, the 1975 paper, and the paper in press.

34. Ickes, Wicklund, and Ferris (1973)

35. Ferris and Wicklund, in Wicklund (1975)

36. Carver (1975)

37. As mentioned in the last chapter, unpublished research at the University of Texas had already shown that a mirror has no systematic impact on self-esteem.

38. Scheier, Fenigstein, and Buss (1974)

39. Wicklund's reasons for not using audiences to induce self-awareness are stated in his 1975 paper.

40. Regardless of whether my interpretation is correct, an audience and a mirror did produce the same effect. For this reason, I did not discuss this experiment in the last chapter—that is, in itself it neither strengthens nor weakens self-consciousness theory.

41. Another, perhaps obvious, example of a difference between public and private standards concerns honesty. When others are watching, most people do not cheat, even if there is no penalty for getting caught. They simply do not wish to be observed committing a dishonest act. But when no one is watching, as in the honor system for examinations, those who refrain from cheating do so because of private scruples—internal standards concerning one's own intrinsic honesty.

42. I am referring mainly to the private part of self-consciousness theory. The public part does take into account both social norms and idealized self-images. More of this later.

43. Scheier (1976)

44. Buss (1966)

45. Scheier and Carver (1977)

46. Gibbons, Scheier, Carver, and Hormuth (1979)

47. Carver (in press) has amended Wicklund's theory by assuming that a standard is always present during self-awareness because of the way our cognitive processes work. This assumption, however, makes it extremely difficult to obtain evidence that opposes the theory.

LOOKING BACKWARD AND FORWARD

As the title suggests, this chapter is oriented in two directions: what we know already and implications for future research and understanding. What do we know and need to know about the transient states of private and public self-awareness, the traits of private and public self-consciousness, and the interaction between these states and traits?

After these questions are answered, we shall see how the private–public distinction can be used as a conceptual tool. Then the implications of this distinction for body awareness, self-disclosure, and other aspects of the self will be discussed. Finally, we shall see how public self-awareness is closely linked with social anxiety. The chapter closes with an introduction to four varieties of social anxiety, the topic of the next section of the book.

Limits of self-consciousness theory

When you refer to yourself with your name or the pronoun *I* or *me*, which aspect of the self is involved, private or public? There is really no way to decide. Such terms refer to you as a whole, not to any particular aspect of you. Suppose you take responsibility for an action, attributing causality to yourself; is this private or public? The best answer may be both. Generalized self-attributions and terms of self-reference fall under the heading of *the undifferentiated self.* The self as a whole is relevant, not specifically private or specifically public aspects. It follows that any manipulation, private or public, can cause a generalized, undifferentiated self-focus.

In one study, college students were asked to read a foreign language and fill in blanks whenever these appeared in the text.[1] It was suggested that pronouns would be appropriate for the blanks. Compared with a control condition, both a mirror and a television camera elicited more personal pronouns.

In another experiment, college women read hypothetical situations such as, "you're driving down the street about five miles over the speed limit when a little kid suddenly runs out chasing a ball and you hit him."[2] For each situation, the subjects stated to what degree they were causal. Compared with a control condition, a mirror caused more self-attributions. In follow-up research, people high in private self-consciousness made more self-attributions than lows; public self-consciousness had no effect.[3] Greater self-attribution is also caused by videotape feedback.[4] And in a three-person group, whether they are accepted or shunned, high public self-conscious women attribute more causality to themselves than do Lows.[5]

In brief, both private and public states and traits cause more self-reference and more attribution of causality to the self. What is the relevance of these findings to self-consciousness theory? None. The theory starts by distin-

guishing between private and public aspects of the self. If
these two cannot be distinguished—if the relevant behavior concerns only a generalized, undifferentiated self—
self-consciousness theory does not apply. All theories have
a range of application, beyond which they are not relevant.
Self-consciousness theory applies only to situations that
engage either the private self or the public self. And, as described in Chapters 2 and 3, each aspect of the self is defined in terms of its own domain, inferred processes, inducers, and disposition.

FACTS AND NEEDED FACTS

Transient states

There is good evidence that a small mirror induces private
self-awareness and that being observed and receiving feedback induce public self-awareness.[6] In virtually all previous
research, private and public manipulations were not compared in the same experiment.[7] What we need now is research that contrasts the effect of a mirror or instruction to
introspect with the effect of an audience, television camera, or feedback from a videotape or tape recorder. In addition to the knowledge accrued, such research would test
several hypotheses that derive from self-consciousness
theory, as follows.

1. A mirror has been found to increase resistance to
persuasion (increase reactance) and to increase resistance to
the suggestions that accompany an inert drug (placebo).[8]
My interpretation of these findings assumes that a mirror
induces private self-awareness; privately aware subjects
should know themselves better and therefore resist attempts at persuasion and false suggestions. But self-
consciousness theory states that publicly aware subjects do
not know their private selves better. It follows that such
public self-awareness manipulations as a television camera,

a videotape, or an audience would not induce subjects to resist persuasion or false suggestions.

2.   Tape recordings and videotapes of subjects have been found to diminish their self-esteem. These are manipulations that induce public self-awareness. Both manipulations involve perceptual feedback, which according to self-consciousness theory should diminish self-esteem. Two hypotheses follow from the theory. First, the presence of a television camera, with no video feedback, should result in little or no drop in self-esteem. Second, a private manipulation—mirror or instruction to introspect—should yield no change at all in self-esteem.

3.   One's tape-recorded voice and video image induce conformity to the views of a group. These effects are interpreted as being caused specifically by public self-awareness. Greater awareness of yourself as a public object should motivate you to move closer to the group's position. Two hypotheses follow from the theory. First, nonfeedback public manipulations, such as an audience or television camera, should also produce conformity. Second, private manipulations, such as a mirror or instructions to introspect, should not induce conformity; rather, they should lead to resistance to conforming.

4.   There is strong and consistent evidence that a small mirror induces private self-awareness, as suggested by self-consciousness theory. The theory also suggests that a large, three-sided clothing mirror induces public self-awareness. This hypothesis could easily be tested by comparing the effects of the two kinds of mirror in the same experiment.

Traits

There is clear and consistent evidence that both private and public self-consciousness are determinants of how we behave in situations involving self-awareness.[9] Despite a moderate correlation between these two traits, they affect behavior in different ways. When one trait is effective and

Highs behave different from Lows, the other trait is not effective. Or, when one trait affects behavior in a particular direction, the other affects behavior in the opposite direction. For example, in several studies high private self-conscious subjects made accurate self-reports of behavior, but Lows did not. At the same time, low public self-conscious subjects made accurate self-reports, but Highs did not. In brief, the distinction between private and public self-consciousness, which originated in factor analyses of the self-consciousness questionnaire, has been validated by laboratory research.[10]

What next? When two people are conversing or when one is interviewing the other, each person is both the observer and the observed.[11] Public self-consciousness should be especially relevant here. The prediction is clear-cut: In any two-person situation or conversational group, people high in public self-consciousness would feel more observed than would Lows.

Public self-consciousness also has implications for therapeutic techniques that occur in group settings. Some therapists have their clients take the role of different people. Other therapists carry this procedure to its endpoint and actually stage a brief play, a technique called psychodrama.[12] Two predictions can be made here. First, public self-conscious clients will find it hard to participate, and second, the therapy will diminish their public self-consciousness.

Another set of techniques for altering behavior, called consciousness-raising, is usually done in groups. In such groups, the participants are encouraged to ventilate their feelings of love, hate, anxiety, annoyance, jealousy, and so on. To the extent that the participants are encouraged to "get in touch with the inner self, the real you," their private self-consciousness will increase. But such groups also encourage their members to tell how they feel about each other, so that each person can discover how he or she is coming across to other people. This procedure surely increases public self-consciousness.

What about insight therapies, which range from the mild uncovering of feelings that occurs in Rogerian therapy to the near-total reconstruction of childhood that occurs in psychoanalysis? Such therapies continually direct clients' attention to their inner selves: thoughts, feelings, images, dreams, motives, and moods. This self-directed attention, repeated over months or even years, surely makes the clients more privately self-conscious. Clients who start insight therapies being low in private self-consciousness pose a special challenge to the therapist. Such Lows, by definition, tend not to reflect about their motives, feelings, or moods, and so would have difficulty in revealing their inner selves—not necessarily because of resistance but because of habitual inattention to such matters. Highs, of course, would be prime candidates for insight therapy.

We have some information about private and public self-consciousness. To discover more about each of these traits, we need to use both simultaneously in selecting subjects. Such selection would yield four groups of subjects: those who were high in both, those who were low in both, and two groups who were high in one and low in the other.

Consider first those who are high in both traits. Their being high in private self-consciousness means that they tend to be introspective. Knowing themselves well, they furnish accurate self-reports and react strongly to restriction of choice and pressure to change beliefs or attitudes. They focus on their affects and motives and so tend to react more intensely when they become emotional. But they are also high in public self-consciousness, which means that they are concerned about their appearance, manners, and style. Being concerned about others' opinions, they are easy to sway, tend to conform, and tend to make self-reports they think will please others, which renders their self-reports less accurate.[13] It would not be unfair to say that people high in both private and public self-consciousness are self-centered. Certainly they are more concerned about themselves than most of us.

People low in both private and public self-consciousness,

in contrast, rarely attend to themselves at all. Not knowing themselves, their self-reports tend to be inaccurate. Relatively unaware of their emotional states, they have duller emotional reactions. At the same time, they are unconcerned about themselves as social objects, so they are unlikely to worry about the immediate social consequences of their appearance or style of behaving. They may or may not conform; if they do, it is not because they are concerned about others' opinions, but because they do not know their own minds.

Now consider the other two contrasting groups, people high in one trait but low in the other. Those high in private and low in public self-consciousness tend to react strongly to emotional situations and to express their emotions because of their relative unconcern about themselves as social objects. Because they know themselves and because they worry less about the social impact of what they say, their self-reports are the most accurate of any of the four types of people being described here. If there is any group of people who would gladden the hearts of personality researchers, many of whom rely on self-reports, it is those who are high private, low public.

In contrast, the self-reports of those low in private and high in public self-consciousness are not worth much. Having reflected very little about themselves, they do not know themselves well. Being concerned about what others will think, they tend to distort their self-reports, behave as they think others expect them to behave, or both. As a result, there is little or no correlation between what they say about themselves and how they behave.

Though these four descriptions have been stated as though they were facts, they are best regarded as hypotheses. True, parts of these hypotheses have already been confirmed (see Chapter 4). In only one experiment, however, were subjects in all four groups studied in numbers large enough to yield reliable facts.[14] So the present status of the above descriptions is that of hypotheses or predictions that derive from self-consciousness theory.

States and traits

What is the relationship between the states of self-awareness and the traits of self-consciousness? In Chapter 3 it was suggested that private self-consciousness might not have any particular impact on the way people react to inducers of private self-awareness. There has been only one relevant experiment.[15] In a study mentioned several times before, men were angered by an experimental accomplice, who then received electric shock from the subjects he angered. The presence of a mirror resulted in more aggression (higher shock levels) in both high and low private self-conscious subjects. This study confirms my suggestion, but one experiment is obviously not a sufficient basis for drawing a firm conclusion.

It was also suggested that public self-consciousness would affect the way people react to inducers of public self-awareness. Again there is confirmation. High public self-conscious subjects reacted more intensely to shunning than did Lows.[16] And again one study is insufficient for making a generalization.

Why has there been so little research in which each kind of self-awareness and the matching self-consciousness are varied in the same experiment? There may be two reasons. First, self-consciousness theory is not well known, and most researchers are unaware of the private–public distinction; some researchers simply ignore it. Second, to vary both a state and trait simultaneously, a researcher needs four groups of subjects: an experimental and a control group for the state, and a high and a low group for the trait.

The burden of four groups may also explain why subjects are not divided by both kinds of traits into High–High, High–Low, Low–High, and Low–Low groups. Regardless of the burden, however, such research needs to be done. It may prove especially rewarding. In one case, it will tell us more about how each trait interacts with its matching state, a matter of keen interest in the last decade. In the other case, it will tell us more about people who are

selected on the basis of not one but two traits simultaneously. The use of more than a single personality dimension
to select people and study them must be regarded as an
important step forward in personality research.

THE SELF: PRIVATE AND PUBLIC

The private–public distinction is relevant to the way we
regard our bodies and what we are willing to disclose about
ourselves, identity, self-esteem, and morality. These matters properly belong under the heading of the *self.*

Body

Private aspects. Every day of our lives each of us is aware of
bodily sensations that cannot be experienced by anyone
else. Your stomach may gurgle, your scalp may itch, you
can feel muscles tense or relax. In a quiet room you can
hear your heart beat, feel your pulse pound, or even hear
your breath whistling through your trachea. These *neutral*
bodily sensations are in the minority; most sensations are
either pleasant or unpleasant. Few internal sensations are
positive; a moderately full stomach and sexual arousal are
pleasant for most of us. But we are often pleasantly aware
of skin sensations: warming cold hands, cooling the body
with a shower or a swim, or being caressed or massaged.
The most frequent bodily sensations are *negative:* muscle
cramps, aches in teeth, joints, head, or stomach, as well as
the familiar unpleasantness of a hangover.

Also private is the reaction each of us has to drugs and
similar kinds of stimulation. Some people are especially
sensitive to drugs—for example, the same amount of al-
cohol that leaves one man in reasonable control of his
faculties may be enough to stagger another. People also
vary considerably in their physical response to sexual
stimulation; some are easily aroused, others not. And our
autonomic nervous systems are differentially reactive,
especially the sympathetic division.[17] A threatening

stimulus may activate sweating and heart pounding in one person while leaving another relatively tranquil.

Finally, we regard the private aspects of our bodies in different ways. Some people regard their bodies as weak and not dependable—unable to fight off disease or recover quickly from lack of sleep. Others have a positive evaluation of their bodies: as strong and as a part of oneself that can be relied on momentarily in stress and in the long run in fighting off disease and recovering from fatigue. These various categories of the private aspects of the body— awareness, reactivity, and evaluation—are summarized in Table 7.1.

Public aspects. As a social stimulus, the body's most obvious and important characteristic is its *appearance.* Obese and extremely thin people tend to conceal their bodies; those with beautiful bodies exhibit them. Some people are virtual neuters in terms of sexual attractiveness; others are sexually stimulating. And psychological research has confirmed that attractive children and adults are liked more and treated better.[18]

TABLE 7.1

Private aspects of the body

Category	Examples
Awareness	
Neutral	Itching, stomach gurgling
Positive	Pleasantly full stomach
Negative	Pain, muscle cramps
Reactivity	
To drugs	Easily activated, quieted
To sexual stimulation	Easily aroused
Autonomic nervous system	Easily distressed, frightened
Evaluation	Strong–weak
	Dependable, not dependable

In concentrating on the appearance of the body as a social object, we have neglected how the body *functions* as a moving object. Some of us are clumsy, awkward, and uncoordinated; others of us are lithe, graceful, and coordinated. Some people blunder their way through life like a bull in a china shop; others are as deft as a fawn. Though the body's appearance is a more potent stimulus than its movements, we should not underestimate grace and coordination (or lack of these) as an important determinant of the body as a social object.

Bodily *modesty* is learned during the process of socialization. Boys and girls discover which parts of their bodies they can expose to whom. They also learn which parts of their bodies can be touched by their mothers, fathers, and friends of either gender.[19] By the time we reach maturity, all of us know that certain parts of the body are not available for inspection by most others and know that it would be even worse if these parts were touched by others.

Finally, there is the issue of *self-control* in public. Some people blush easily, an embarrassment that continually worries them. Others sweat easily, and they are concerned about their shining faces or moist palms. A minority of children and a few, rare adults have trouble controlling their bladders, which causes a nagging fear of wetting themselves in the presence of others. Some girls, for instance, cannot laugh excessively without risk of a relaxation of the bladder sphincter.

In brief, there are four different aspects of the body as a social stimulus. In addition to the most obvious one, *appearance*, there are *bodily movement, modesty,* and *self-control.* These public aspects stand in sharp contrast to the private aspects of the body: awareness of inner sensations, reactivity to drugs, sexual stimulation and threatening stimuli, and evaluation of the body's strength and dependability.[20]

Individual differences. Seymour Fisher, who has investigated various aspects of the body, stands almost alone as a student of individual differences in body awareness.[21] Of particular relevance here is his *body prominence* measure. Subjects are asked to list 20 things they are aware of at the moment. Both direct and indirect references to the body are scored: not only "My skin tingles" and "I am cold" but also "I can see my reflection in the glass case" and "My dress is green." Clothes are included as indicating body awareness because Fisher believes they are closely linked to the body. Surely it would be of interest to divide answers about the body into two distinct categories, one private and the other public.

In light of the novelty of the private–public distinction, we should not be surprised to discover that no prior measure of body awareness has used it. An obvious next step would be to develop a measure of body awareness specifically designed to distinguish between the private and public components of the body. This is precisely what two colleagues and I attempted.[22]

We made up a set of items that, taken at face value, seemed to tap into awareness of either private or public aspects of the body. The items were administered to several samples of college men and women. In this preliminary research, we found few gender differences, so we combined the data for men and women. As expected, the factor analysis yielded two factors.

The private factor is shown in Table 7.2.[22] Notice that some of the items refer to awareness of specific bodily reactions, such as a dry mouth, heart beating, or stomach con-

TABLE 7.2

Private body awareness factor

1. I am sensitive to internal bodily tensions.
2. I know immediately when my mouth or throat gets dry.
3. I can often feel my heart beating.
4. I am quick to sense the hunger contractions of my stomach.
5. I'm very aware of changes in my body temperature.

tractions. Other items refer to awareness of more generalized body changes, such as tensions or changes in temperature. But whether specific or general, the internal stimuli are entirely private.

The public factor is shown in Table 7.3. Again there are two subgroups of items. One set refers to grooming: appearance of hands, skin, and hair. The other set refers to enduring features of one's face or body: worst or best feature, waist size, body build, and posture. But whether the awareness concerns grooming or more enduring features, all these stimuli are open to observation by others. In brief, the private–public distinction needs to be taken into account when we study body awareness.

Disclosure

In everyday conversations we talk not only about politics, sports, and violence but also about ourselves. We ordinarily reserve the more intimate details about ourselves for our closest friends or spouses, though occasionally we reveal secrets about ourselves to total strangers on an airplane or train, especially to people we shall never see again. In the past decade, starting with Sidney Jourard, psychologists have become intensely curious about disclosure.

TABLE 7.3

Public body awareness factor

1. When with others, I want my hands to be clean and look nice.
2. It's important for me that my skin looks nice—for example, has no blemishes.
3. I'm very aware of my best and worst facial features.
4. I like to make sure that my hair looks right.
5. I think a lot about my body build.
6. I'm concerned about my posture.
7. I get concerned as soon as my waist gets bigger.

Jourard compiled lists of self-disclosure topics and scaled them for intimacy.[23] One list contains such items as the town you were born in, present physical maladies, attendance at church, and your father's occupation. Another list includes your personal religious views, what you are most sensitive about, your most frequent daydream, the feelings you have the most trouble controlling, and your strongest ambition. The first set of topics concerns behaviors or events that can be observed by anyone who knows you: the facts that are available to any diligent searcher but are not necessarily known to any present listener. I label them *public* for the same reason that I call any other aspect of the self public: they are open to observation.

The second set of topics, called *private,* consists of feelings, private concerns, secret ambitions, and daydreams. Unobservable by anyone else, they will remain private unless you divulge them.[24] The topics I call public, on the other hand, can be discovered by anyone with the time and energy. In brief, private topics are not known to others because they are intrinsically private. Public topics may be unknown at the moment, not because they are unavailable, but because they are presently inaccessible.

This division of topics about oneself has several implications for disclosure. For instance, which topics are more intimate? Presumably, private topics are more intimate because they are more central to oneself and therefore more revealing. If our private feelings and thoughts, secret ambitions, and especially our present "crush" were revealed to another person, their exposure would cause embarrassment. Worse still, accidental self-disclosure of an especially intimate topic to a stranger or casual acquaintance might cause embarrassment to both speaker and listener. We share the most private aspects of ourselves only to those close to us: husband or wife, understanding parent, or intimate friend. If another person disclosed the private matters that we would reveal to only our closest confidants, we would be embarrassed. This would be an instance of "leakage," which is a prime cause of embarrassment in adolescents and in some adults.

If public topics are less intimate, why are they not disclosed? In general, public topics are more likely to be revealed than private topics. There are, however, public behaviors and events that would cause shame if they were known: sexual acts regarded as immoral or perverse; previous failures, such as having flunked out of college or being fired from a job; having been in jail or on probation for commission of a crime; a blot on the family history, such as insanity or mental retardation; the circumstances of one's birth, such as having been adopted or born out of wedlock; and so on. These are topics that would tend to cause shame if other people were informed. Therefore they are revealed only to those we trust—people who can keep a secret.

These differences between private and public topics are summarized in Table 7.4. If you reveal a private topic to someone, this person now knows things about you that you have uttered to no one else or perhaps to only a select few. Such knowledge is bound to enhance intimacy and cement the social bond. If a private matter about you were revealed by another person, your initial reaction would be embarrassment. Such disclosure would surely weaken any friendship or stop one from developing.

Self-disclosure of a public topic would tend to increase your trust in the other person, assuming he or she did not tell your secret to anyone else. There are professional

TABLE 7.4

The results of disclosure

Topic	By self	By others
Private	More intimacy	Embarrassment
Public	More trust	Shame

people who must be trusted if they are to serve us: physicians, lawyers, clergymen, and therapists. If another person were to reveal a public topic about you, you would likely be ashamed. The assumption is that any public topic that you have kept secret must be something you are ashamed of. And you would distrust and be angry with anyone who disclosed your shameful secret.

In summary, private topics are assumed to be more intimate (more revealing of oneself) than are public topics. Disclosure of private topics has quite different consequences than does disclosure of public topics. Finally, it is a reasonable hypothesis that, other things equal, people high in private self-consciousness tend to disclose more about themselves (private topics) simply because they have more to disclose.

Identity

The answer to the question "Who are you?" involves identity. The most widely known theoretical approach to identity is Erik Erikson's,[25] but all approaches share a dual definition. One part of identity is *private:* that which is me, mine, and personally, uniquely mine. This is a sense of having idiosyncratic feelings and sensations that cannot be experienced by anyone else. It is a sense of having a unique combination of dispositions, fantasies, past experiences, and plans for the future. And it is a sense of having a particular body, with its unique proportions, scars, and perhaps some parts that are kept hidden from others.

The other aspect of identity is *public:* roles, relationships, and membership in groups. This public identity, by definition, is shared with others. Roles that tend to be crucial in identity are parent, child, husband or wife, and lover. Vocation is a basic part of identity, and one's professional identity—psychologist, for example—tends to be important. Group membership makes its claims on each of us. It may be a local club or charity, a political party, a state or nationality, or a religious or ethnic group.

People vary in the make-up of their identity. For some, the private aspects predominate; for others, the public aspects. I suggest that the balance is determined by self-consciousness. Other things equal, private self-conscious people emphasize the individual aspects of their identity. They attend more to the unshared idiosyncracies of their particular experiences, fantasies, and feelings. Their identity is based largely on *individuality*, a sense of separateness from other living things. This emphasis on uniqueness derives from the focus of their self-directed attention: on the private aspects of self. Loss or lack of identity is felt as being commonplace and deindividuated.

Public self-conscious people tend to identify with groups. The size of the group varies from the dyad of husband–wife to the millions of national, religious, or ethnic identity. They see themselves as social beings, sharing attitudes and affiliations with others. There is deep satisfaction in a feeling of belonging to a large, powerful group, one with continuity beyond one's own life cycle. It is rewarding to be recognized by others as being an American, a member of a sorority, or a physician. These public identities, important for most people, are especially important for people high in public self-consciousness. If they are also low in private self-consciousness, virtually most of their identity will be social. Who they are will be defined mainly by their social roles, their group affiliations, and how they appear to others. Such an identity is strongly supported by a feeling of belonging and a sense of being recognized as a member of groups. Loss of identity is felt as being alienated from others. In a sense, their identity requires them to be identified by others and with others.

Self-esteem

Of the many sources of self-esteem, only one is relevant here: performance evaluated against a standard. Standards may be private or public. A golfer may play alone and try for a lower score than she has ever achieved. A dieter may try to slim down to a weight he finds desirable. These private norms concern only one person, and how well he or she meets them affects self-esteem.

Most standards are of course public: winning a tennis match, getting good grades, attaining a professional degree, winning an election, and so on. Success or failure is seen by others, and self-esteem is elevated or depressed by literal or metaphorical cheers or boos.

It appears that the standards most relevant to self-esteem are determined by the focus of self-consciousness. Private self-conscious people tend to establish their own norms and consider them more than group norms. They must please themselves more than the multitude. For example, a woman might win a tennis match but deprecate her lack of skill in doing so; this would indicate a personal standard higher than the public standard. The point is that people high in private self-consciousness tend to march to their own drummer. They may criticize their own performance when it is successful in public or praise themselves when others regard their work as a failure.

People high in public self-consciousness continually reflect the group consensus. Public norms are their norms, and success and failure are defined only in terms of group standards. As their identity is largely affiliative, so their performance-based self-esteem derives mainly from success in meeting group (public) standards.

Morality

Morality may be based on either private or public standards. Private standards involve moral codes that have been "internalized" in the sense that they are regarded as one's own. Violations of such moral principles lead to a feeling of guilt. No one else need know that an evil or sinful act has occurred. Self-knowledge is sufficient to induce guilt. Violation of public codes of morality causes shame. The crucial element is an audience: being seen or heard. The most common cause of shame is to be caught publicly in a private act.

The relevance of private and public self-consciousness

should be obvious. Private self-conscious people are more likely to suffer from guilt. When moral issues arise, they focus attention on a private code of morality, on principles they alone apply to themselves. Their concern is not with exposure to prying eyes but with violating their own internal standards. The group does not judge them; private self-conscious people tend to judge themselves.

People high in public self-consciousness also judge themselves but only as social objects. Have they failed in front of an audience? Has their cowardice been revealed? Have they been caught in adultery? The common element is public exposure. As people with a strong sense of themselves as social objects, those who are publicly self-conscious must be painfully aware of all public indiscretions. That is, they are especially susceptible to shame.[26]

The various ways that the private–public distinction applies to the self are summarized in Table 7.5.

SOCIAL ANXIETY

The link that connects self-consciousness with social anxiety is public self-awareness. Presumably, when people are socially anxious, they are in a state of acute public self-awareness. There are several kinds of social anxiety, each with its particular observable behavior, feelings, causes, and consequences. But regardless of how they differ, all the social anxieties have in common an acute awareness of oneself as a social object.

Social anxiety may be divided into four varieties. *Embarrassment* is marked by blushing, giggling or nervous laughter, and a feeling of foolishness. *Shame* is characterized by feelings of self-disgust and self-abasement, as well as looking dumbstruck and mildly depressed. *Audience anxiety* is revealed by the presence of tension, disorganization, worry, and a feeling of panic. *Shyness* is inferred from an inhibition of expected social behavior, together with feelings of tension and awkwardness.

TABLE 7.5

The private–public distinction applied to the self

	Private	Public
Body	Inner sensations	Appearance or coordination
Self-disclosure	Of thoughts, of feelings, ambitions	Behavior or events not currently known
Self-knowledge	Good in Highs; poor in Lows	Better in Lows than in Highs
Identity	Individual	Social
Self-esteem	Personal standards (self-reward)	Social standards (reward by others)
Morality	Guilt	Shame

These sketchy descriptions are meant only to introduce each of these negative social affects. The next section of the book contains a chapter on each of them. In each instance, the emotional reaction, causes and consequences, and theoretical approaches will be discussed. Finally, an integrative chapter will compare and contrast the four social anxieties.

NOTES

1. Davis and Brock (1975)

2. Duval and Wicklund (1973)

3. D. Buss and Scheier (1976)

4. Liebling (1975)

5. Fenigstein (1979)

6. The evidence was reviewed in Chapter 5. In addition to the previously mentioned research on public self-awareness, there are also studies of how small groups and audiences can induce embarrassment, shyness, and audience anxiety—all of which

contain elements of public self-awareness. This research will be reviewed in the chapters on social anxiety.

7. The exception is the experiment in which men aggressed women (Scheier, Fenigstein, and Buss, 1974). In that experiment, private and public standards had the same effect on behavior for reasons discussed in Chapter 6.

8. The facts mentioned in this section were reviewed in Chapter 5, so I shall not repeat the reference citations made there.

9. This evidence, reviewed in Chapter 4, need not be repeated here.

10. The private–public distinction has been accepted for self-consciousness, and researchers are using the Private Self-Consciousness scale as a measure of the disposition to be self-aware. But there has been no general acceptance of the private–public distinction for self-awareness—a reluctance that is puzzling when we consider that the distinction is the same for both the transient state and the enduring trait.

11. Argyle and Williams (1969)

12. Moreno (1946)

13. The self-reports of public self-conscious people tend to be less accurate mainly when they are asked about matters that may be viewed positively or negatively by others. But when asked about neutral topics, such as how sociable they are, people high in public self-consciousness are expected to be as accurate in their self-reports as Lows.

14. Scheier (1978)

15. Scheier (1976)

16. Fenigstein (1979)

17. Mandler, Mandler, and Uviller (1958)

18. Berscheid and Walster (1969)

19. Jourard (1966)

20. Several bodily reactions can be both private and public. When a man's penis swells, he is immediately aware of the erection. But this private event may also be public if, for example, the man is in a shower or locker room with other men. Or, when the man is fully dressed, it can be even more embarrassing if the tell-tale bulge in the man's pants can be seen by any women who are present.

In the late states of pregnancy, a woman experiences a variety of internal events, including the movements of her fetus. In addition to these private aspects of pregnancy, there is of course the obvious abdominal bulge that announces the pregnancy to anyone with eyes. Pregnant women react differently to their swollen bellies. Some are proud of their fertility and imminent motherhood; others are distressed at their bloated figures and try to conceal the tell-tale bulge as long as possible; failing that, they may remove themselves, as far as possible, from public view.

And there is menstruation, which, until only a few decades ago, had the stigma of uncleanliness. Even in today's relatively enlightened social climate, menstruation is an event to be concealed from others, its discovery often an embarrassment. And these public aspects of menstruation contrast sharply with the private sensations of bleeding and (in some women) abdominal cramps.

21. Fisher (1970, 1974)

22. Miller, Murphy, and Buss (1979).See this paper for details of the factor analysis.

23. Jourard (1971). See Cozby (1973) for a review of literature.

24. As this book was going to press, I discovered a paper that used a concept similar to my concept of disclosure of private events. The authors called it *inwardness*, which they defined as "...to what extent is the speaker disclosing personal experience as opposed to impersonal observations." (Carpenter and Freese, 1979, p. 79).

25. Erikson (1963)

26. Shame and the distinction between it and guilt will be discussed further in Chapter 9.

EMBARRASSMENT

This chapter and the next three in this section on social anxiety are organized in the same way. Each starts with a description of the behavior under scrutiny. These various social anxieties share a problem common to all emotion: there is an *expressive component* that can be observed by others and a *feeling component* that is known only to the experiencing person. Emotions tend to be expressed freely early in childhood, but children learn to suppress and conceal their fear, rage, and social anxiety. When older children and adults inhibit the expression of their emotions, scientific observers are faced with the serious problems of identifying whether an emotional reaction is occurring and, if so, which one. The presence of a particular emotional reaction can be determined in three ways. First, we can observe cues that are too small or subtle to be suppressed by the person having the emotion. Second, we can infer the emotion on the basis of the immediately preceding stimulus or situation and the subsequent behavior of the person. Third, we can simply ask the person whether he or she is experiencing the emotion. Each of these solutions has its faults, but taken together they provide an accurate estimate of the emotion. Fortunately, there are few attempts to conceal social anxiety, and in some instances—blushing, for example—none of us can suppress or inhibit expression of the affect.

In each of these four chapters, the description of the emotional reaction is followed by an account of its *immediate causes.* These causes consist of stimuli that are part of social contexts, the actions of other people, and the actions of the experiencing person himself.

The next section of each chapter consists of *enduring causes:* the physical attributes, attitudes, beliefs, and traits that predispose the person to become socially anxious. Next, there are the *consequences* of social anxiety, both for immediate and long-term behavior. Each chapter closes with the *theoretical approaches* that others have offered for the social anxiety being examined.

In organizing the available facts into the orderly sequence just described, I have added my own hypotheses to fill in gaps in knowledge. In several instances, my hypotheses have led to original research, presented here for the first time. My suggestions may have resulted in a neater picture of the state of our knowledge than really exists. We possess little scientific knowledge about the various social anxieties, and much of what is contained in these chapters consists of hypotheses that must be subjected to empirical test. Finally, there is offered a developmental account of how the social anxieties originate. Because this theory is broader and more speculative than the narrower, more easily testable hypotheses of these four chapters, it is placed in a separate chapter: the final, speculative chapter of the book.

THE REACTION

The hallmark of embarrassment is blushing. The cheeks become pink or even red, and some people blush from scalp to neck. The only other observable features specific to embarrassment are a silly smile (often called an "embarrassed smile") and a nervous giggle or laugh. Accompanying these facial expressions is a feeling of silliness. Embarrassed people report that they feel foolish, ridiculous, and uncovered (in the sense that something private has been made public).

In addition to these features specific to embarrassment, there are features shared by other social anxieties. There is an acute feeling of being observed, an awareness of oneself as a social object. Gaze aversion is also common. Embarrassed people tend to break off eye contact, look down or to the side, or even cover their eyes or entire face. Acute public self-awareness, gaze aversion, and covering of the face or eyes occur in several of the social anxieties, so they cannot be used to identify embarrassment.

Embarrassment can be identified only by the features specific to it. Mentioned earlier, they are: blushing and a silly smile (observed) and a feeling of foolishness (reported). Blushing is the surest sign of embarrassment, but what if someone blushes and at the same time denies being embarrassed? We know that some people, defensive about their own emotions, tend to deny feelings they actually experience. Some people, especially those low in private self-consciousness, are poor in perceiving their moods, feelings, and inner states. The answer, then, is to assume that blushing means embarrassment even when the person refuses to admit it. The same answer applies to a silly smile or a giggle: it usually signals embarrassment.

Another problem—no blushing but a self-report of embarrassment—is more complex. Why would a person who is not blushing report being embarrassed? One reason may be confusion about how to label inner experience. The person may be fearful, shy, ashamed, or merely publicly self-aware, but he declares that he is embarrassed. Such mislabeling occurs because our inner states are diffuse, our verbal labels are imprecise, and our judgment about such matters is often clouded by arousal. Another possibility is misattribution. If the situation usually leads to embarrassment, the person may attribute embarrassment to himself solely because of the context. Inferring inner feelings from the context has been demonstrated many times.[1]

Of course, the absence of blushing may be more apparent than real. Some people turn beet red when they blush; others merely show a little pink. The blush of dark-skinned people is harder to discern because it is more subtle. Thus, when embarrassment is mild, the blush of some people may be so slight as to be missed. This line of reason may appear excusatory—that is, it appears to assert that blushing always occurs in embarrassment even when the blushing is not apparent. There is, however, a way to resolve the issue: use facial temperature as an objective measure of blushing. When a person blushes, the influx of blood raises the skin temperature of his or her face as much as a degree Fahrenheit. Let us use as subjects only people whose skin, because of texture or color, reveals little color change. We would embarrass them in one of several possible ways (to be discussed shortly). Such research would tell us if, in some people at least, skin temperature rises without a blush being detected by others.[2]

Blushing

The most complete essay on blushing was written by Charles Darwin more than a century ago in his book *The Expression of Emotions in Man and Animals.* He began by saying, "Blushing is the most peculiar and the most human of all expressions. Monkeys redden from passion, but it would require an overwhelming amount of evidence to make us believe that any animal could blush."[3] Using his own and others' observations, Darwin also concluded that blushing is universal. It is easier to discern in people with light skin, but even very dark-skinned people blush: "Several trustworthy observers have assured me that they have seen on the faces of Negroes appearance resembling a blush, under circumstances which would have excited one in us, though their skins were of an ebony-black tint. Some describe it as blushing brown, but most say that the blackness becomes more intense."[4]

Human infants do not blush; like monkeys, their faces redden with rage. Darwin reported blushing in children between two and three years of age. There are no developmental norms for blushing (surely a worthwhile research project), but a reasonable guess is that children start to blush during the third year of life. According to Darwin, the blind blush, but the severely mentally retarded do not.

Blushing is limited in most people to the face, neck, and ears. Darwin mentioned rare cases whose blush extended down to the chest, but blushing is normally restricted to the head. The redness starts in one area on each side of the face and spreads to adjacent areas as the color deepens. He suggested that the particular pattern of reddening is inherited, which seems reasonable in light of the inheritance of other aspects of physiology and skin, but there is no empirical evidence for this conclusion.

Knowing little more about blushing today than Charles Darwin knew more than 100 years ago, we are left to wonder why we blush. Consider the available facts. Only humans blush, and virtually all humans do so. Other animals have the physiological capacity—a bed of capillaries close to the skin, which can become engorged with blood—but they redden only when they are enraged or sexually aroused. Infants and idiots surely have the physiological mechanism, but they do not blush. What do older children and adults possess—lacking in animals, infants, and the severely mentally retarded—that is required for blushing to occur? I believe it is public self-awareness. Only when children become aware of themselves as social objects are they capable of being embarrassed and therefore of blushing. Animals, infants, and the severely mentally retarded are not aware of themselves as social objects; they lack a cognitive self and therefore do not blush. If this conjecture is true, blushing should be delayed in children who are moderately mentally retarded.

Regardless of the truth of this hypothesis, we are left without an ultimate explanation for the presence of blushing in humans. Clearly, the reddening of the face is a signal to others that the blusher is embarrassed, but why is it necessary for others to know? What social need is satisfied by having others become aware of your embarrassment? There are no good answers to these questions. If there is no adaptive function for blushing, why is it species-wide and restricted to humans? The puzzle persists.

Physiology

A search of the literature yielded only one laboratory study on the physiology of embarrassment.[5] The subjects, 120 college men, were divided into two groups, one fear and one embarrassment. Members of the fear group were told that they would receive intense painful shocks. The embarrassment group was read these instructions:

> What I will ask you to do is very simple. Here are a number of objects, namely a baby bottle, a breast shield, a pacifier, and a couple of nipples. In a few minutes I'd like you to take each of these objects into your mouth and suck on it for a few seconds. This will allow us to gauge your physiological sensitivity to such oral stimulation.[6]

The subjects waited for two minutes while physiological measures were recorded, and then the experiment ended. No one was actually shocked or required to suck on objects.

The two groups, embarrassment and fear, did not differ in their self-reports along the dimensions of calm–tense, pleasant–unpleasant, and embarrassed–not embarrassed. This failure of subjects to distinguish between the internal feelings of fear and those of embarrassment confirms the point made earlier: subjective feelings are diffuse and difficult to specify.

The two main physiological measures were skin conductance and heart rate. The level of skin conductance rose higher in fear than in embarrassment, suggesting that the fear subjects were more aroused. Heart rate changed little in fear but dropped significantly in embarrassment.

We know that in fear the sympathetic division of the autonomic nervous system stimulates widespread bodily changes in preparation for massive action. The parasympathetic division, in contrast, stimulates less arousal, and bodily changes tend to be more specific. The results of this experiment suggest that embarrassment is physiologically a low arousal condition, marked by a decrease in heart rate. In addition, though it was not assessed in this research, embarrassment is marked by blushing. The pattern of low arousal, lowered heart rate, and blushing suggests that in embarrassment the parasympathetic division is dominant. If this conclusion is correct, it must be difficult to be embarrassed and fearful simultaneously because the sympathetic and parasympathetic divisions ordinarily are opposed.

One study, of course, is a frail basis for conclusions. It would be interesting to repeat it with several additions. A control group should be added—one that is neither scared nor embarrassed. Skin temperature should be measured and blushing observed. Such research would tell us quantitatively the relationship between skin temperature and blushing on the one hand and internal physiological reactions on the other hand.

IMMEDIATE CAUSES

Reflect for a moment, and you will be able to recall several situations that caused you embarrassment. By pooling the recall of a large number of people, we can discover many of the immediate causes of embarrassment. Using this strategy, one researcher compiled a list of several dozen causes and then grouped them into three clusters.[7] The first set dealt with *impropriety:* improper dress or dirty talk. The second concerned *lack of competence:* slips of speech, public clumsiness, or forgetting someone's name. And the third referred to *conspicuousness:* being looked at by the opposite sex or displaying excessive emotion in public. Impropriety and public incompetence are so well known as causes of embarrassment that they require no further comment. Conspicuousness, however, needs to be elaborated.

To be conspicuous is to receive somewhat more than your normal share of attention. You may receive special attention because you are in some way different from others in a public situation: you enter a large elevator filled with people of the opposite sex; you enter a bar frequented only by those of a different sexual persuasion; or you discover that you are the only party-goer dressed formally. You may be singled out in a crowd and asked to stand up and be recognized; or you sit quietly while a colleague introduces you and recites the history of your accomplishments.

You may also be made conspicuous by others ridiculing your appearance, background, or behavior. Teasing and caricature, especially when done in a good humored way, cause discomfort and blushing. When the underlying hostility that characterizes teasing starts to show through, the victim may react by becoming hurt or enraged, or may become abashed merely because others are staring, especially when they are strangers or merely casual acquaintances.

Breaches of privacy

In addition to impropriety, social incompetence, and conspicuousness, there is a fourth category of immediate causes of embarrassment: breaches of privacy by casual acquaintances or strangers. For present purposes, we can distinguish three kinds of privacy. The first involves behavior or parts of the body that should not be seen. In our culture, there is a strong preference for solitude during the elimination of wastes. Women are especially sensitive to being seen, and some cannot complete the act when others are present.

There appears to be a universal human preference for privacy in sexual acts such as coitus and masturbation.

Scrutiny by others causes acute embarrassment in almost everyone—with the exception of those inclined toward sexual exhibitionism.

There is also universal socialization involving exposure of body parts. The standards of modesty vary widely from one culture to the next. In some, only the genitals need to be covered; in others, women are expected to show only their eyes when in public. Exposure of the taboo parts of the body causes acute embarrassment: the typical embarrassment dream involves being caught entirely naked in a public place.

The second kind of privacy concerns what others may touch and how close they may come. In general, others may not touch those parts of the body that should not be seen. In our culture these are the breasts, buttocks, and genitals for women, and the buttocks and genitals for men. When these parts are touched by another person, both people may become embarrassed.

Concerning personal space, an anthropologist has described an *intimate zone* that extends to about two feet in front of the body: "This is the distance of lovemaking, and wrestling, comforting and protecting. Physical contact or the high possibility of physical involvement is uppermost in the awareness of both persons."[8] When a stranger or casual acquaintance moves in closer than two feet, you will start to feel uncomfortable and try to back away. Inability to retreat may cause embarrassment. In a crowded elevator, bus, or train, people generally avoid facing one another; if they must face one another, they avoid eye contact and maintain an uncomfortable silence. Any doubts about invasion of the intimate zone as a source of embarrassment can be resolved by a simple experiment. Ask a casual friend to stand still while you try something. Walk up to this person, stop a foot away, and maintain eye contact for about 30 seconds. One or both of you will be likely to blush.

The first two kinds of privacy involve intrinsically public aspects of the self, which can be seen or touched (or approached); we are trained to conceal them or to prevent them from being touched. The third kind of privacy involves aspects of the self that are intrinsically private. If the person does not share them or allow them to be observed, they will never become public. All of us at times have strong feelings of love, sexual interest, admiration, hatred, jealousy, or even cowardice, which we share with no one or perhaps only with an exceptional other person. These covert affects and cognitions would cause embarrassment if they became public, and so they are rarely disclosed. But Freudian slips do occur, and all of us have at one time or another blurted out an intense feeling that should have been left unspoken. Paradoxically, positive feelings seem to cause more embarrassment than negative ones. Adolescents are particularly susceptible to discomfort when they reveal affection for another person, especially heterosexual affection. And they may reveal, through nonverbal expressions, the positive feelings they have been trying so hard to conceal. In fact, the blush itself may reveal a young person's love for another, in which case the giveaway blush leads to a blush of embarrassment. (When you become aware that your face is red and hot, you may become embarrassed at this leakage of the affect of embarrassment.) The term *leakage* is a deliberate metaphor; presumably the discomfort is caused by a leak in the dam that has been holding back the not-to-be-revealed feelings and aspirations.

There is a bodily parallel to leakage of feelings—one that we need not dwell on. Internal bodily noises, such as stomach rumblings, belches, and other sounds, usually cause embarrassment when others are present and can hear them.

The immediate causes of embarrassment due to breaches of privacy are summarized in Table 8.1. The three categories of privacy have been labeled *unseen*, *untouched*, and *unshared*, and the bodily and behavioral examples should make clear the meaning of each category.

TABLE 8.1

Breaches of privacy that cause embarrassment

Category	Examples	
	Body	Behavior
Unseen	Genitals	Defecation
Untouched	Buttocks, genitals	Personal space (intimate zone)
Unshared	Digestive noises	Intimate feelings

Overpraise

Most adults have been embarrassed at least once by being overpraised in public. Having experienced the discomfort resulting from excessive compliments, we accept the fact as entirely reasonable. But there is a paradox: compliments, which should make you feel good, make you blush and feel uncomfortable.

Perhaps the paradox can be resolved by invoking conspicuousness. Overpraise does make you conspicuous, but so does praise that merely reflects your accomplishments. For example, if you have received a scholarship, won a prize, or received a promotion, praise for these achievements would make you just as conspicuous as would overpraise, without causing the awkwardness that overpraise does. Perhaps the cause lies in a discrepancy between your achievements and the evaluation you receive, whether the discrepancy is positive or negative.

Conspicuousness and discrepancy, as explanations of why overpraise causes embarrassment, were evaluated in an experiment by Laura Buss.[9] She used college women who rated themselves for attractiveness and sensitivity to others. Several weeks later they participated in an experiment that ostensibly studied first impressions. Another subject (really an experimental accomplice) rated the subject lower, the same as, or higher than she had previously

TABLE 8.2

Number of subjects (out of 20) who blushed, giggled, or avoided eye contact

	Overpraise	Accurate praise	Underpraise
Blushing	19	7	3
Giggling	16	5	0
Gaze avoidance	20	16	18

rated herself. In all three conditions—underpraise, accurate rating, and overpraise—the subject was conspicuously the center of attention.

The experimenter (not the accomplice) scored each subject for presence of blushing, giggling, and gaze avoidance. For half the subjects, the experimenter was aware of to which experimental group they were assigned; for the other half, not. Knowledge of experimental condition made no difference; the observations were about the same in each case.

The results are shown in Table 8.2. Almost all the overpraised women blushed, and most of them giggled. Only a small minority of women in the other conditions blushed or giggled. Regardless of condition, most subjects avoided eye contact while they were being evaluated, but we do not know whether this avoidance was caused by their being evaluated, their being conspicuous, or both.

Since accurate praise resulted in essentially no embarrassment, we conclude that merely being conspicuous during an evaluation does not account for the overpraise effect. Since underpraise yielded almost no embarrassment, we conclude that it is not just any discrepancy that accounts for the overpraise effect. Clearly, it is only a positive discrepancy, overpraise, that leads to embarrassment.

One explanation is leakage. In our society, children are socialized to be modest, or at least to appear modest. We are not supposed to admit that we are good; positive self-evaluations are to be kept "inside." This situation appears to be another instance of a public–private distinction of the kind listed in the bottom row of Table 8.1. Presumably, overpraise tempts you to believe that you are really that good. Such immodest thoughts have been the object of teasing and ridicule, much as feelings of love have been ridiculed. If these assumptions are true, the possibility of public exposure of your conceit (that is, leakage) would cause you embarrassment. Even if you had no immodest thoughts, you would still be concerned that others (the overpraiser or other observers) would infer that you did. Such concern parallels what occurs in leakage of feelings of love: you are concerned that others believe you are in love, regardless of whether you are.

In brief, the explanation for the paradoxical discomfort caused by overpraise may lie in leakage (actual or feared) of immodest thoughts and feelings. Like exposure of hidden affection, being complimented excessively causes a mixed state: you are both pleased and uncomfortable. The pleasant part is a rise in self-esteem; the unpleasant part is embarrassment.

ENDURING CAUSES

There has been only one attempt to develop a measure of embarrassment as a personality trait: a 26-item embarrassability questionnaire.[10] College men were asked to rate how embarrassed they would become in a variety of situations. The responses to the various questions were intercorrelated, and a factor analysis yielded five factors:

1. Accidental foolishness.

2. Inability to respond.

3. Being the passive center of attention.

4. Watching someone else fail.

5. Inappropriate sexual encounters.

There are no published norms for either the five factors or the entire 26-item questionnaire. We do not know whether the five factors are related to one another, and the questionnaire has been used only with men. Evidently, no one else has used the questionnaire, so we have virtually no information about its usefulness.

It may be futile to pursue a broad trait of embarrassability because there are several different causes of embarrassment. An alternative strategy is to ask which kinds of people are likely to become embarrassed most frequently.

One class of people consists of those who blush easily. Perhaps they have a richer capillary bed underlying the skin of the face—in other words, a biological tendency to become embarrassed.[11] The remaining dispositions that might cause embarrassment are all psychological.

Consider the four situational causes of embarrassment: conspicuousness, impropriety, breaches of privacy, and temporary incompetence. Perhaps there are classes of people who tend to be caught more frequently in these embarrassing situations.

The tendency to be aware of oneself as a social object is probably a dispositional cause of all the social anxieties. Concerning embarrassment, public self-consciousness tends to make the person feel exposed to the scrutiny of others. Other things equal, this feeling of being observed should make people feel conspicuous. And being the center of attention appears to be an immediate cause of embarrassment.

People who are socially clumsy tend to blurt out statements that should not be said, to call people by wrong names, and, in general, to lack poise and polish in their interactions with others. Lacking social skills, they repeatedly make the small mistakes that cause them to feel foolish, silly, uncomfortable—in a word, embarrassed.

Some adults are extremely reluctant to reveal their bodies, even to friends. In our culture, women have been

TABLE 8.3

Dispositional causes of embarrassment

Disposition	Specific immediate cause it is likely to lead to
Public self-consciousness	Conspicuousness
Social ineptness	Impropriety
Excessive modesty	Breach of body privacy
Being a "closed person"	"Leakage" of private sentiments

traditionally more embarrassed by their own nudity than men. Some women even refuse to use public showers or dressing rooms. This concern about nakedness may be the result of training by extremely strict parents or of an adolescent concern with the sexual connotations of the naked body. Whatever the cause, such people tend to become embarrassed whenever they must disrobe—in a locker room, a physician's office, or perhaps even in the bedroom with a loved one.

People may be aligned along a dimension of expressiveness that is anchored at one end by openness and a willingness to disclose ambitions, affections, hostilities, and all the various private affects and cognitions that fall under the heading of feelings. The other end of the expressiveness dimension is represented by a reluctance to disclose private feelings, especially those involving self-esteem or affection for others. People who keep such feelings from others should be especially susceptible to leakage. They are more likely than most to become embarrassed when overpraised or when teased about crushes or juvenile ambitions.

These four psychological dispositions are summarized in Table 8.3. Public self-consciousness can lead not only to embarrassment but also to shame, audience anxiety, and shyness.

CONSEQUENCES

Embarrassment evokes divergent reactions in others. They may offer sympathy and warm reassurance to help you through your predicament. More often, others turn away, probably for two reasons. First, they wish to spare you the further embarrassment of their scrutiny; their ignoring you temporarily makes you less conspicuous. Second, they may be discomfited by your embarrassment. Most adults have a capacity for empathy; their shared feeling of embarrassment, though dilute, may be enough to make them wish to escape from the situation.

The worst reaction of others, mercifully less common, is laughter or scorn. Others' laughter at your embarrassment doubles your discomfort by making you even more conspicuous. And laughter and ridicule are, of course, immediate causes of embarrassment. In brief, the reactions of others can intensify your embarrassment or help to alleviate it.

One consequence for yourself may be a temporary drop in self-esteem. Embarrassment does not always lower self-esteem. With the exception of situations involving over-praise and leakage of positive feelings, however, embarrassment usually lowers your self-evaluation, at least temporarily.

Another transient consequence is an awareness that you are blushing. Unfortunately, this public self-awareness is itself a cause of further embarrassment. In fact, just being told that you are blushing—whether you are or not—usually makes you blush.

An uncomfortable state, embarrassment motivates attempts to escape from the aversive situation. College students whose voices were poor were asked to sing for money; the longer they sang, the more money they made.[12] The students were sufficiently embarrassed by their bad voices to cut short their singing even though it cost them money. One consequence of embarrassment, then, is an attempt to escape.

Finally, because embarrassed people usually feel foolish, one consequence is an attempt to save face by engaging in prosocial behavior: "Embarrassed individuals should be especially susceptible to requests for help, since by helping someone they can counteract the threat to face of the embarrassing incident. They can show others what fine people they are and demonstrate, thereby, that the embarrassing incident did not accurately represent them."[13] One group of college men (embarrassed) were asked to sing and also to imitate a five-year-old child having a temper tantrum; a control group was not embarrassed. Then the embarrassed subjects and controls were asked to volunteer for an experiment that could last for 20 days. The embarrassed subjects volunteered for three times as many days of the experiment as did the control subjects. Evidently, embarrassment does lead to greater compliance in the service of saving face.

In summary, embarrassment causes several different reactions:

1. Self-awareness of blushing.

2. A temporary drop in self-esteem.

3. Attempts to escape from the situation.

4. Attempts to save face—for example, by greater compliance.

THEORETICAL APPROACHES

The opinion of others

Charles Darwin started by assuming that self-attention causes embarrassment, but he emphasizes that self-awareness is not sufficient: "It is not the simple act of reflecting on our own appearance, but the thinking what others think of us, which excites a blush."[14] After suggesting several different causes of embarrassment, such as breaches of etiquette and modesty, Darwin concluded that they all depend on the same principle, "this principle being a sensitive regard for the opinion, more particularly for the depreciation of others, primarily in relation to our personal appearance, especially of our faces; and secondarily, through the force of association and habit, in relation to the opinion of others on our conduct."[15]

Darwin's principle appears reasonable, but it must be at least partly incorrect. We saw earlier that overpraise—but not underpraise or realistic praise—caused people to be embarrassed.[16] If a sensitive regard for the opinion of others were the basic cause of embarrassment, underpraise would surely cause blushing; it does not.

Darwin also tried to explain why attention from others causes blushing. He speculated that "attention closely directed to any part of the body tends to interfere with the ordinary and tonic contraction of the small arteries of that part. These vessels, in consequence, become at such times more or less relaxed, and are instantly filled with arterial blood."[17] It follows that if someone stared at your hand, it would become red. Surely, this speculation is wrong. Blushing is limited mainly to the face; in fact, facial blushing can occur when other parts of the body are stared at. Though Darwin was undoubtedly wrong in his explanation, no one else has offered any other explanation of why we blush when embarrassed.

Self-presentation

Viewed sociologically, embarrassment is a disruption of the normal flow of social give-and-take. This is the approach of Erwin Goffman, who starts by describing the components of social encounters:

> During interaction the individual is expected to possess certain attributes, capacities, and information which, taken together, fit together into a self that is at once coherently unified and appropriate for the occasion. . . . The elements of a social encounter, then, consist of effectively projected claims to an acceptable self and the confirmation of like claims on the part of others.[18]

When something unexpected happens that throws doubt on these claims, at least one participant becomes embarrassed. In Goffman's terms, embarrassment is caused by the projected social self being discredited. Embarrassment, in turn, causes a loss of poise, and the entire encounter is ruined. The participants can no longer continue to play their appropriate social roles because they are too uncomfortable and because the assumptions underlying such roles have been violated.

Goffman's approach has been applied to encounters in a nudist camp.[19] In the camp, nudity caused no embarrassment, but if a person's membership in the camp became known at his church, he became embarrassed: his role as a church-goer was partially discredited. And in the camp the presence of a penile erection was extremely embarrassing, presumably because it discredited the man's role as a nonsexual social partner.

André Modigliani added self-esteem to Goffman's formulation, suggesting a three-step process: (1) an event undermines or discredits self-presentation, (2) the person senses that others are aware of this discrediting, and (3) this awareness causes a loss of situational self-esteem.[20] Certainly, in the majority of instances, embarrassment causes a temporary drop in self-esteem, especially when the embarrassed person has, through clumsiness or impropriety, brought it on himself.

Socialization

Neither Charles Darwin's more-or-less biological approach nor Erwin Goffman's sociological approach pays much attention to how children are socialized. Nor do they attempt to relate the goals of socialization to how embarrassment develops. We know that humans have a built-in biological mechanism for blushing, but blushing evidently does not occur during the first few years of life. It follows that the process and content of the socialization of children are likely to be important determiners of the development of embarrassment. (This theme will be elaborated on in Chapter 13.)

NOTES

1. The influence of context on the labeling of emotions has been demonstrated in a now-classical experiment by Schachter and Singer (1962). In a study to be discussed in Chapter 13 (Buss, Iscoe, and Buss, 1979) some parents reported that their children reacted to teasing with embarrassment when the parents' own descriptions of the child's behavior indicated that the children were angry, not embarrassed. For some people, the fact that teasing occurs is sufficient for them to label the reaction embarrassment even in the absence of any observable sign of embarrassment.

2. Using a thermistor to measure skin temperature would also tell us whether redheaded people tend to blush more (a frequently heard observation) or their blushes are easier to see.

3. Darwin (1873, p. 309)

4. Darwin (1863, p. 318)

5. Buck, Parke, and Buck (1970)

6. Buck and Parke (1972, p. 145)

7. Sattler (1965)

8. Hall (1966, p. 110)

9. L. Buss (1978)

10. Modigliani (1968)

11. An alternative to a richer capillary bed is a translucent skin, an issue discussed earlier in the chapter.

12. Brown and Garland (1971)

13. Apsler (1975, p. 147)

14. Darwin (1863, p. 325)

15. Darwin (1873, pp. 336–337)

16. L. Buss (1978)

17. Darwin (1873, p. 337)

18. Goffman (1967, pp. 105–106). See also his 1956 paper.

19. Weinberg (1968)

20. Modigliani (1968). See also his 1971 paper.

SHAME

Shame is related to embarrassment. There are similarities in the observed reaction of each, and they share certain immediate causes. For these reasons, the experiencing individual may be unable to distinguish between shame and embarrassment, and some authors have lumped them into a single category.[1] Nevertheless, shame and embarrassment are different in certain respects. Unlike embarrassment, which is trivial and momentary, shame is serious and enduring. Embarrassment carries no moral burden; shame does. The opposite of embarrassment is *poise;* the opposite of shame is *pride.*

THE REACTION

The observable components of shame are similar to those of embarrassment, except that shame does not involve blushing. If this assertion is true, how can we account for the fact that ashamed people sometimes blush? We must assume that they are simultaneously ashamed and embarrassed. Surely no one would deny that two separate affects can occur at the same time. We can be simultaneously enraged and afraid, happy and sad, relieved and upset. And we can be embarrassed or ashamed, or both simultaneously. The combination, however, is rare; usually we are either embarrassed (trivial) or ashamed (serious), not both.

The ashamed person cannot look another person in the eye. Gaze is averted, or the face is covered with the hands. Sometimes there is a stricken look, sometimes expostulations or even sobbing. Severe shame looks very much like depression.

The feelings in shame are primarily those of self-disgust or self-disappointment. There is inevitably a sharp drop in self-esteem, as the person verbally attacks himself or feels let down by himself. Shame is the only variety of social anxiety that always involves a decrease in self-esteem. There are intense feelings of regret or mortification, which are hard to verbalize. The ashamed person wishes he could sink into the earth, away from those who have observed his shameful behavior. He assumes that their low opinion of him matches his own. Such self-condemnation, with overtones of moral decay, are largely absent in the other social anxieties.

IMMEDIATE CAUSES

Our society emphasizes achievement and success in competition. Those who achieve or win in competition feel proud; those who fail often experience shame. Shame-inducing failure may take one of several forms. Suppose that you have set a high standard of performance for yourself, a standard that is realistic in light of previous performance. The activity might be presenting a talk or playing a tennis match. If your public performance is well below your standard, you may feel discredited because your fail-

ure was there for all to see. Such shame might occur even if
others thought your talk was good or if you won the tennis
match. The failure would be in your eyes only. Such personal shame is less frequent than the more common public
shame; performance that the audience recognizes as inferior. Why should a single poor performance cause shame?
I suggest that it is awareness of the audience's inference
that you are unintelligent, poorly trained, lacking in
ability—in brief, in some way inferior. This kind of shame
is caused by the attribution of flawed character: of an enduring, inherent baseness of the person.

The problem is compounded by the societal push for
winning. Even if you play well, losing in competition may
induce ignominy. And the chagrin is especially keen if you
or your team represents an institutional entity such as a
high school, college, or city.

A different kind of failure involves sexuality. Among
consenting adults, men are expected to be potent, women
to be arousable. Temporary impotence tends to cause
humiliation in men; somehow their entire masculinity is
placed in jeopardy. Frigidity among women is a weaker
cause of shame, presumably because the criteria for femi-
ninity are neither as clear nor as crucial for women as the
criteria for masculinity are for men.[2]

The machismo kind of masculinity is so strongly established in many men because failure to conform tends to be
followed by shame. The ideal man, as portrayed in movies
and on television, is a hero who brooks no insults, stands
up for his rights, and above all demonstrates courage in the
face of threat. Police stories and westerns, the staples of
television and movies, portray the male hero as someone
who defends his honor with fists or guns. Those who lack
the courage to risk injury or death are shown to slink away
in disgrace.

For many of us, such an ideal is a perversion of masculinity. Nevertheless, no one objects to both boys and girls
being socialized to be courageous and unselfish. Anyone
who demonstrates unequivocal cowardice or selfishness

tends to be censured. We shame children who make no attempt to cope with their fears (of the dark, of being left
alone, and so on). We scorn and reject children who do not
share their goods with others when sharing is the norm. In
sum, the milder forms of cowardice and the stronger forms
of selfishness often lead to shame. To avoid such disgrace,
we may display more courage than we feel, more charity
than we might otherwise.

The most intense shame arises from acts that have been
branded immoral. In our puritanical culture, forbidden sexual acts or their consequences are especially shameful. We
have always condemned homosexuality, and, even in the
more enlightened era of the present, many homosexuals are
ashamed of their sexual preference. In church and school
premarital or extramarital sex has been branded as shameful, though only a minority of people, especially young
women, feel debased by such sexual behavior. Venereal disease and pregnancy outside of marriage are still regarded by
many people as badges of dishonor. The days of "Never
darken my doorway again" may be past, but there are
enough residuals of our earlier strictness in these matters
to make some pregnant unmarried women and those with
gonorrhea or syphilis feel stigmatized and debased. The
least shameful sexual act, masturbation, remains a cause
of shame for a minority of adolescents and adults. Some
people are merely embarrassed when their self-manipu-
lation is discovered; others are deeply ashamed.

Whether any of these proscribed sexual acts lead to
shame when they are disclosed depends on the current
morality of the people involved. There has been a shift during the last few decades from a stern moral position on sex
to a position that regards sex as not a moral issue but a
personal one. If sex is the concern of no one but the people
involved, there is obviously no shame attached to it. But if
certain kinds of sex are regarded as reflecting depravity, the
exposure of such acts inevitably causes shame.

Immorality is of course not limited to forbidden sexual
behavior. Lying, cheating, and stealing form a continuum

of increasing immorality. For most of us, it is not the acts themselves that cause shame but the discovery and exposure of the acts. The discovery of a lie is a borderline case. If it is a "white lie" or a lie involving good manners (telling the hostess that her tasteless dinner was delicious), exposure tends to cause embarrassment. If the lie is more serious—say, a claim of possessing a PhD or an MD or of being unmarried when the opposite is true—disclosure usually causes shame.

Discovery of cheating usually elicits more intense shame than exposure of lying. Some kinds of cheating, however, seem to be exempt. Cheating on income tax or attempting to avoid excise duties is not considered disgraceful, and only rarely is anyone ashamed when caught. Cheating on exams was once universally condemned; now only a minority of students would feel dishonored if their cheating were discovered. On the other hand, cheating one's friends, failing to pay debts when money is available, duping others into surrendering goods or money—all such acts, it is generally agreed, are shameful. For most of us, disclosure of such cheating would cause us to feel deep shame.

Stealing, robbing, and murdering—the more extreme end of the crime dimension—are obvious causes of shame when they are discovered. Only a minority of the population can admit to such antisocial acts without feeling debased or depraved. For most of us, even being charged with a serious crime, whether we are guilty or not, would be a sufficient disgrace.

In summary, there are four major categories of self-initiated causes of shame (see Table 9.1). These events are likely to cause shame only among the majority, who have undergone the normal socialization of our culture. A minority of people, however, experience little or no shame. Whatever their label—*psychopath* and *sociopath* are two common names—such people suffer no regret or repentance when they display cowardice, irresponsibility, or immorality.

TABLE 9.1

Causes of Shame

Category	Subclasses
Failure	To perform well To win in competition
Disappointment	To oneself To family or friends To teammates
Lack of prosocial behavior	Machismo (for men) Cowardice Selfishness
Immorality	Forbidden sex Venereal disease Forbidden pregnancy Lying, cheating Stealing, murder

ENDURING CAUSES

Which people are likely to become ashamed? One enduring cause of shame may be public self-consciousness. People who continually examine themselves as social objects and worry about the impression they make tend to be more susceptible to any of the immediate causes of shame.

Another enduring cause of shame is the presence of a *stigma*. The stigma may be a physical defect easily seen by others: the absence of an arm or leg, deformity of body proportions, or severe scarring of the face. The shameful defect may be a body problem that can be concealed. The absence of body parts as a result of radical surgery (mastectomy, castration) causes shame in some people. Similarly, some young women are so concerned about the small size of their breasts that they refuse to be seen in swim suits. Very fat or very thin people may be ashamed of being seen in revealing clothes or naked in public showers or locker rooms.

The term *stigma* refers not only to bodily defects but also to black marks on people's identity. Illegitimate children, whether branded by themselves or others, feel degraded in comparison with other children. A stain on the family's honor spreads to all members of the family: when the father is a criminal or a traitor, when the mother is a prostitute, or when an adolescent comes out of the closet and publicly declares his or her homosexuality. When offspring are upwardly mobile, they may try to conceal the lower class status or ethnic ways of their parents and extended family out of a fear of being tarred with the same brush.

Shame can derive not only from familial defects but also from a person's own past history. Some prostitutes and pimps, some thieves and embezzlers, some cheats and liars do reform and attempt to take their place in society as upright, law-abiding citizens. If unrevealed, their past acts continually lurk in psychological dark corners as potential threats to their new identity. For such people, the shame of their earlier life is compounded by an enduring fear of disclosure. And many of them feel a continuing sense of inferiority because of the base behavior which, though in the distant past, remains as a permanent stain on their honor.

The disposition of low self-esteem can be a cause of shame. By definition, people who feel inferior are more ready to admit incompetence, cowardice, and blame for letting others down. It follows that such people more readily experience shame whenever any of the immediate causes of shame happen to occur.

Finally, the interaction between enduring and immediate causes of shame, though implicit in the last several paragraphs, needs to be stated explicitly: any person who has an enduring reason for feeling shame will be more susceptible to the immediate causes of shame. Consider "all the president's men," the lawyers and politicians responsible for the Watergate break-in, its cover-up, or systematic illegal acts against political opposition. Some of these men felt humiliated and mortified at their illegal acts; they have publicly announced their shame and their wish to lead a better life. Others have denied any serious wrongdoing and apparently have never felt any shame about any of their actions. As this example demonstrates, whether an immediate cause of shame induces chagrin and humiliation depends on whether there is any enduring disposition to be susceptible to shame.

CONSEQUENCES

For the experiencing person, the consequences of shame are all bad. There is a strong sense of responsibility either for failure to perform or for immoral acts. Such negative self-attributions cause a precipitous drop in self-esteem. The ashamed person feels unworthy because either inability or immorality has been exposed. This kind of self-blame may have enduring consequences: a continuing sense of one's own inferiority.

Having been discredited and humiliated, the ashamed person may subsequently avoid those who have witnessed his disgrace. If continued contact is inevitable, the disgraced person is likely to become shy and inhibited in social contacts. When new friendships occur, the ashamed person may fear disclosure of his previous shameful behavior. This kind of secret knowledge is a dreadful burden to carry into new relationships.

The foregoing comments may appear too dramatic. Indeed, they apply mainly to the shame that follows disclosure of especially disgraceful actions. The milder varieties of shame are likely to have less dire consequences. Self-esteem is diminished, not shattered; the sense of inferiority is not so intense; subsequent shyness is not so extreme; and there is little or no burden of secret knowledge. And there is always the possibility of returning to the good graces of others. A cowardly act can be reversed by a courageous act; causing the team to lose one game can be wiped out by winning for the team in the next game; and immoral acts can be undone by appropriate public confession, penance, and later acts of high morality.

What are the consequences of a person's shame for family, friends, acquaintances, and co-workers? There is an immediate drop in their esteem and respect. Admiration may change to ridicule, friendship to hostility. They are likely to display their disappointment and negative feelings directly or by shunning or rejecting the disgraced person. Such reactions occur mainly when the shame involves immorality. But when the cause of shame is inability or a lapse in performance, others may show sharply divided reactions. Some people may react as described above. Others may offer sympathy and help. In brief, whether the reaction is negative or positive would seem to depend on the nature of the relationship (family versus acquaintances or bystanders), the nature of the shameful act (immorality versus ineptitude), and the degree of ignominy (mildly shameful acts versus depraved acts).

Finally, the reaction of others depends on the kind of attribution they make. If they believe that the shameful act was an unusual or unique instance, largely situational, they would probably be sympathetic. If they believe that the shameful act was typical, something to be expected from such a base person, they would probably shun the person. In brief, a situational attribution would yield sympathy and a personal attribution, rejection.

THEORETICAL APPROACHES

Of the various approaches to shame, two can be dealt with briefly. Charles Darwin equated shame with embarrassment; his approach to shame has already been discussed in the chapter on embarrassment. In contrast to our Western view of shame, Orientals see it as essentially a loss of face.[3] In Japan and traditional China, shame is more important both as a means of social control and as an experienced affect. It has been suggested that in these countries shame persists like a psychic scar, with less possibility of healing than guilt has.

Dynamic

Classical psychoanalytic theory, as formulated by Sigmund Freud, had little to say about shame. For Freud, shame would occupy a stage of development somewhere between a child's anxiety and an adult's bad conscience. The classical Freudian position has been modified by Piers and Singer,[4] who provide a larger role for shame.

In this modified psychoanalytic theory, shame is differentiated from guilt. Guilt is believed to arise from parents' punishment and hostility. Parental inhibitions somehow become internalized to form the *conscience*. Guilt is the result of a conflict between the ego and conscience. Conscience demands that the ego suffer for transgressions of the moral code. Thus guilt is, in a way, hatred from within.

Shame, in contrast, involves a conflict between the ego and the ego-ideal. The *ego-ideal* is formed through identifying with parents and peers, thereby adopting their goals and aspirations for oneself. When the ego fails to attain these goals, the ego-ideal makes the ego aware of the discrepancy. The ego fears contempt from the ego-ideal, perhaps followed by abandonment. *Shame* is a fear of abandonment; *guilt* is a fear of castration.

Shame and guilt are linked to society's requirements for self-control:

> Guilt transfers the demands of society through primitive parental images. Social conformity achieved through guilt will be essentially one of *submission*. Shame can be brought to the individual more readily in the process of comparing and competing with peers (siblings, schoolmates, gang, etc.). Social conformity achieved through shame will be essentially one of identification.[5]

Lynd presents a similar position.[6] In contrast to Piers and Singer, she links guilt with anxiety, and shame with inferiority. Lynd assumes that guilt involves specific transgressions; overcoming guilt produces self-righteousness. Shame is concerned with the broader realm of achievement (attaining goals); overcoming shame leads to identity and freedom.

Innate negative affect

Shame is regarded as one of the major negative affects by Silvan Tompkins.[7] His approach to shame is embedded in a broad theory of imagery, affects, and consciousness, and a full exposition of his position would take us too far afield. The following brief account attempts merely to offer the flavor of his approach, mainly through quotations.

Tompkins makes no distinction among shyness, shame, and guilt as affects, though he concedes that they are experienced differently. His two crucial assumptions are that shame is innate and that it is linked to enjoyment:

> Shame is an innate auxiliary affect and a specific inhibitor of continuing interest and enjoyment.[8]

Shame occurs because interest or joy is incompletely reduced so that the person still hopes to revive the former, pleasant feelings. Whatever slows down enjoyment will somehow induce shame:

> The most general sources of shame are the varieties of barriers to the varieties of objects of excitement and enjoyment which reduce positive affect sufficiently to activate shame, but not so completely that the original object is renounced: "I want, but . . ." is one essential condition for the activation of shame.[9]

It is generally conceded that shame is closely linked to the self, but no one has asked why this linkage exists. Tompkins asks the question and answers it:

> Why is shame so close to the experienced self? It is because the self lives in the face, and within the face the self burns brightest in the eyes.[10] The shame response is literally an ambivalent turning of the eyes away from the object toward the face, toward the self.[11]

SHAME VERSUS GUILT

Since shame is the only social anxiety to involve morality, it is important to distinguish it from the other major moral affect, guilt. In *guilt* the feeling is of sin or evil ("I am bad; I have transgressed"). In *shame* the feeling is one of exposure ("I am ugly; I have failed; I have been caught cheating"). In brief, guilt involves *self-hatred;* shame involves *social anxiety*.

Except for religious dogma, there is only one kind of transgression that leads to guilt: harming someone else. The damage can be direct and the victim a single person, or it can be indirect and the victim a large group. The transgression that usually causes the most intense guilt is hurting a loved one. Shame, on the other hand, is triggered by such acts as cheating, cowardice, or sexual indiscretion. Certain immoral acts, such as lying or stealing, usually cause shame only if the person is caught. There are also situations involving failure while being watched—for example, missing the two foul shots that could have won the basketball game.

The public–private dichotomy offers the clearest distinction between guilt and shame. Guilt is essentially private. The best test of guilt is whether anyone else knows of the transgression. In true guilt, no one need know. It is private, a matter of your own conscience, and therefore there is no escape. Shame is essentially public; if no one else knows, there is no basis for shame. And if your action is seen, you can diminish shame only by running from the group. Perhaps this is why ashamed people cast their eyes down or avoid looking at others.

How is the stigma removed? The problem for guilty people is to convince themselves of their worth by reforming. Children are taught early that evil must be punished. Self-punishment not only evens the score ("an eye for an eye") but also serves to reform the evil-doers. The problem for ashamed people is to convince others of their worth. This is accomplished by succeeding when previously they

TABLE 9.2

Guilt versus shame

	Guilt	Shame
Feeling	Sinfulness, evil	Regret, self-disgust
Basis	Harming someone, violating a religious code	Disappointing the group; cowardice, sexual indiscretion
Inner-outer	Private, no escape	Public, escape by hiding
Atonement	Self-punishment (convincing self of worth)	Succeeding, being competent (convincing others of worth)
Basis of social control	Submission to authority	Conformity to (peer) group

had failed, by showing skill and competence when previously they had been clumsy and incompetent.

Finally, guilt involves submission to authority, the appeal being to the authority of legal codes or to a "higher law." Shame involves submission to the appropriate reference group, usually one's peers. Doing one's duty and being competent are actions judged by the group, the issue being conformity, not submission. These various contrasts between guilt and shame are summarized in Table 9.2.

In theory, guilt is more effective than shame in insuring self-control. People who harm others presumably will feel guilty whether or not they are caught. Incompetent or clumsy people will not experience shame unless they are exposed; so long as they avoid being caught, they are safe. Thus, shame does not lead to self-control in private.

Nevertheless, in our society, shame is probably a stronger force for self-control than guilt. With the waning of religion as a moral force, most people easily rationalize their transgressions. Even murder and torture can sometimes be reconciled with conscience. The Nazis who sent Jews to the gas chambers said that they were "just following orders"; the barbaric treatment received by prisoners in some penitentiaries is justified by the belief that they deserve it. In addition, there is a wide-spread tendency to believe that the world is a just one in which the good are rewarded and the bad are punished. Thus, when a victim suffers and an observer can do nothing about it, the observer tends to blame the victim for his misfortune.[12]

Most of us are trained to fear censure from groups. The most severe punishments are being laughed at, being pitied, and being rejected as failures. All these punishments involve shame: a failure to be competent or to keep private acts from being made public.

One drawback to shame and guilt as deterrents is that they ordinarily occur after the forbidden responses have been made. The problem is the familiar one of the timing of punishment—in this case, self-punishment. The solution may lie in cognitions. The person must think of the transgression he is about to commit and then imagine the self-punishment. If these negative feelings can be linked with the anticipated act, the feelings may inhibit the act.

SHAME VERSUS EMBARRASSMENT

Some writers have made no distinction between shame and embarrassment, perhaps because the two affects have certain similarities. Common to both are gaze aversion, covering of the eyes or face, discomfort, and parasympathetic reactivity. Both affects may be caused by a person's own acts or by the scrutiny of others. Both may result from disclosure of socially unacceptable behavior or from ridicule by others. And both cause a drop in self-esteem.

Shame and embarrassment may be aligned on a dimension of severity. The person's own acts are more unacceptable in shame than in embarrassment. The actions of others are milder in causing embarrassment (teasing) than in causing shame (scorn). And the ensuing drop in self-esteem is sharper in shame than in embarrassment. In brief, shame is a more serious and a more severe social anxiety than embarrassment.

If shame and embarrassment have similarities and differ only in severity, why distinguish between them? Shame and embarrassment have different reactions, immediate causes, and consequences.

Embarrassment and shame are both reactions to specific events in a social context. Blushing, smiling, or giggling are part of embarrassment but not of shame. The embarrassed person feels foolish or silly; the ashamed person, regretful and depressed. There is also a difference in self-attribution: in embarrassment, a mistake; in shame, a personal defect.

Embarrassment has many immediate causes and therefore occurs more frequently than shame. A breach of etiquette may cause embarrassment but not shame. Being teased, overpraised, or merely scrutinized by others can cause embarrassment but not cause shame. On the other hand, letting the group down or being caught in an immoral or cowardly act causes shame but not embarrassment. Embarrassment occurs because of leakage or disclosure of affection or other positive feelings; shame occurs because of disclosure of baseness or strongly negative feelings or attitudes.

Finally, the consequences of shame and embarrassment are different. There is merely a temporary loss of self-esteem in embarrassment, but an enduring loss in shame. And an embarrassed person is likely to be laughed at, accepted, and consoled afterward, whereas an ashamed person is likely to be rejected, shunned, and scorned.

These various differences are summarized in Table 9.3. The most important difference between these two social anxieties is that shame has moral implications but embarrassment does not. In a sense, all the other differences derive from this initial distinction. Thus the reaction in shame is one tinged with regret and depression, whereas embarrassment consists more of feelings of foolishness or awkwardness. And the consequences of shame are serious, whereas the consequences of embarrassment are trivial. It

TABLE 9.3

Embarrassment versus shame

	Embarrassment	Shame
Reaction		
Blushing	Yes	No
Smiling, giggling	Sometimes	Never
Feeling	Foolish	Depressed
Self-attribution	Mistake	Personal defect
Immediate causes		
Breach of manners	Yes	No
Conspicuousness	Yes	No
Teasing	Yes	No
Overpraise	Yes	No
Letting the group down	No	Yes
Public immorality	No	Yes
Leakage/disclosure	Of affection	Of baseness
Consequences		
Self-esteem	Temporary loss	Enduring loss
Reaction of others	Laughter	Scorn
	Acceptance	Rejection

would border on the unethical to induce shame in the laboratory because of its seriousness, but it would seem to be ethical to induce embarrassment. This ethical consideration and the practical problems of attempting to induce shame are the major reasons why shame has been so little studied and why we have so little reliable knowledge about it.

NOTES

1. Goffman (1956), Zimbardo (1977)
2. During childhood, for example, it is worse for a boy to be called a sissy than for a girl to be called a tomboy.
3. Ho (1976)

 4. Piers and Singer (1953)
 5. Piers and Singer (1953, p. 36)
 6. Lynd (1958)
 7. Tompkins (1963)
 8. Tompkins (1963, p. 123)
 9. Tompkins (1963, p. 185)
10. Tompkins (1963, p. 133)
11. Tompkins (1963, p. 136)
12. Lerner and Simmons (1966)

AUDIENCE ANXIETY

Most people do not habitually speak or perform before audiences. Though such occasions are infrequent, audience anxiety is the most frequently reported fear among adults.[1] When people are required to give a speech, many of them worry, find excuses not to perform, or even become sick. A college teacher reports the following phenomena:

> several students fainting while giving a speech, dozens of students who "disappeared" when their first speech was due, similar dozens who cowered in the back of the room when called on, claiming not to be "ready," absences on days when speeches were due that were too numerous to count, instances of students vomiting when called on to speak, and even one attempted suicide allegedly brought on by fear of a speech due the next morning.[2]

Audience anxiety, which consists of fear, tension, and disorganization in front of an audience, may be regarded as one extreme along a dimension of public performance. The middle of the dimension is marked by a relaxed, calm, assured demeanor, which results in communication or performance that is organized and coherent; the speaker is doing his job with minimal attention to himself as a participant. At the other extreme is exhibitionism, in which the speaker deliberately calls attention to himself; instead of focusing on performing or communicating, he says in effect, "Look at me." Exhibitionists are usually so obvious in their attempts to capture an audience's attention that their motive quickly becomes known to the audience. Of course, if the exhibitionist is especially skillful and offers a particularly appealing personality, he may attain the special status called *charisma*; such spellbinders are especially welcome in politics and revivalist forms of religion.

THE REACTION

The observable features of audience anxiety may be divided into expressive, physiological, and instrumental signs. The *expressive* component is easy to see because the person is standing in front of an audience: a scared look, rapidly shifting eyes, skin pallor, quaking, and a shaky voice.

The *physiological* component is the same as in all fear: sweating, rapid breathing, elevated blood pressure, and a pounding heart. When a person gets up to speak, his heart rate immediately accelerates.[3] These various bodily reactions are due to activation of the sympathetic division of the autonomic nervous system. Such sympathetic arousal in audience anxiety stands in sharp contrast to the parasympathetic dominance that occurs in embarrassment and shame.

The *instrumental* component appears mainly as a disorganization of ongoing behavior. The speaker may forget his speech, stammer, lose his place, laugh nervously, fumble with papers—all revealing a deterioration of performance. The fear may become so intense that the speaker shortens his performance by omitting material or even bolting from the room in the midst of a sentence. And some speakers have opted out by fainting.[4]

The expressive and instrumental components are relatively easy to observe. Two speech researchers[5] have listed these observable aspects of audience anxiety and classified them into five groups:

1. Verbal Fluency—stammering, vocalized pauses ("Ah," "um"), speech blocks, hunting for words.

2. Voice—quivering, tense, speech too fast or too slow, monotonous.

3. Facial Expressions—lack of eye contact, peculiar eye movements, grimaces, twitches, "deadpan" expression.

4. Arms and Hands—rigid, tense, fidgety, motionless, lack of appropriate gestures.

5. Body—swaying, pacing, shuffling feet.

The reported feelings of audience anxiety are similar to those of any strong fear: anguish, tension, and apprehension, which at times reach the intensity of panic and terror. There are two kinds of worry. One is simply *evaluation anxiety*, a fear of performing poorly and of failing. This fear of failure is common to all situations involving evaluation: a job interview, a test, or a school or work assignment. The dread specific to audience anxiety is failing in front of a group.

The second kind of worry is that of *being rejected as a person*. The speaker is concerned mainly about whether he will be liked and appreciated. An audience might approve of a speaker's performance but find him unattractive, cold, or even hostile. Or, an audience might give him low marks for performance but approve his appearance and demeanor. The point here is that a public speaker is usually subject to two kinds of scrutiny by the audience. One kind, causing him to focus on his performance, may cause evaluation anxiety. The second kind, causing him to focus on himself as a person, may cause acute public self-awareness, a concern over his appearance or behavior.

IMMEDIATE CAUSES

Suppose that after listening to a talk, you rise to ask the speaker a question. As part of the audience, you are anonymous and unnoticed; as a standing questioner, you are suddenly conspicuous. You may become tense and anxious, but your fear quickly dissipates as soon as you sit down. The speaker, unfortunately, has no comparable retreat. He must remain on stage, the center of the audience's attention. Being so conspicuous, he may become acutely aware of himself as a social object. He may focus attention on himself so intensely that he forgets his lines and his performance deteriorates. Public speaking and stage performance require close attention to the task at hand. Acute public self-awareness distracts the person from his performance, and his realization of this distraction and his failing efforts may throw him into a panic. Thus, *conspicuousness* can cause audience anxiety.

Another cause, perhaps less obvious, is *novelty*. We are all more relaxed in familiar surroundings. An unfamiliar room, lecture hall, or stage tends to cause a wariness that may lead to audience anxiety. Even if the room is familiar, the perspective of the speaker may be entirely novel. I regularly teach in a hall that holds 500 students, and occasionally I bring a student on stage. Almost without exception, such students become tense and inhibited, and they are surprised how different the view is from the stage in contrast to the familiar view from the audience. Such novelty is obviously enhanced by the presence of an audience of strangers, in contrast to an audience of friends.

The speaker's or performer's role may also be novel. The novice actor tends to be more scared on stage than is the veteran; the newly-minted teacher suffers more from audience anxiety than the aging professor. When a speaker or performer is unsure of his lines and insecure in his new profession, he tends to carry the apprehension onstage where, added to perceptual novelty, it becomes audience anxiety.

One cause of audience anxiety, almost by definition, is *properties of the audience. Size* is important. Teachers at ease in a small class may have strong qualms about teaching a large class. Rookie baseball players tend to be awed when they first play in Yankee Stadium. I remember vividly the first time I stepped into an auditorium to face 500 tightly packed students. Despite years of previous teaching, I felt oppressed by the mass of people whose attention was focused on a single point, me. Fortunately, the moment passed, my experience took over, and I soon habituated to lecturing to large classes. Inexperienced speakers, however, find it difficult to cope with larger audiences and tend to shorten their presentations to escape the aversive situation.[6]

The *status* of the audience also determines the intensity of the anxiety. Adult speakers are usually relaxed when the audience consists of children. Fellow students or colleagues may induce moderate tension in a speaker. But if the audience includes people of higher status than the speaker's— teachers when a student speaks or nationally known scientists when a new PhD speaks—the speaker tends to be shaky and apprehensive. Status is related to formality: other things equal, the higher the status of the audience, the more formal the context. And formal occasions, because they imply higher standards for socially correct behavior, are more likely to induce social anxiety.

Whether the audience is *familiar* is also important. The teacher who is relaxed with his students toward the end of the semester may be tense on the first day of class. The sight of friends, relatives, or colleagues in the audience tends to reassure the speaker; the sight of strangers tends to escalate anxiety. Closely related to familiarity is the *similarity* between speaker and audience. Consider how a man feels when talking to an audience of women, or an Anglo woman speaking to an audience of Chicanas. Such speakers would be at least wary lest they inadvertently offend the audience, and at most, panicky because of uncertainty and worry about how they are performing. In brief, the less

TABLE 10.1

Immediate causes of audience anxiety

Cause	Example
Conspicuousness	Being onstage in the spotlight
Novelty	
Of perspective	Audience appears different when viewed from the stage
Of role	New teacher lectures for the first time
Kind of audience	
Size	Large auditorium or stadium filled with people
Status	Student speaks before professors
Familiarity	Institutional host welcomes visiting audience
Similarity	Woman speaks to male athletes
Behavior	Audience is apathetic

similar and the less familiar the audience, the more likely is audience anxiety.

Finally, the *behavior* of the audience obviously affects the speaker. Suppose, in a small room, the audience avoid eye contact with the speaker, never smile, show no signs of approval, and become restless and preoccupied; surely the speaker would become upset. In contrast, a speaker would be at ease if the audience looked at the speaker, smiled, nodded, and became relaxed and attentive. When these contrasting audience behaviors were manipulated, speakers' heart rates rose much higher in response to an inattentive audience than to an attentive, approving one.[7] Such objective evidence, obtained under controlled laboratory conditions, is all to the good. Nevertheless, even without further laboratory evidence we know from everyday life that any negative audience's reaction is likely to intensify the speaker's anxiety.

In summary, the immediate, situational causes of audience anxiety have been discussed under the headings of conspicuousness, novelty, and audience properties. These various causes are listed in Table 10.1.

AUDIENCE ANXIETY AS A TRAIT

People vary considerably in audience anxiety. Some dread public speaking and avoid it at all costs. If forced to speak, they tend to panic in front of a group. Others have qualms about being on stage, but the fear is mild enough to be tolerated. And a fortunate minority are sufficiently relaxed to enjoy public speaking and perform well.

These variations in the trait of audience anxiety can easily be observed, and each of us knows approximately where he or she stands on this dimension. It is simple, therefore, to devise a self-report questionnaire about the disposition. Unfortunately, most of the questionnaires tap not only audience anxiety but other social anxieties as well. The Social Anxiety scale I helped devise contains only two items specific to audience anxiety and four others on shyness and embarrassment.[8] A speech researcher has developed an excellent self-report instrument on communication anxiety, but it contains not only audience anxiety items but also shyness items.[9] These and similar questionnaires will be discussed in the Social Anxiety chapter. This leaves the only two questionnaries that are unconfounded measures of audience anxiety.[10]

The first was constructed for research on various therapies.[11] It consists of 30 items, 15 true and 15 false. Representative items are:

I am in constant fear of forgetting my speech.

I always avoid speaking in public if possible.

I perspire and tremble just before getting up to speak.

I am terrified at the thought of speaking before a group of people.

The scale was evidently used in only a single study on therapy, and no one has used it since.

The other scale was designed for elementary school children.[12] It consists of only five items, the contents of which are:

Afraid people will laugh.

Embarrassed when singing.

Knees shake when reciting.

Afraid of mistakes.

Scared in front of a group.

Children who scored high on this questionnarie tended not to volunteer for a classroom skit. The scale correlated $-.55$ with an Exhibitionism scale and .74 with a Test Anxiety scale. Clearly, children high on the trait of audience anxiety are not exhibitionists, and they are fearful of test results.

We need research with similar instruments on college students and other adults. At present the only studies on adults that link the trait of audience anxiety with public speaking performance have used the confounded questionnaries mentioned earlier. For example, in a sample of college students high in communication anxiety, from 50 to 70% dropped courses in public speaking; for the Lows, the range was from 5 to 10% dropping courses.[13] If we possess this kind of knowledge, why insist on a questionnaire specifically on audience anxiety? Because we want to ensure that our self-report measure be specific and limited to social anxiety. It is entirely possible, for instance, that people who are highly emotional also avoid public speaking, as they avoid a wide range of fear-arousing situations. On the other hand, at least some people with intense audience anxiety are probably not at all fearful in nonpublic or nonsocial situations. We need to separate the personality traits specific to audience anxiety from more general personality traits.

A THEORY OF AUDIENCE ANXIETY

A search of the literature revealed no theory designed specifically to explain audience anxiety. My own approach separates the immediate situational causes of audience anxiety from the enduring dispositional causes. As such, the theory integrates the previous material in the chapter. For this reason I am deviating from the chapter plan common to the chapters in this section of the book and presenting my own theory here.

Immediate causes and processes

Let us begin by dividing audience anxiety into a sequence of three time intervals. The first is the time preceding the speech or performance. This period can last a day or so (in extreme cases, longer), but for simplicity, let us say that this interval is the period just prior to the performance (say, a few minutes to an hour). This is the time for worry, dread, and apprehension about what will happen once the spotlight points at you.

The following interval is just the first minute or two of the speech or performance: you have just been introduced, or you have just appeared on stage. These are the moments when you are under the closest scrutiny by the audience. Knowing this, you are likely to suffer an acute public self-awareness. Perceiving that all eyes are on you, you may feel terribly exposed and vulnerable.

The last time interval is the remainder of the performance. As the performance continues, you are likely to concentrate more and more on what you are saying or how you are performing. This shift in attention necessarily reduces public self-awareness. Your level of anxiety, however, may remain high because of the continuing novelty of the situation.

Which interval is the worst for someone afraid of speaking or performing in public? Most likely it is the time period when two causes of audience anxiety occur. This is the first minute or two, when the performer is conspicuous and the situation is most novel. There are data consistent with this suggestion.[14] The heart rate of subjects giving a talk were recorded at time intervals matching the three that have been described. The heart rates, in beats per minute, were as follows:

just before	114
at the start	124
later in the talk	114

Just prior to the speech, heart rate had risen to 114 beats per minute, presumably because of worry. Heart rate peaked at the start of the speech, probably because the subjects were conspicuous (public self-awareness) and aroused by novelty. Presumably, as the talk proceeded and the subjects became involved in the content of the speech, their public self-awareness dissipated, and their heart rate dropped to the pre-speech level. This level was still well above normal (the post-speech heart rate was 98 beats per minute), perhaps because of arousal caused by novelty or perspective and of role.

This analysis of the sequence of audience anxiety into three time segments has implications for the course of the anxiety over months and years. Most people habituate to audiences and eventually are less tense and scared when speaking or performing. One assumes that this habituation and the diminution of fear occur backward in the three-part sequence. After a few performances, most speakers relax as they get into their speech, even though they are tense at the start and worried beforehand. Gradually, with continued experience, the anxiety present at the start of a speech wanes and may disappear, even though there is still apprehension just before the performance. The last component of audience anxiety to disappear is the prior worrying.

What causes audience anxiety to dissipate? Why does it diminish backward through the time sequence? To answer these questions, we must consider three causes of audience anxiety: novelty, conspicuousness, and evaluation anxiety.

Let us proceed backward through the time sequence. During the speech or performance, novice speakers or performers contend with novelty of both perspective and role. The room and the audience are strange, and the role is unfamiliar. As performance follows performance, however, such novelty wears off. The room or auditorium soon becomes the same old place, and the role of speaking or performing becomes as practiced as any repeated motor act. Such habituation occurs gradually and may require many performances. But for most people the novelty eventually wanes and no longer causes audience anxiety.

Now consider the first minute or two. When a person rises to speak, he immediately becomes conspicuous. The audience scrutinizes his appearance and behavior, inducing an intense awareness of himself as a social object. As long as he remains in this state of acute public self-awareness, he will remain at a peak level of audience anxiety. As soon as his attention shifts from himself, his anxiety level drops sharply. What causes such a shift? As he concentrates on what he is saying or doing and "gets into" the speech or performance, his attention focuses on the content of what he is doing. He may show a slide, write on the blackboard, ask a question, start a discussion, or even tell a joke. However his attention is diverted from himself, once he stops feeling conspicuous, his anxiety diminishes. After this initial minute or two, the only remaining problem is novelty.

The last component of audience anxiety to dissipate is the one that occurs first in the time sequence: the apprehension that occurs just prior to going on stage. Long after people have habituated to the novelty of public speaking and after they no longer feel conspicuous when they start a speech, they may still worry beforehand. What are they worried about? Failing! Their concern is with how well they will perform. And they will continue to experience this evaluation anxiety until they are eventually reassured by positive feedback from audiences or their own recognition of success. At that point they can anticipate public speaking or performing with confidence, and there is no longer any need to worry.

Let me review these complex issues involving remedia-

TABLE 10.2

Processes and remediation of audience anxiety

Time sequence	Major cause	Remediating cause	Routine outcome
Just before First minute or two	Evaluation anxiety Conspicuousness (public self-awareness)	Positive feedback about performance Attention shifts away from self	Confident anticipation Attention to performance
Remainder of performance	Novelty (arousal, uncertainty)	Habituation of perspective and role	Relaxation, lack of inhibition

tion of audience anxiety using Table 10.2 as an aid. The remediation of audience anxiety starts with habituation. After only a few performances, perhaps sooner, the perspective and the role are no longer novel, and the speaker can be relatively relaxed and uninhibited. Each time the speaker appears onstage, however, he again becomes conspicuous and publicly self-aware. This self-awareness can be wiped out by a shift in attention to the performance itself. It takes time to develop the ability to launch immediately into a speech without considering oneself as a social object, so the audience anxiety of the first minute or so tends to persist longer; eventually it disappears. But prior worry over failure may continue after all the onstage anxiety has dissipated. Such apprehension is relieved only by recognition of success, which in turn leads to confidence. In brief, the sequence of remediation of audience anxiety proceeds backwards over time: first, most of the time onstage; then, the first minute or so; and finally, the few minutes just prior to performance.

Such remediation represents a benign cycle: anxiety→ experience and habituation→relaxation and confidence→ lack of anxiety. But there can also be a vicious cycle, in which the experience of speaking or performing leads to either no decrease in audience anxiety or an intensification. The major determinants of a vicious cycle may be several dispositions.

Dispositions

Which personality traits can make people more vulnerable to audience anxiety? A partial answer is: traits involving a chronic concern with one's self as a social object. There appear to be three such personality dispositions.

The first is *low self-esteem*. Those who have a low opinion of themselves assume that they will perform poorly. No one wants to fail in public, so such people avoid the spotlight. Why do some people have low self-esteem? There are several reasons,[15] but one possibility is recognition of

one's own lack of ability. Suppose you have trouble thinking on your feet; suppose you have had no practice at
speaking before groups; suppose you stammer, lisp, or have
trouble pronouncing *l*s or *r*s; or suppose you have a foreign
accent or a peculiar regional speech accent. Any of these
"defects" might cause you not only to devalue your communication skills (low self-esteem) but also to avoid speaking in public (audience anxiety).

   Shy people also tend to be scared of audiences. *Shyness*,
as we shall see in the next chapter, is a broad disposition
that includes both inhibition of social behavior and avoidance of others. And shy people are less likely to develop the
social skills needed for speaking in public. There is only a
single published study relevant to this point, and it is
confirmatory. In contrast to college students who are not
shy, shy students report more anxiety and are judged more
anxious when delivering speeches.[16]

   Finally, acute *public self-consciousness*, which is presumed to underlie the other varieties of social anxiety, can
also cause audience anxiety. Items on the Public Self-
Consciousness scale include concern about what others
think, self-presentation, appearance, and style of behaving.
All these concerns would be enhanced when a person is on
stage being scrutinized by an audience.

   The above hypotheses were first stated in an early draft
of this book. To test them, a colleague and I developed
self-report measures of these traits and correlated them
with a self-report of audience anxiety. The Audience Anxiety scale consisted of five items.[17] Some were borrowed;
some were newly written; all were designed to measure
various aspects of this fear:

   I feel very relaxed before speaking in front of a group.

   I feel anxious when I speak in front of a group.

   I am very nervous while performing in front of people.

   My voice never shakes when I recite in class.

Sometimes my body trembles when I speak up in class.

Notice that the content of the scale includes fear before and during performance, both speaking and performing, and also the expressive components of voice and body.

The Self-Esteem scale consists of seven items that tap opinions of self-worth—for example, "I have a low opinion of myself." The Shyness scale consists of nine items that tap the various ways a person might be shy.[18] A typical item is, "I feel inhibited in social situations." (The Public Self-Consciousness scale was described in Chapter 4.)

The correlations between the Audience Anxiety scale and the other three traits were in the predicted direction. For Self-Esteem, the correlation was −.34. It appears that people who lack self-esteem tend to worry about public speaking and become tense when they perform.

For Shyness, the correlation was .48. Presumably, shy people, being excessively tense and inhibited socially, would be panicky in front of a group. And for Public Self-Consciousness, the correlation was .21. Audience anxiety, like the other three social anxieties, must involve an acute sense of oneself as a social object.[20]

In interpreting these three correlations, I have inferred that each of the three traits (low self-esteem, shyness, and public self-consciousness) is a cause of audience anxiety. No scientist is allowed to infer the direction of effects from the mere presence of a correlation. This particular direction of causality is assumed on theoretical grounds. Self-esteem, shyness, and public self-consciousness are all generalized tendencies, whereas audience anxiety is specific to situations involving an audience. It is hard to believe that being scared in front of audiences would make a person shy in two-or three-person groups, or that audience anxiety would cause tendencies as pervasive as low self-esteem and public self-consciousness. Therefore, it appears that the traits of low self-esteem, shyness, and public self-consciousness are causes of audience anxiety.[21]

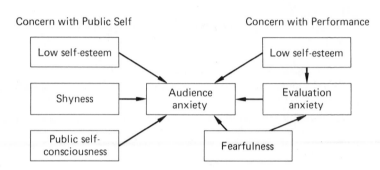

FIGURE 10.1

Dispositional Causes of Audience Anxiety

One final question concerning the above three correlations: could they have occurred because audience anxiety would correlate with almost any other trait? No, audience anxiety does not correlate significantly with either Sociability (wanting to be with others) or with Private Self-Consciousness.[22]

The relationships just discussed are shown on the left side of Figure 10.1, which deals with a concern about one's public self. The right side of this diagram portrays the traits related to an excessive concern about success or failure in front of an audience. *Evaluation anxiety* must be listed as a prime cause of audience anxiety. Test anxiety, one form of evaluation anxiety, correlates .74 with audience anxiety in children.[23]

It appears that people with *low self-esteem* tend to be more anxious about being evaluated; thus low self-esteem can heighten evaluation anxiety. But even if a person with low self-esteem is not anxious about being evaluated, he will expect to perform poorly in front of an audience; thus low self-esteem can directly cause audience anxiety.

Finally, *fearfulness*, the general tendency to become upset and scared, must be included. It is placed in the middle of Figure 10.1 because fearfulness is more general than the specific concern with your public self or performance. As a generalized tendency, fearfulness contributes directly to audience anxiety, and indirectly by intensifying evaluation anxiety. Not surprisingly, fearfulness correlates .42 with audience anxiety.

The dispositions portrayed in Figure 10.1 may explain the vicious cycle of the maintenance of audience anxiety—that is, why so many people do not habituate even after considerable practice in public speaking. If a speaker has low self-esteem, he expects others to devaluate both his performance and himself (appearance and personality). If he is shy, he will tend to be tense and inhibited in all social situations. If he is high in public self-consciousness, he will be unable to shift the focus of attention away from himself. If he is panicky with fear, he will be unable to habituate to either the novel perspective or the novel role. And if his public self-awareness and anxiety level both remain high, his performance will be disorganized and perhaps even incoherent. As a result, he will fail and be aware of his failure. Or, he may become so anguished that he bolts from the stage; thereafter the stage would constitute a conditioned stimulus for a powerful avoidance response. In summary, the dispositions diagramed in Figure 10.1 might so predispose a speaker to tension, failure, and avoidance that the entire experience might be regarded as a trial of traumatic avoidance conditioning. If these assumptions are correct, any attempt at therapy would require dealing with these dispositions before even starting on the relief of stage fright.

NOTES

1. Bruskin Associates (1973)
2. McCroskey (1977, pp. 90–91)
3. Behnke and Carlile (1971)
4. McCroskey (1977)

5. Mulac and Sherman (1974)

6. Levin, Baldwin, Gallwey, and Paivio (1960)

7. Bassett, Behnke, Carlile, and Rogers (1973)

8. This social anxiety factor, part of the Self-Consciousness Inventory (Fenigstein, Scheier, and Buss, 1974), is discussed in Chapter 4.

9. McCroskey (1977)

10. This statement refers to published questionnaries. I helped to devise an unpublished questionnaire which will be discussed shortly.

11. Paul (1966)

12. Paivio, Baldwin, and Berger (1961)

13. McCroskey (1970)

14. Porter (1974). I discovered this research after I formulated my hypothesis about the three-step sequence of audience anxiety.

15. See Buss (1978, Chapter 23)

16. Pilkonis (1977)

17. The coefficient of internal consistency (alpha) for these items is .73, entirely adequate for a short scale. My collaborator was Jonathan Cheek.

18. The Shyness scale will be described in more detail in Chapter 11.

19. The correlations all had the same sample size, 579 college men and women.

20. I had originally thought that the correlation between Audience Anxiety and Public Self-Consciousness would be somewhat higher than .21. On reflection, I realized that (1) the latter scale correlates only in the twenties with the general Social Anxiety scale (one factor of the Self-Consciousness Inventory) and (2) that audience anxiety is an extremely common social anxiety, afflicting even some of those who are below average in public self-consciousness.

21. It is also possible that these relationships are caused by still another personality trait, as yet unspecified. This possibility, however, is too vague to consider here.

22. That audience anxiety correlates significantly with public but not with private self-consciousness is merely another fact

that shows the difference between the two kinds of self-consciousness.

23. Paivio, Baldwin, and Berger (1961). In this research the subjects were elementary school children. In elementary school, speaking before an audience is closely linked with being graded, hence the very high correlation between test anxiety and audience anxiety. I suggest that in adolescents and adults test anxiety can be distinguished from the more generalized anxiety over any evaluation and that there would be a lower correlation between test anxiety and audience anxiety.

SHYNESS

When a stranger greets an infant or when two adults are introduced, the participants are expected to make social responses. There are norms for greeting behavior and the interaction that follows. Each person is expected to speak, listen receptively, look at the other person, and, in general, respond as a social being. Normally, both members of a dyad hold up their end of the interaction, but when one of them is quiet, retiring, and inhibited, we label such behavior *shyness: the relative absence of expected social behaviors.*[1]

THE REACTION

Shyness consists of both instrumental and affective components. The *instrumental* component is marked by an absence or diminution of social behavior. There is little eye contact, as the gaze is directed downward, sideward, and sometimes even upward—anything to avoid looking directly at the other person's face or eyes. There is a tendency to shrink back from the other person as if there were safety in distance. Shyness is revealed in a classroom by taking a seat far from the lecturer, and in a small conversational group by remaining on the fringe of the group and listening rather than talking. Even acutely shy people tend to remain in the presence of others, their shyness revealed as a reluctance to become involved. But, occasionally, a desperately shy person may bolt from the room, and a shy child may try literally to hide behind its mother's skirts.

Communication is severely restrained. Less speech is emitted, longer pauses ensue, and volume is down, as if the person were fearful of offending others merely by speaking in a normal voice. I recall introducing a young psychologist to a well-known, shy, older psychologist at a party. I left immediately, but the younger man later recounted the experience. He was too awed to initiate any talk, and the older psychologist was evidently too shy. The latter rocked back and forth on his feet for a few minutes of interminable silence and then merely wandered off.

This example is of course an extreme case; even when intensely shy, most people can manage to stammer out a few words. The constraint carries over to the nonverbal aspects of communication. There are few head nods, exclamations, gestures, or other displays of interest or animation. Smiling is notably absent, except for an occasional sickly smile. In general, the picture is one of timidity, inhibition, and strain.

The strain and tension are part of the *affective* component in shyness. When shy, most people report an intense awareness of themselves as social objects. They may feel naked and revealed. They may be concerned about being seen as ill-mannered, clumsy, intrusive, or too loud. (The latter presents an interesting paradox: an inhibited person worrying about being too effusive). They may worry about saying the wrong thing or appearing foolish. Or they may worry about being ignored or rejected by the other people present.

These apprehensions are future-oriented: the shy person fears what might happen. Such worry is unlike the parasympathetic reactions of embarrassment and shame, in which the person reacts to an event that causes acute public self-awareness. Rather, shyness is more like audience anxiety in its anticipation of disaster. Like the person suffering from stage fright, the shy person is often scared. His heart may race, his breathing rate speed up, and his blood pressure rise—all part of arousal of the sympathetic division of the autonomic nervous system. Notice the use of the subjunctive. The shy person *may* worry, *may* have a strong sympathetic reaction. But if he is only a little shy, he may be socially inhibited without any sympathetic reaction.

Social behavior can also be inhibited by fatigue, illness, and moodiness. When people are sleepy, ill, or melancholy, all responsiveness is diminished, not merely social responsiveness. These conditions are excluded as examples of shyness because the inhibition of behavior is nonspecific and generalized. This exclusion is not arbitrary. We define learning, for example, as a change in behavior due to experience. It is then necessary to exclude changes in behavior caused by fatigue, illness, sensory changes, and changes in motivation. By the same token, when we define shyness as the inhibition of social behavior, we must exclude such inhibition when it is caused by generalized, nonsocial conditions such as fatigue and illness.

If there are instances of apparent shyness that we exclude, are there also instances of apparent nonshyness that we include? Yes, people who are shy but compensate by being overloud, brash, and socially intrusive. How can we distinguish between such people and undersocialized extraverts? One way is to ask them. Another is to check for consistency: the truly shy person cannot maintain a facade of extraversion either within a given social context or across situations. In any event, shy compensators are rare, and we should be cautious in labeling brash, overbearing behavior as a compensation for shyness.

IMMEDIATE CAUSES

The most frequent and important situational cause of shyness appears to be novelty.[2] It is well known that a strange context induces caution. Most people need to feel secure before they explore and initiate social contacts. The best evidence for this need for security comes from research on infants,[3] but everyday experience appears to confirm that the same need exists in older children and in adults. We do seem to be cautious and inhibited in novel environments.

The novelty may be physical or geographical. Both venturing into a new neighborhood and visiting a distant city or country induce wariness. So does starting at a new school or job, or moving to a new home.

Novelty also occurs in social contexts. When we meet strangers, we are usually cautious and inhibited, hiding our typical social behavior behind a facade of formality, politeness, and cliches. The sense of strangeness is more intense when a person is introduced to a group of people who know each other or to people who belong to an organized group, such as a club or a work group.

Perhaps the most important kind of novelty—in terms of personality development—is *role* novelty. As children mature, they are required to adopt new roles—for instance, from being the baby of the family to being an older sibling. Adolescence is a period of especially rapid shifts in roles, as young people start assuming adult roles. Each time a new role is assumed, the novelty usually causes shyness. The adolescent on a first date is typically unsure, cautious, and inhibited. A man or woman, on being promoted to a supervisory position, feels uncomfortable in the new role and tends to be tentative and somewhat shy in initial contacts with others.

Whenever there is novelty—of geography, social context, or role—there is an initial conflict between the motives of security and exploration. In each instance, adaptation to the new situation requires exploratory, instrumental behavior. At first, such behavior is inhibited by the strangeness of the situation; the need for security predominates. As the new surroundings, people, and roles become familiar, the person attains a measure of security. Now shyness dissipates, and instrumental social responses are made more freely and in a more relaxed manner.

Two kinds of social contexts tend to induce intense shyness. When the situation is *formal*—as at a wedding, funeral, anniversary dinner, inauguration, or similar celebration—some of the participants may not know all of the ritual behavior expected of them. As a result, they tend to remain quiet and shrink from contact with others.

Shyness may also be intense when the stranger holds *high status*. Many people are uncertain about how to act with a president, a king, a Nobel prize winner, or even a famous actor. Again, a common outcome is gaze aversion, shrinking from close contact, and an inability to converse normally—in brief, shyness.

Being *conspicuously different* from others can also inhibit social behavior. Consider the plight of the only boy in a room full of girls, of a Chicano in a room full of Anglos, or of a basketball center surrounded by jockeys. Such singularity of a person's gender, ethnic group, or appearance tends to make him acutely aware of himself as a social object. The usual outcome is a sharp drop in social initiative and responsiveness, avoidance of others, and a search for the exit.

Though shyness may occur because of the mere presence of others, their actions are more likely to cause shyness. Others may make you conspicuous by staring or making personal comments. Or they may single you out by shunning you when at least minimal social interaction is the norm. Both excessive and insufficient social attention commonly cause acute awareness of oneself as a social object, one outcome of which is an inhibition of speech and an absence of attempts at social contact.

TABLE 11.1

Immediate causes of shyness

Category	Example
Novelty	
Physical	New school
Social	Meeting strangers
Role	Job promotion
Presence of others	
Formality	Funeral
Status	Meeting royalty
Conspicuousness	Only man among women
Actions of others	
Excessive attention	Being stared at
Insufficient attention	Being shunned
Intrusiveness	Others are too intimate

On the other hand, another person may be overfriendly and excessively intimate. He may try to talk about very personal topics and ask for revealing confidences. Such *intrusiveness* tends to make the listener back off and exhibit the typical signs of shyness: wariness, reduction of speech and expressive behavior, formality, and even a physical retreat.

In summary, the immediate causes of shyness include novelty, the presence of others, and their actions. These causes, together with examples of each, are listed in Table 11.1.

ENDURING CAUSES

Shyness as a trait

On personality inventories, shyness appears as a factor or a scale, usually associated with low sociability or anxiety. People who have little motivation for mixing with others tend to be shy, and timidity is an aspect not only of shyness but also of wariness and fearfulness. So it is not surprising that on personality inventories shyness is linked with either low sociability or fearfulness. But this linkage merely confounds shyness with other dispositions, a confounding that should be avoided in future research.

Shyness has also been represented in speech anxiety questionnaires. As we discovered in the last chapter, one of the better communication anxiety questionnaires, though consisting mainly of audience anxiety items, also contains several shyness items.[4]

Two speech experts, breaking with tradition, have described a trait called *reticence*, which appears to be identical to shyness.[5] They list "symptoms" of reticence:

1. Maladroit socially; do not talk much and are silent in the classroom.

2. Misperceive social situations; uncertain about obligations and wait for others to make the first move.

3. Confused and uncertain about the nature of their problem.

4. Do not know what communication really is.

5. Do not listen well.

6. Are low in self-esteem.

So far we have been discussing shyness as a trait in normal people, but many psychiatric patients are also hesitant, wary, and socially uncertain. One factor that emerged from the self-reports of psychiatric outpatients was called *social timidity*.[6] The eight items comprising the factor are excellent examples of various aspects of the disposition to be shy:

1. I usually feel awkward with strangers.

2. I usually feel uncomfortable when with a crowd of people I do not know.

3. I usually feel nervous when speaking to someone in authority.

4. I find it difficult to ask other people for information.

5. I always feel uncomfortable when I do not know what is expected of me.

6. I am usually in doubt whether to greet someone I know only slightly.

7. I am sometimes afraid of expressing myself in case I make a foolish mistake.

8. I feel generally uncomfortable when eating or drinking in front of others.

In describing men who score high on this factor, the authors wrote: "The typical man of this group is solitary, rarely or never enjoys going to parties and describes himself as being the sort of person who thinks much and speaks little."[7] The typical woman "is socially ill-at-ease, uncomfortable if she has to greet someone in the street, finds it difficult to speak in public, and is bothered if watched at work."[7] Social timidity was the mildest and most normal of the social anxieties of these psychiatric patients. Indeed, social timidity is common in most populations, and the above descriptions would apply to any shy person.

The most extensive research on the disposition of shyness was a dissertation by Paul Pilkonis, a student of Philip Zimbardo. The dissertation, published as two papers,[8] combined self-reports with objective measures of behavior. College men and women rated themselves for shyness and filled out several personality questionnaires. Shyness correlated $-.38$ with extraversion, and had roughly the same negative relationship with sociability.[9] There were several gender differences. A higher percentage of men reported being shy. Public self-consciousness was moderately correlated with shyness in men ($r = .27$) but not in women ($r = .06$). Pilkonis suggested that his sample of Stanford University women may be less shy than most women: "Women who successfully compete for places at a selective, private university may be relatively more assertive and socially competent than their male peers."[10] For both genders, the correlation between shyness and private self-consciousness was, as expected, nearly zero.

Pilkonis had his subjects become acquainted with other subjects (really experimental accomplices) while observers rated the subjects' social behavior. Observers' ratings of shyness correlated substantially with subjects' self-reports ($r = .58$). Shyer subjects (self-reported) were observed to be less willing to break silence, either initially or in the middle of an interaction, and they spoke less frequently. Once the conversation was initiated by the confederate, however, shy subjects did respond. Nonverbal behavior was also observed, and there was a gender difference:

> Shy females, anxious to make a good impression but constrained by a somewhat passive role, attempted to achieve their goal through frequent nodding and smiling. Among men, social anxiety created a reluctance to talk, look, or make eye contact; among women, anxiety created a need to be pleasing that was expressed through nodding and smiling.[11]

Pilkonis also had his subjects fill out a brief shyness questionnaire. From their self-reports he extracted two clusters of shy people. In the first cluster were those who reported avoiding social situations, not responding when with others, and being awkward socially. The second cluster consisted of people who reported internal discomfort and fear of negative evaluation. If these two clusters have a familiar ring, it is because they are similar to the two components of the shyness reaction, described earlier. The first cluster corresponds to the instrumental component, and the second cluster, to the affective component of the shyness reaction.[12] In brief, in some shy people the instrumental component predominates, their main focus being on their own social behavior. In other shy people, the affective component predominates, their main focus being on their subjective discomfort (sympathetic arousal?) and worry over rejection by others.

Sociability and shyness

Is shyness nothing more than low sociability? If a person is low in sociability, is he or she necessarily shy? Can a low sociable person be unshy? Are some high sociable people shy? These questions can be answered by correlating sociability with shyness. If shyness is nothing more than the low end of the trait of sociability, the correlation should be high—say, −.60 or above. Pilkonis reported a correlation of −.38, but there were problems with his subject sample and his measures.[13]

As far as can be determined, all published measures of sociability—including my own—also tap shyness. To correct this confound, a colleague and I developed a short self-report measure of sociability: the need or preference for being with others.[14] The following items were rated on a scale from 1 (extremely uncharacteristic) to 5 (extremely characteristic):

I like to be with people.

I welcome the opportunity to mix socially with people.

I prefer working alone rather than with others. (reversed)

I find people more stimulating than anything else.

I'd be unhappy if I were prevented from making many social contacts.

The shyness measure was designed to tap inhibition and feelings of tension, discomfort, and awkwardness in social situations. The nine-item scale[15] had one item reversed (the last one):

I feel tense when I'm with people I don't know well.

I feel inhibited in social situations.

I am socially somewhat awkward.

I am often uncomfortable at parties and other social functions.

When conversing, I worry about saying something dumb.

I feel nervous when speaking to someone in authority.

I am more shy with members of the opposite sex.

I have trouble looking someone right in the eye.

I don't find it hard to talk to strangers.

Notice that these shyness items refer to feelings and behavior that occur during social interaction. The sociability items, in contrast, refer to the need or desire to be with people. In other words, there is no built-in overlap between the two scales.

For a sample of almost 1500 college men and women, the correlation between sociability and shyness was $-.33$.[16] This correlation is large enough to indicate that low sociable people tend to be shy. It appears that the reason for this relationship is the preference of low sociable people for being alone. Their frequency of social contact has two consequences. First, they tend not to habituate to the novelty of social contexts and therefore remain aroused. Second, they are less likely to learn the social responses appropriate to mingling with others and therefore feel awkward and clumsy.

The meaning of a correlation of $-.33$, however, should not be exaggerated. This correlation is too modest to equate shyness with low sociability. Though obviously related, the two traits must be regarded as distinct. It should not be too hard to find low sociable people who are not shy, as well as high sociable people who are shy.[17]

In suggesting how low sociability might lead to shyness, I have attributed causality to sociability. But shyness might just as readily cause low sociability. If shy people feel nervous and awkward in social situations, they might start to avoid being with others to avoid discomfort. Thus, concerning the relationship between shyness and sociability, each might just as easily cause the other. In some people at least, it is possible that a positive feedback cycle occurs: if shyness is increased by low sociability, the greater shyness might diminish the desire to be with others.

Which is more important in determining how people behave in social situations, shyness or sociability? Sociability, bear in mind, refers to a need or preference for being with others; shyness refers to feeling tense or awkward when with others. Given these definitions, it is a reasonable prediction that shyness is the more important determiner of what people do when they find themselves in social situations.

To answer this question, Jonathan Cheek selected college women who were high or low in sociability and high or low in shyness.[18] Thus there were four groups of subjects: High–High, High–Low, Low–High, and Low–Low. Pairs of subjects who were matched on the two personality variables (High–High with High–High, High–Low with High–Low, and so on) were asked to get acquainted. The setting was a waiting room in which video and sound components were stored. The subjects were surreptitiously recorded for five minutes, yielding a frequently used measure of social interaction, total amount of talking. Regardless of sociability, low-shy women talked more than high-shy women. Sociability did not affect amount of talking.

In interpreting these findings, we should not forget that the subjects were matched on both personality variables. They might have behaved differently if they were talking with someone who differed in either shyness or sociability, or if the other member were a man. Perhaps the results would have been different if the subjects had been men. These are matters for further research to decide. Meanwhile, within the limits of the study, it appears that shyness, not sociability, is an important determiner of social behavior once people are actually in a social situation.

Sociability is undoubtedly important when people are deciding whether to join others or to remain alone, but this issue is beyond the scope of the present discussion.

Self-consciousness and self-esteem

In my approach to social anxiety, public self-consciousness is a prominent component. This assumption applies to shyness as much as to the other varieties of social anxiety. In these terms, it makes sense for shyness to correlate with public self-consciousness, though there is no reason to suspect a correlation between shyness and private self-consciousness.

Pilkonis' dissertation, mentioned earlier, confirmed these hypotheses.[19] Shyness did not correlate with private self-consciousness. Shyness correlated with public self-consciousness for men but not for women (for a reason already mentioned). Jonathan Cheek and I repeated these correlations on our sample of almost 1500 students, using our measure of shyness.[20] Shyness correlated near zero with private self-consciousness and .26 with public self-consciousness. There were only trivial gender differences, and our .26 correlation virtually duplicates the .27 correlation between shyness and public self-consciousness obtained by Pilkonis.

If you possess at least an average amount of self-esteem, you tend to expect that most people will like you or at least not reject you. But what about those with low self-esteem? Lacking confidence, they are unsure of how they will be received or perhaps even expect to be ignored or rejected by others. They are afraid to commit themselves with gestures of friendliness and liking because they expect that such gestures will not be reciprocated. What is more unpleasant than to have your handshake ignored or your smile be greeted by a "stone face"? It is safer to initiate nothing and remain behind a facade of reserve and indifference. Small wonder, then, that people low in self-esteem tend to be shy—that is, shyness and self-esteem are negatively correlated.

The last paragraph was part of an earlier draft of this chapter. To test the hypothesis that shyness and self-esteem are negatively correlated, Jonathan Cheek and I used our self-report measure of shyness and a self-esteem measure.[21] Using almost 1500 subjects, we found a correlation of −.51, which confirms the hypothesis that shy people lack self-esteem.

Remember, however, that a correlation does not indicate the direction of causation. Shyness might just as easily cause low self-esteem as the reverse. Because shy people tend to feel awkward, tense, and inhibited in social situations, they might infer from such behavior that they are not worth much. Again, a feedback cycle is possible; low self-esteem—shyness—lower self-esteem—still more shyness.

Stigma and social skills

One reason that some people are high in public self-consciousness or low in self-esteem may be that they have been stigmatized. The stigma may involve physical appearance. A person who has been scarred in face or body, someone who has been crippled, or someone who has a pronounced speech stammer—such people have good reasons for believing that others are uncomfortable or embarrassed in their presence. In addition to such defects of appearance or behavior, there is the stigma of identity. Criminals, those labeled as having committed crimes against humanity (Nazis, for instance), those labeled as deviates (child molesters and, in some places, homosexuals), and often the children or other relatives of such people are commonly branded as unfit for human companionship. Like those who have been scarred or crippled, these stigmatized people realistically fear shunning or rejection by others. Consequently, they tend to shrink from strangers, initiate few social contacts, and inhibit social responsiveness when with others—in brief, they are shy.

Shyness may also be the result of a lack of experience in new social situations or a lack of social skills. The two lacks are obviously connected, for social skills can develop only through social contacts. *Inexperience* means that each contact with unfamiliar people is relatively novel. As we saw earlier, novelty is a major immediate cause of shyness. A lack of experience prevents people from habituating to strangers or to new social environments, and this failure to habituate maintains shyness.

Even someone with a history of repeated social contacts may fail to learn appropriate social skills. Perhaps the person was too self-conscious or too low in self-esteem or sociability; perhaps the models were inappropriate or absent. Whatever the reason, some of those who have had the opportunity nevertheless failed to learn how to deal with strangers and casual acquaintances. Aware of their lack of social skills, these people tend to avoid others; or, when social contacts are made, they show wariness and a lack of social responsivity.

The lack of social skills can establish a vicious cycle: lack of skills leads to inhibition and a failure to try out social responses, and therefore results in no acquisition of social skills. And the lack of experience can establish its own vicious cycle: inexperience leads to a tendency to retreat from or to avoid social contacts with unfamiliar people, which, in turn, prevents a person from habituating to novelty and from acquiring the social experience that would compensate for the lack.

CONSEQUENCES

The timidity and unresponsiveness of the shy person may arouse several different reactions in other people. Others may respond with warmth and sympathy. One way to overcome shy people's reticence is to tread softly, as one would approach a timid animal. A gentle acceptance of the shy people's reserve may well be the best thing that can happen to them.

Unfortunately, most strangers and casual acquaintances either do not appreciate shy people's problems or are too involved with their own affairs. Thus, the most common reaction to shyness is indifference or perhaps even shunning. Sympathy and help are usually reserved for good friends, and are not distributed freely to strangers or casual acquaintances. Remember, too, that the others in the social situation are not there as therapists. They, too, may be shy or lack social skills. We can visualize with sympathy the awkwardness of two shy people who have just been introduced.

The reaction of others may be even worse than shunning: it may consist of teasing and ridiculing the shy person. Such hostility, whether direct or veiled in humor, surely adds to the aversiveness of social interaction already experienced by the shy person. Others may also mistakenly try to coax or coerce shy people into greater involvement by calling attention to their shyness. Such attempts, however well-meaning, make shy people conspicuous, which must intensify their discomfort.

Shyness also has consequences for shy people themselves. As we have seen, social inhibition leads to an absence of social rewards, to being ignored by others, or perhaps to scorn and ridicule. In the face of such outcomes, shy people may become melancholy or bitter. Surely their self-esteem will be battered. And a major consequence may be either of the vicious cycles, described above, that maintain shyness through inexperience or lack of social skills.

A THEORETICAL APPROACH: ATTRIBUTION AND CULTURAL VALUES

Until now, the only psychologist to theorize about shyness has been Philip Zimbardo.[22] He suggests that shy people can be aligned along a continuum. At the low end are *in-*

troverts who prefer solitude to the company of others. In the broad middle range are people who feel *awkward*, possess few social skills, and lack confidence. And at the high end are those whose social anxiety is so intense that they are *neurotic* in their escape from and avoidance of social contacts. This continuum consists of three different kinds of shy people: low sociable people, who prefer to remain alone and are comfortable with their preferred way of behaving; people of average sociability, who like social contacts but are inhibited and frightened of social interaction; and people with serious adjustment problems.

Why do people become shy? Zimbardo offers two reasons: attribution and cultural values. Shy people, he argues, label themselves as shy and are so labeled by others. When they act timid or bashful, they attribute causality to themselves rather than the situation. Yet, we know that in some contexts, especially formal ones, most people are reserved and inhibited. Shy people blame themselves, but unshy people blame the situation. As a result, unshy people may try to change the situation, whereas shy people accept things as they are and remain shy.

But even before the labeling process begins, cultural practices and values may help induce it. Zimbardo lists ten ways in which a society may promote shyness:

1. Valuing rugged individualism (making it on one's own, doing it my way).

2. Promoting a cult of the ego (narcissistic introspection, self-absorption, and self-consciousness).

3. Prizing individual success and making failure a source of personal shame in a highly competitive system.

4. Setting limitless aspirations and ambiguous criteria for success, while not teaching ways of coping with failure.

5. Discouraging expressions of emotions and open sharing of feelings and anxieties.

6. Providing little opportunity for intimate relations between the sexes and strict taboos on most forms of sexual expression.

7. Making acceptance and love contingent on fluctuating and critical social standards of performance.

8. Denying the significance of an individual's present experience by making comparisons to the unmatchable glories of past times and the demands of future goals.

9. Fostering social instability through mobility, divorce, economic uncertainty, and any other way possible.

10. Destroying faith in common societal goals and pride in belonging to the group.[23]

Any of these ten practices and values might have negative consequences for young people being socialized in any society, but the practices and values would seem to have such broad effects on behavior that it is hard to see how they would specifically cause shyness. The first two, for example, might yield self-centered, rugged individuals who were not at all shy. The sixth appears to characterize Chinese society today; but as Zimbardo and others have commented, today's Chinese may be among the least shy people on earth. In brief, Zimbardo's ten societal practices do not all necessarily lead to shyness, and they appear to be too broadly conceived to be antecedents of the more specific problem of shyness.[24]

NOTES

1. This definition applies to shyness in animals and human infants, as well as in older children and adults. This chapter deals only with shyness in older children and adults. (Shyness

in animals and especially in human infants will be discussed in Chapter 13.)

2. In this chapter, as in previous ones, I am stating generalizations based on casual observations of everyday life or on sparse laboratory evidence. These statements are really hypotheses, but to say so each time I present one would make this book dull and tedious.

3. This evidence is more relevant to development, so it will be mentioned in Chapter 13.

4. McCroskey (1977)

5. Phillips and Metzger (1973)

6. Sandler, deMonchaux, and Dixon (1958)

7. Sandler, deMonchaux, and Dixon (1958, p. 25)

8. Pilkonis (1977a,b)

9. Unfortunately, both the extraversion and sociability self-report measures contained items that also tapped shyness. The sociability measure, for instance, contained this item: "Do you suddenly feel shy when you want to talk to an attractive stranger?" We would expect that unconfounded measures would yield a lower correlation between sociability and shyness.

10. Pilkonis (1976, p. 25)

11. Pilkonis (1976, p. 66)

12. The idea of two components of shyness (instrumental and affective), part of an earlier draft of this chapter, predates Pilkonis' research. His research suggests that the distinction has merit.

13. Pilkonis (1976). The women in his sample tended to be unshy, and there was at least one shyness item in his measure of sociability (see Footnote 9).

14. Cheek and Buss (1979). An attempt to factor analyze the five-item scale, using correlations from a sample of 1492 subjects, yielded only a single factor. The measure of inter-item consistency, alpha, was .72; this is entirely adequate for such a short scale.

15. Again, a factor analysis revealed only a single factor. The alpha was .78, suggesting adequate inter-item consistency. For the correlations between each item and the total scale for both the shyness and sociability measures, see Cheek (1979).

16. The gender differences here and in other correlations to be reported were so small that we combined the men's and women's data.

17. In fact, it was not hard to find such subjects for a study that will be reported shortly.

18. Cheek (1979)

19. Pilkonis (1976)

20. Cheek and Buss (1979)

21. Our self-esteem measure consists of seven items, all on the same factor. The coefficient of item consistency was .75 for 1492 subjects. In the following list of self-esteem items, the starred ones are reversed:

> I have a low opinion of myself.*
>
> I often wish I were someone else.*
>
> Things are all mixed up in my life.*
>
> I'm fairly sure of myself.
>
> There are lots of things about myself that need to be changed.*
>
> I am a failure.*
>
> I am basically worthwhile.

22. Zimbardo (1977)

23. Zimbardo (1977, pp 211–212)

24. A developmental theory that is specific to shyness is presented in Chapter 13.

SOCIAL ANXIETY

The last four chapters have described embarrassment, shame, shyness, and audience anxiety, and suggested the immediate and enduring causes of each. These four affective reactions comprise *social anxiety*, which is defined as *discomfort in the presence of others*. The discomfort is not a fear of harm. *Fear* is an entirely appropriate word for worry about being attacked or punished, or merely being the victim of accidental harm or illness. *Social anxiety* has a more limited meaning: being upset or disturbed by others' scrutiny or remarks, or merely because others are present.

When we talk to strangers or casual acquaintances or when we are looked at by others, we tend to become aware of ourselves as social objects. This self-awareness can become so acute that we are disturbed and uncomfortable— that is, we are socially anxious. The major difference, then, between social anxiety and public self-awareness is that social anxiety involves mild or intense discomfort.

Acute public self-awareness and discomfort are present in all four varieties of social anxiety. What else? Attempts to escape from the situation, or at least to avoid the scrutiny of others. Gaze aversion, inhibition of ongoing speech or other social behavior, and disorganization of behavior (stammering, slips of speech, and clumsiness) are also frequent.

COMMON CAUSES

The four varieties of social anxiety share several causes. True, certain causes favor the occurrence of embarrassment, others the occurrence of shyness, and so on, but the events to be cited are general enough to be called common causes of social anxiety. These are divided into two main categories: characteristics of social contexts and behavior of others.

Social contexts

People get together in so many different situations that we would have trouble organizing them into meaningful patterns. Fortunately, the kinds of social contexts that bear on social anxiety are more limited. I have classified the appropriate dimensions into five dichotomies.

The sheer number of people is an important dimension, ranging from two persons to a large group. Starting a conversation with one other person may entail mild trepidation; initiating talk with a group of people involves somewhat more apprehension. Larger groups of people make most of us more nervous than smaller groups, and we tend to be more at ease with just one other person.[1]

The number of people in the group is closely related to how much attention they offer. When only you and another person converse, you each take turns talking and listening. Such give-and-take usually occurs in a relaxed atmosphere. When you are part of a larger social group, one of two things can happen. You may remain part of the audience, a passive listener who suffers no social anxiety. Or you may be asked a question or be singled out for your clothes or lack of attention. In a larger group, when it is your turn to speak or respond, or merely when others focus on you, you are much more on-stage than when you are dealing with only one other person. Being the center of this larger attention ordinarily evokes a fair degree of social anxiety.

The familiarity of the social context is an important determiner of social anxiety. We tend to be relaxed with friends, wary with strangers. A strange country or city, a new college or job, a new building or home, a new group of potential friends or associates—any of these novel contexts is likely to raise our level of social anxiety.

Familiarity tends to be linked to informality. With those we know, we can let our hair down. With strangers, we tend to adopt company manners and other formal behavior. But even with friends or relatives, the occasion may be formal enough for us to become acutely aware of ourselves as social objects: weddings, funerals, graduations, receptions, and formal dinners. At such affairs we are careful of our dress, demeanor, and behavior. We are keenly aware of ourselves as social objects, and the general level of public self-awareness may be high enough to spill over into social anxiety.

Finally, most social occasions contain no element of evaluation, at least not explicitly. Most of the time when you are talking to one person or participating in a group, no one is sizing you up or grading you. Encounters with others may raise or lower your social stock, but evaluation is usually not an inherent part of the interaction. But there are important exceptions. You may interview for a job, audition for a part, or meet your future spouse's parents. You may attend a dance to meet a social partner or gamble on a blind date. In these social encounters, others are scrutinizing you for faults and virtues. Is your dress appropriate, manners acceptable, appearance pleasing, speech correct, conversation knowledgeable? Evaluation anxiety, a fear of the consequences of the present test, intensifies any social anxiety already present.

TABLE 12.1

Features of social contexts that cause social anxiety

Feature	Less social anxiety	More social anxiety
Size	Two-person	Group
Amount of attention	Give-and-take	On-stage
Familiarity with the people	Familiar	Novel
Formality	Informal	Formal
Extent of evaluation	Neutral	Evaluative

These five dimensions, arranged as dichotomies of social contexts, are summarized in Table 12.1. Some of these dimensions are related, and none is mutually exclusive. When the more socially anxious ends of each dichotomy are combined, the result is a situation that will surely induce social anxiety. Thus, if you are at all susceptible to social anxiety (as most of us are), be warned about being in a *formal* situation with a *large group* of strangers who are *scrutinizing* you closely with an eye toward an eventual *evaluation*.

Behavior of others

Groups of people can induce social anxiety without saying a word, merely by paying too little or too much attention to a person. If they steadfastly refuse to talk at all, the shunned person is likely to become embarrassed, shy, or perhaps even ashamed. If he is merely not noticed at a party or other gathering, the ignored person tends to withdraw and inhibit social responses.

The opposite end of the dimension of social attention—close observation or staring by the group—also causes social anxiety. The conspicuous person is likely to show signs of embarrassment, shyness, or audience anxiety.

These negative reactions are especially likely to occur when the group scrutiny occurs suddenly and unexpectedly—for instance, when all conversation at a party stops and a single voice is suddenly the only one heard.

Too little or too much social attention induces a generalized social anxiety, in which you do not focus on any particular aspect of your public self. But people may make remarks about your appearance, manners, or style of behaving. Entirely neutral statements, by directing attention to one's hair, face, body, clothes, speech accent, gestures, and so on, can induce embarrassment or shyness. Sudden changes of appearance are especially noticed, and the person who decides to alter the way he looks had better be prepared for both staring and exclamations from friends, acquaintances and even strangers. I know. Several summers ago I shaved my head completely. That fall, when friends, relatives, colleagues, and students saw my hairless pate, the staring and banal remarks continued for weeks. When a busload of schoolchildren visited the campus, a boy suddenly yelled, "Hey, Kojak." I soon habituated to all this attention, all those repetitive remarks, but for a week or so I blushed more often and was much more aware of my impact on strangers.

The comments of others are not restricted to the friendly or neutral variety; they may be barbed references to another's public self. Laughter, ridicule, and mocking jests are usually sharp enough to pierce our social skin and cause embarrassment, shyness, or perhaps even shame. Scornful sneers and contemptuous glances add hostility to excessive social attention, adding insult to social injury. Paradoxically, the open hostility of others may diminish the victim's social anxiety. He may be too angry to become socially anxious: the intensity of his private affect (rage) may displace his attention from his public self (the object of the taunts).

Other people can also cause social anxiety accidentally or at least without intending to cause harm. When you discover that a third person has overheard an intimate conversation or a juicy piece of gossip you are passing on, you tend to react with embarrassment or shame. Strangely enough, you may react the same way when it is discovered that you are the person who has accidentally overheard a private conversation.

Similarly, you might stumble onto a pair of people coupling or another person unclothed in the bathroom; or the positions might be reversed. Usually, no matter the role—intruder or victim—all those involved tend to become embarrassed or ashamed, and subsequently shy in relation to the others involved.

Another breach of the private–public distinction involves disclosure. In talking to a friend, you might accidentally reveal something about him that you were not supposed to know. His reaction might make you embarrassed or ashamed, and he might well share your social anxiety. Or a casual acquaintance might tell you intimate details of his own fantasies or life history, secrets that are ordinarily shared only by close friends; no one would be surprised if you became embarrassed or socially inhibited and tried to withdraw. A sudden declaration of love from someone you barely knew might prove embarrassing. And for the majority of people, such a declaration or proposition from a person of the same gender would surely induce strong social anxiety.

People can also cause problems merely by disrobing. Many women become upset when another woman strips naked to shower or change clothes. Many men are made uncomfortable at the sight of a mother baring a breast to nurse her infant. And there are still some adults who become upset by others' nudity or near-nudity at public beaches.

In brief, many different behaviors of others can cause social anxiety. A group may shun or ignore you, or scrutinize you excessively. Others may make neutral remarks that draw attention to your public self, or they may make nasty, hostile remarks. Finally, others may unintentionally violate the private–public distinction by overhearing conversations, intruding on private acts, or disclosing too much private self or body.

DIFFERENTIATING FEATURES

Though the four varieties of social anxiety share certain common causes, each variety has its own specific causes. For instance, overpraise can cause embarrassment but not cause any of the other three social anxieties. The four social anxieties also differ in the details of the reaction itself, details described in the last four chapters. The sequence of those chapters was no accident. Shame followed embarrassment because the two have more in common than they do with the other two social anxieties; similarly, audience anxiety and shyness tend to be linked. This section reflects this more or less natural division of social anxiety as embarrassment–shame and audience anxiety–shyness.

The differentiating features that emphasize this two-way split are listed in Table 12.2. Consider first the various reactions that occur in social anxiety. When people are embarrassed or ashamed, they tend to cover their faces, but do not when they suffer from stage fright or shyness. There is often autonomic nervous system reactivity in social anxiety; in embarrassment and shame the parasympathetic division predominates; in audience anxiety and shyness the sympathetic division predominates. Self-blame occurs in embarrassment and shame and not in the other two social anxieties. Finally, we can talk about individual differences in the traits of audience anxiety and shyness; neither embarrassment nor shame, however, appears to possess much consistency over time or across situations, so we cannot regard these as traits.

Now consider three immediate causes of social anxiety. Conspicuousness tends to elicit shyness or audience anxiety. It rarely elicits embarrassment, and never elicits shame. Audience anxiety and shyness are triggered by novelty and evaluation anxiety; embarrassment and shame, by disclosure.

TABLE 12.2

Features that link embarrassment with shame and audience anxiety with shyness

	Embarrassment	Shame	Audience anxiety	Shyness
Reactions				
Cover face	Yes	Yes	No	No
Parasympathetic dominance	Yes	Yes	No	No
Sympathetic dominance	No	No	Yes	Sometimes
Self-blame	Yes	Yes	No	Sometimes
Trait	No	No	Yes	Yes
Causes				
Conspicuous	Sometimes	No	Yes	Yes
Novelty	No	No	Yes	Yes
Disclosure	Yes	Yes	No	No
Evaluation anxiety	No	No	Yes	Sometimes

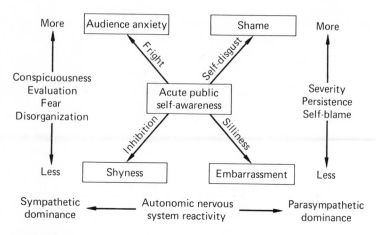

FIGURE 12.1

The Varieties of Social Anxiety in Relation to Public Self-Awareness

In brief, the overall pattern of reactions and causes listed in Table 12.2 is clear: embarrassment and shame share certain features, and other features are common to audience anxiety and shyness. That these two linkages emerge from the table should not surprise anyone, for the table includes only the reactions and causes consistent with this neat split. There are, of course, other characteristics of social anxiety that differentiate among the four varieties of social anxieties.[2]

Nevertheless, in thinking about social anxiety, it helps to remember the embarrassment–shame and audience anxiety–shyness linkages. They provide a basis for a classification of social anxiety, which is shown in Figure 12.1. As this figure shows, social anxiety starts with acute public self-awareness and is completed by a feeling of discomfort. If the person is on-stage and becomes frightened, he suffers from audience anxiety. If the social interaction involves only two or several people and the person becomes socially inhibited, he suffers from shyness. The sympathetic division of the autonomic nervous system predominates in both. Conspicuousness, evaluation, fear, and disorganization are common to both, but these four tend to be more intense in audience anxiety than in shyness. People seem to be much more scared in front of an audience than when dealing with only a few others. On the other side of Figure 12.1, self-disgust is associated with shame, and a feeling of silliness is linked to embarrassment, but both of these social anxieties share parasympathetic dominance. Shame is clearly the more intense affect. More severe, it endures longer and involves greater self-blame than embarrassment.

If shame is stronger than embarrassment, and audience anxiety is more intense than shyness, can we also compare the affects on the left side of Figure 12.1 with those on the right side? No, there is no basis for such a comparison, even of the two stronger affects. When most ashamed, we are depressed and full of self-recrimination; when at the height of audience anxiety, we are panicky and disorganized. We might as well compare apples with pears.

SOCIAL ANXIETY AS A TRAIT

The social anxiety scale

One self-report questionnaire of social anxiety was discussed briefly in Chapter 4. This is the six-item scale derived from the same factor analysis that yielded the private and public self-consciousness factors. The six items inquire about embarrassment, audience anxiety, and shyness; no questionnaire, including this one, contains items about shame.

This Social Anxiety scale correlates moderately with public self-consciousness (the coefficients range from the teens to the thirties) but not with private self-consciousness (the coefficients range from −.06 to +.14).[3] As expected, social anxiety correlates negatively in the forties with sociability, partly because in most questionnaires of sociability there are some social anxiety items. Aside from these correlations, there has been only pilot research with the social anxiety scale.

Avoidance and evaluation

An earlier questionnaire divided social anxiety into Social Avoidance and Distress (SAD) and Fear of Negative Evaluation (FNE).[4] Some representative SAD items are: "I try to avoid situations which force me to be very sociable," "I am usually nervous with people unless I know them well," and "I am seldom at ease in a large group of people." The items on this scale seem to tap a mixture of low sociability and social anxiety.

Some representative FNE items are: "I become tense and jittery if I know someone is sizing me up," "I am often afraid that I may look ridiculous or make a fool of myself," and "I worry a lot about what my superiors think of me." This scale, which concerns evaluation anxiety in social contexts, correlates about .50 with SAD.[5]

Nevertheless, the SAD scale does relate to social behavior. College students participated in a group discussion and then were allowed to choose whether to return to it or to work alone; those who scored high on the SAD chose to be alone.[6] In another study, subjects were videotaped while role-playing an interview; SAD correlated .47 with talking and .28 with amount of eye contact while talking.[7] Perhaps we should be cautious in interpreting these relationships. Sociability items are present in the SAD, which correlates −.76 with a measure of sociability. Perhaps SAD measures sociability as much as social anxiety.

Communication anxiety

McCroskey devised a communication anxiety scale that consists mainly of audience anxiety items ("I am fearful and tense all the while I am speaking before a group of people") but also contains some shyness items ("I'm afraid to speak up in conversations").[9] Communication anxiety must be a pervasive disposition, for scores on this questionnaire relate to a variety of behaviors. Those who score high:

1. Describe themselves as introverted, emotionally immature, and lacking in both self-control and self-esteem.[9]

2. Talk less in class.[9]

3. Avoid college classes in public speaking at a 50–70% dropout rate, compared to a 5–10% dropout rate in those low in communication anxiety.[10]

4. Disclose less when the amount of talking is controlled.[11]

5. Prefer large lecture classes to small classes, where they might be called on to recite.[12]

6. Avoid the central seating positions in the middle or front of lecture halls.[13]

7. Prefer housing remote from the center of interaction in dormitories.[14]

8. Avoid occupations that require more communication with other people and prefer occupations with less social contact.[15]

Clearly, the combination of shyness and audience anxiety is a powerful determinant of the social behavior of college students across a wide range of situations. Having experienced fear and discomfort in contexts that require them to speak up, they avoid these situations, even at the cost of occupying worse niches in classrooms and dormitories. Avoidance is precisely what we expect of those high in audience anxiety and shyness, but remember that this pair comprises only half of social anxiety. We do not know whether those high in communication anxiety would be more embarrassed or ashamed once they were involved in social situations. A reasonable guess is that they would not, because their dominant affect is on the sympathetic (fear) side of autonomic reactivity rather than the parasympathetic (embarrassment) side. True, some people are so high in social anxiety that they tend to be both shy and embarrassed. But surely there are others who may avoid social contact (shyness) but do not necessarily become embarrassed once they are with people, and others who seek out social contact but become embarrassed easily.

Inheritance

Is there an inherited component in social anxiety? On the basis of a factor analysis, three researchers produced a 13-item scale of social anxiety.[16] One item dealt with audience anxiety, and the remaining dozen were divided between shyness and embarrassment items. To determine heritability, the scale was administered to a sample of twins. The considerably higher correlation between identical twins (.61) than between fraternal twins (.30) is clear evidence for an inherited component.

One explanation for the heritability of social anxiety may lie in *temperaments*, innate personality dispositions. Two relevant temperaments are emotionality (tendency to become distressed) and sociability (desire to be with others). The heritability of these two is well documented.[17] In a sample of 258 college students, the social anxiety factor of the Self-Consciousness Inventory correlated .31 with emotionality and −.39 with sociability. The correlation between sociability and emotionality is very low, which means that each temperament probably makes a unique contribution to social anxiety. In other words, the above correlations suggest that the more emotional and the less sociable a person is, the more socially anxious he will be. It is entirely possible, then, that inheritance of social anxiety can be explained by its links with emotionality and sociability, whose inheritance has already been established. The presence of inherited components of social anxiety, however, does not deny that there are also learned components; undoubtedly there are.

Psychiatric patients

Social anxiety can become so intense that it interferes with adjustment to everyday life situations. In factor analyzing a questionnaire filled out by outpatients at a psychiatric clinic, three English researchers discovered a general social anxiety factor and four subfactors: (1) fear of not knowing how to behave, (2) fear of loss of bodily control, (3) fear of being conspicuous, and (4) fear of being judged negatively by others.[18] These subfactors consist of the same kinds of problems that normal people worry about but not to the same degree. Uncertainty, conspicuousness, and evaluation have all been mentioned as causes of social anxiety. Loss of bodily control has not been mentioned because most of us have sufficient control; perhaps it is only psychiatric patients who are so tense that they must realistically worry about losing control of bowels, bladder, or other body parts.

In a more descriptive vein, a psychiatrist listed several frequently occurring features in a group of psychiatric patients with severe social anxiety.[19] The most common complaints were sensitivity, fear of criticism, expecting disapproval, low self-esteem, rigid notions of appropriate social behavior, intense worry, fear of scrutiny, and fear of being trapped in social situations. Thus social anxiety, like any other fear, can intensify to the level of a phobia.

Most phobias are rooted in experiences during childhood, and social anxiety is no exception. Late in the first year of life a small minority of children develop severe stranger anxiety. Whatever the cause of this extreme fear—high emotionality, low sociability, or an absense of contact with

strangers—such children may well be predisposed to develop severe shyness and other social anxieties later in
childhood or adulthood.

Children who receive too much teasing, ridicule, or scorn
are also especially susceptible to social anxiety. Such early
experiences might make them more likely to feel embarrassed or ashamed in the presence of others. One solution
for such children is to avoid potential embarrassment or
shame, either by staying away from people, or when such
avoidance is not feasible, to remain passive and inhibited
when with others.

The most "normal" phobia is, of course, audience anxiety. Children who rarely recite or speak before an audience
are fighting an uphill battle against novelty, which induces
a state of high arousal. How can they habituate to a high-
arousal situation they have rarely been exposed to? And
those who have suffered being laughed at or corrected
while on stage tend naturally to avoid reciting or speaking
in public.

In brief, both the intense phobias of psychiatric patients
and the milder social anxieties of normal people probably
originate in negative childhood experiences or the lack of
exposure to certain contexts.[20] The development of social
anxiety and self-consciousness are the topics of the next
chapter.

NOTES

1. This statement is acceptable as a generality, but there are exceptions. Similarly, there are exceptions to the generalization
that people are more at ease in informal than in formal social
situations. In this chapter, however, I am trying to say what
commonly occurs, and the reader can fill in any exceptions I
omit. To include the exceptions in every instance would lead
to a dull exposition.

2. These different reactions, causes, and consequences have been
discussed in the previous four chapters.

3. Fenigstein, Scheier, and Buss (1975)

4. Watson and Friend (1969)

5. This high correlation suggests considerable overlap between the Social Avoidance and Distress and the Fear of Negative Evaluation scales. A factor analysis would help, but the items on the scales have not been factor analyzed.

6. Watson and Friend (1969)

7. Daly (1978)

8. See Table 4 in Watson and Friend (1969)

9. McCroskey (1977)

10. McCroskey (1970)

11. Hamilton (1972)

12. McCroskey and Andersen (1976)

13. Weiner (1973)

14. McCroskey and Leppard (1973)

15. Daly and McCroskey (1975)

16. Lykken, Tellegen, and Katzenmeyer (1973)

17. Buss and Plomin (1975)

18. Dixon, deMonchaux, and Sandler (1957)

19. Nichols (1974)

20. The hypothesis of a developmental origin of social anxieties does not necessarily contradict an inherited component. Children higher in the temperament of emotionality, for instance, are likely to react more intensely to rejection, scolding, and teasing than are children low in emotionality. Put another way, a temperamental disposition might easily amplify the negative consequences of anxiety-provoking experiences in childhood.

CHAPTER

DEVELOPMENT 13

Our discussion of private and public self-consciousness did not cover the origins of self-consciousness in childhood; that topic will be covered in this chapter. In the social anxiety section of the book, nothing was said about the development of social anxieties; this topic too will be treated in this chapter. My nondevelopmental theory of audience anxiety has already been given (see Chapter 10).

Like no other chapter except the Introduction, this chapter treats a variety of topics. It starts with the development of private self-consciousness, the least understood of all these issues. Then the development of shyness, shame, and embarrassment, will be discussed, in that order. The first appearance of embarrassment plays a special role in marking the onset of public self-consciousness, the next topic. There follows a schema that attempts to pull together public self-consciousness and early- and late-developing social reactions. All these previous topics are relevant to the special case of adolescence, the next topic. The chapter closes with some comments on the way we socialize our children.

PRIVATE SELF-CONSCIOUSNESS

Private self-consciousness may be one of the outcomes of a developmental trend toward covertness. Infants are uninhibited in their expression of emotion. When distressed, fearful, or enraged, they scream and thrash about. As children mature, they learn to suppress the observable aspects of their emotions. They still become frightened, but with each passing year, they are more reluctant to admit fear, and they cry less when upset. They still become jealous and enraged, but temper tantrums diminish throughout childhood. The gradual dampening of emotional expressivity does not mean the end of emotional reactivity. Older children and adults still become scared and angry, but these emotions are less observable. A placid exterior may conceal intense, private emotion. Awareness of such emotion is one aspect of private self-consciousness.

We are also socialized to be modest in our self-evaluations and ambitions. Most people react negatively to others engaging in self-praise, and they label as childish such assertions as "I am the greatest" by the boxer, Muhammed Ali. Similar conceit in children is usually punished, at least verbally, by parents. As a result, most older children and adolescents learn to keep to themselves their exalted self-evaluations and ambitions. But if I nurture a secret ambition, the very fact that it is unshared must increase my consciousness of a private self.

The play of children is a precursor of fantasy. The play of infants is entirely overt, consisting of handling objects and playing such simple games as peek-a-boo. Gradually, young children introduce elements of fantasy into their play. A stick is used as a horse, or a child may gallop on an imaginary horse. Later, children play cops-and-robbers, cowboys-and-Indians, or more recently, space-ship adventures in which their advanced fantasy is even more essential. For some children, play can sometimes become entirely covert and consist only of fantasy. Wishfulfilling daydreams, common in childhood, reach a peak in adolescence. Not all daydreaming concerns oneself but most does, and fantasies about oneself are certainly part of private self-consciousness.

In the second year of life all normal infants start to talk. During the next year or so all their speech is overt, directed toward other people. But young children also start talking to themselves. This self-directed speech gradually becomes more covert, and few adults move their lips when they talk to themselves. What do we talk to ourselves about? Mainly about current problems, emotions, decisions, motives, choices, and so on. Thus, most of covert speech must be considered as another aspect of private self-consciousness.

Four different components of a developmental trend toward covertness have been discussed. The expression of affects is inhibited, ambitions are not disclosed, some play becomes wholly fantasy, and some speech becomes entirely covert. Each of us is aware of feelings, ambitions, fantasies, and private speech that are unobservable to others. Such private self-consciousness would seem to originate in the development of advanced cognitions and the trend toward covertness.

Individual differences

Internal bodily stimuli are the most directly perceived components of the domain of private self-consciousness (see Table 2.1 in Chapter 2). When these stimuli are intense, they demand attention. The children who have frequent stomachaches will naturally attend more to the inside of their bodies. So will children who have any chronic or frequently occurring bodily ills that are painful or uncomfortable. Such children are not only made more aware of internal comfort; they also learn to be alert to symptoms that may require medical attention. In other words, children with a history of frequent illness are likely to attend more closely to internal bodily stimuli and, as a result, have a relatively higher level of private self-consciousness. And it is a reasonable guess that this bodily private self-consciousness can develop earlier than any other variety.

Another influence on private self-consciousness would appear to be introversion.[1] Introverts, by definition, tend to focus more on their own perceptions, thoughts, feelings, and fantasies. Such a focus is necessarily part of private self-consciousness. But fantasies and thoughts can also be directed toward the environment: composing music, planning a bridge, or solving a puzzle. Thus, not all introverts are necessarily high in private self-consciousness. Nevertheless, other things equal, introverts surely score higher in private self-consciousness than do extraverts.

Individual differences in private self-consciousness may also be caused by richness of imagery and covert speech. Though all children are subject to the developmental trend toward covertness, some children are pulled inward more strongly by their own vivid imagery and inner speech. If what is going on "inside" is more interesting than external events, one's focus will surely be directed inward. Who has not drifted off into self-revery in the middle of a dull lecture? If imaginative people are more likely to be high in private self-consciousness, there should be at least a moderate correlation between the two. There is.[2] Imagery and private self-consciousness correlate .30.

Private self-consciousness may be intensified in imaginative children who are socially isolated. Children reared in remote settlements, or for whatever reason denied friendships with other children, tend to conjure up their own "special friend." Such imaginary companions would seem to substitute for missing peers, and it is known that imaginary companions are more frequent among blind children.[3] It is merely a short step from imaginary companions to fantasies and thoughts about oneself and therefore a safe prediction that children who have imaginary companions will turn out to be high in private self-consciousness.

If this list of determinants is short—consisting of only bodily ills, introversion, rich imagination, and social isolation—it is because private self-consciousness is a covert tendency. How can we induce children to focus on their "insides"? There is no easy way, and no one really tries. As a consequence, private self-consciousness appears to be determined largely by dispositions already present in children and perhaps by relative isolation from peers. In marked contrast, public self-consciousness is strongly shaped by parents, teachers, and other socialization agents.

SHYNESS

One may make a distinction between early-developing and late-developing shyness. The earlier kind starts during the first year of life and may continue right through most of adulthood. It is also seen in animals. The later variety starts about the fifth year of life—a rough estimate consistent with other aspects of the development of the public self—and it is seen in no other animal.

Early-developing shyness

Compare the descriptions of adult shyness with the descriptions of stranger anxiety in infants, and you will be struck by the similarity. When strangers approach year-old infants, many infants react with a "wary brow," a "cry face," gaze aversion, and an accelerated heart rate.[4] Infants are usually curious about strangers but are also wary; infants vocalize less, withdraw more, and some even start to cry when a stranger approaches. These reactions to strangers are comparable (allowing for age differences) to the inhibition, withdrawal, and fear that we label shyness in adults.

Despite some dispute about the reality of stranger anxiety in infants—it has even been renamed *wariness*—there is solid evidence for its existence: "The findings of various researchers are quite consistent in showing the emergence of negative reactions as a common response in standard stranger approach situations between about 7 and 9 months, with a continued increase in frequency of wariness across the first year."[5] The wariness of the infant is caused by novelty. With continued contact, the stranger gradually becomes familiar, causing the child's wariness to diminish and eventually disappear. This habituation to novelty is aided by the presence of the mother, who represents the child's secure base. Infants are less shy when their mothers are close and available for reassurance.

Young children are especially upset by spatial intrusion. The presence of a stranger usually elicits only wariness; if the stranger advances, touches, or picks up the infant, it is likely to cry.

Infants vary considerably in how upset they become with strangers. Why? One personality disposition that may contribute to individual differences in wariness is the temperament of emotionality.[6] As a temperament, emotionality is defined solely as a negative affect. Its primordial form is distress, which differentiates first into fear and later into anger. There is abundant evidence that emotionality has a genetic component,[7] and babies differ in degree of distress as early as the second day of life.[8] It seems reasonable to assume that infants high in the temperament of emotionality should be more wary and upset by strangers and take longer to habituate to them.

Another relevant temperament that appears early in life and has a genetic component is sociability.[9] Low sociable people need others less, initiate fewer contacts, respond less, and avoid others more than do high sociable people. As the initial wariness of new social contacts wanes and disappears, children tend to fall into patterns of social behavior that more or less match their sociability temperament. Low sociable children, in the long run, are likely to be on the inhibited, shy end of the continuum of social interaction.

The two temperaments, emotionality and sociability, may account for the individual differences found in a study of infants' social behavior over a period of several years. Concerning the infants' reactions to novelty, the authors wrote: "In their differing inclinations to be cautious in unfamiliar contexts the babies proved moderately con-

sistent throughout the second year across a variety of assessment situations; such differences in wariness have
been noted previously and seem to be associated with early
differences in temperament."[10] The temperament is likely
to be emotionality.

Concerning the behavior that may be strongly influenced
by sociability, there were two other findings:

> First, over repeated exposures to a series of four-baby play
> sessions the individual babies became increasingly differ-
> entiated, and increasingly consistent, in their inclination to
> either withdraw from or engage in the situation. Since the
> cumulative exposure was roughly similar for all babies, the
> growing firmness of their differing reactions indicates that
> some sort of within-baby disposition was determining their
> individual evaluations. Second, the attitudes that developed
> toward the play session experiences were fairly predictive of
> peer behavior shown in a nursery school setting a year and
> a half later.[11]

The individual differences shown by these infants appear to
match emotionality and sociability. Highly emotional children are more likely to be wary and distressed in a novel
situation—in this case, the presence of three other babies.
As months pass, the other three babies become familiar,
wariness habituates, and individual differences in emotionality wane in importance. Eventually, the infants settle
down to consistent patterns of social behavior, which are
determined to a significant extent by individual differences
in sociability.

In brief, it appears that shyness early in life is caused by
novelty (unfamiliar social contexts), high emotionality
(tendency to be wary and distressed), and low sociability
(tendency to withdraw from others).

The just-mentioned individual differences in shyness
may endure, perhaps even into adulthood, but no one has
tried to trace such behavior longitudinally. We do know
that by the preschool years, a small minority of children is
already chronically shy and socially isolated. Observations
of the social behavior of preschool boys and girls from three

to five years of age were cluster analyzed to yield five clusters of children, one of which, "had the lowest means on peer acceptance and were high on a set of shy, anxious, and fearful behaviors. This group seems to best fit the construct of the shy, socially anxious child who also is neither accepted nor rejected, but rather is ignored by peers."[12]

Late-developing shyness

Novelty, high emotionality, and low sociability probably cause shyness as much in older children and adults as in infants. After roughly five years of living, however, children are susceptible to new causes of shyness. Their socialization is well under way, and their training in how to fit in with others continues. They learn that others are watching them, that appearance and cleanliness are important. They learn the rudiments of manners, especially "company manners." Standards for appearance and style of behaving are established. In these various ways, children learn to become aware of themselves as public objects. In the ensuing months and years, children develop varying degrees of public self-consciousness, and these individual differences are relevant to shyness. Children high in public self-consciousness are, by definition, more sensitive to the impact of their own behavior and personality on others. This sensitivity tends to make them socially cautious and wary until they can establish what is "correct" social behavior—that is, other things equal, initially they tend to be shy.

With each passing year, school-age children have more contacts with other children, and parental influence gradually wanes. Most peer contacts occur in the absence of parents; the mother is usually not available as a security base. When confronted by challenge or by the novelty of new playmates, new contexts, or new roles, children can no longer run to mother. Instead they must rely on themselves in calling upon at least rudimentary social skills and past experience. Above all, they need confidence, which in psychological terms translates into self-esteem. Children with little self-esteem, few social skills, or little experience tend to be shy. They simply cannot anticipate success in social interactions and may even expect rejection. As a result, in their social contacts they are tentative, timid, and inhibited—in a word, shy.

Remember, too, the residuals of their experiences with parents and other children. If children are teased, scolded, or ridiculed for their appearance or style of behaving, they are likely to respond by escape or avoidance. When stuck in a novel social context and required to respond, they are likely to be fearful. Thus social punishment can make children shy.

Concerning the presumed dispositional causes of shyness, there is a real difference between early- and late-developing shyness. High emotionality and low sociability are important starting the first year of life, but high public self-consciousness and low self-esteem affect only late-developing shyness—that is, shyness that develops starting in the fifth year of life.

SHAME

How do children come to experience shame and guilt? The following formulation, though speculative, is consistent with the facts of socialization. The issue may be framed in terms of a question: if we deliberately set out to produce shame, how would we proceed?

Consider the reward systems used by parents in socializing their children. The major rewards parents can bestow on a child are their attention and affection, and these can be given unconditionally or conditionally. The earliest common parental response, especially by mothers, is to love their children unconditionally—not for what the children do, but simply because they are. To the extent that children imitate their parents, children learn that they are worthwhile regardless of what they do or fail to do. Later, when training begins, conditional love is employed, the parents bestowing affection only if the children are good or if they achieve. If conditional love is begun too early or is too pervasive, children learn by imitation that they are not intrinsically worthwhile but of value only for what they do. Their esteem will always depend on being good or on achieving the goals set by parents. Thus, to the extent that conditional love predominates, children will be predisposed to develop excessive guilt and shame.

The first step in developing shame[13] is to institute a regime of conditional love as early as possible. Children are taught that their parents' affection depends on what the children do: precocity in motor development, obeying rules, toilet training, and so on. This teaching makes the children dependent on parental support to maintain their self-esteem; later their self-esteem will depend on what they achieve. Thus, allowed to develop little intrinsic self-esteem, they have to achieve and obey rules or suffer from feeling a lack of worth.

Second, the parents set lofty goals for their children, goals difficult, albeit possible, to attain. The children are placed on a schedule of low percentage of reward for achieving the parental goals, a schedule that maintains behavior for a long time. They learn that the goals are within their reach and that reaching them is the major avenue of parental affection, and later, of self-esteem. Similarly, the parents establish a strict code of social conventions, with many restrictions and complex rules to follow. Third, failure to achieve and failure to be socially correct are punished by withdrawal of affection and by ridicule. The ridicule is essential because the children must learn that the parents not only temporarily do not love them but are also disgusted with them. The children are held up to scorn, and their disgrace is observed by others; thus, they are humiliated; they learn that failure to achieve or a breach of conduct leads to scorn and debasement. If the standards are so high that they cannot always be obeyed, then children cannot conform to parental expectations.

Therefore there will be many occasions when they are labeled *inept, dirty, stupid,* or *clumsy,* and they will feel shame. So long as children are held in the parental bind—needing love for self-esteem and later needing to fulfill parental goals taken over as their own—they cannot escape a pervasive feeling of shame. They must continually doubt their own worth and feel that they do not measure up to their parents' standards.

Pseudoshame and true shame

In everyday life, shame has been reported in very young children and even in pet animals. Some parents are certain that their two-year-old, shrinking and cringing after having been caught in a forbidden act, is reacting with shame. Some owners of pets are equally certain that their dog, who has relieved himself on the living room rug, is ashamed because he lowers his head and whines. Such attribution of shame to very young children and pet animals is based on the implicit assumption that they are just as capable of shame as are older human children and adults. It appears that this inference is wrong and that there is a simple explanation for the shamelike behavior of young children and pets. They fear punishment. Their forbidden behavior has been punished in the past, and they anticipate being punished again. Their submissive behavior is a mixture of fear and an attempt to placate the punisher, thus forestalling or minimizing the punishment. In other words, the emotional reaction is fear, not shame.

In my approach, shame can occur only in children old enough to have developed an advanced, cognitive self.[14] Starting approximately at five years of age, children have a sense of themselves as social objects. Having been socialized to regard themselves as unworthy when certain kinds of wrongdoing are revealed, they are capable of experiencing shame when they are caught. The cringing, submissive behavior seen in very young children and animals is really *pseudoshame*: fear and an attempt to reduce punishment.

Only when there is evidence of an advanced cognitive self
—say, a self-directed negative response such as remorse—
can we infer the presence of true shame.

EMBARRASSMENT

My approach emphasizes socialization practices. All children are taught the ways of their group through various
kinds of learning. Prosocial behavior by the child is rewarded by goods, status, affection, and so on. Behavior that
opposes or ignores the goals of socialization is punished
physically or verbally. The most potent verbal punishment
consists of laughter, teasing, and ridicule. Such acts by
others tend to make the child embarrassed. Not all behaviors are socialized through ridicule; only certain kinds of
acts are especially subject to teasing and laughter. And
there may well be a developmental sequence in the areas of
behavior that are socialized at least in part by embarrassment.

The earliest class of behavior to be treated with teasing
concerns self-control. During the second year of life, children are initiated into toilet training. By the third year of
life, they are often teased for "accidents" involving bladder
or bowels.

Laughter and ridicule also start early in the area of modesty. Children are taught to conceal certain body parts in
public and to reserve nakedness for certain occasions (bath)
and certain rooms (bathroom, bedroom). When children
violate the taboo, they are often made to feel silly and
foolish. Somewhat later in childhood, usually starting with
grammar school, children are teased and ridiculed for
another kind of immodesty: bragging and conceit. In our
society, well-socialized people do not tout their own accomplishments. If they do, others react with raucous
laughter, sarcastic remarks, and caricature—all of which
tend to cause embarrassment.

Starting at grammar school age, children are also introduced to manners and etiquette. They are taught appropri-

ate social behavior in more formal contexts, and they quickly learn about "front-parlor" and "eating out" manners. Again, the penalty for mistakes is often ridicule and teasing, and children become embarrassed when others laugh at them.

Finally, children learn about two kinds of privacy. They learn that certain activities must be clandestine: plotting and scheming with others, masturbation, and reading about, talking about, or viewing sexual behavior. For example, a child caught with a copy of *Playboy* will be chastened, but his or her reaction to being caught will usually be embarrassment about being caught in public in a private act (rather than shame).

The other kind of privacy concerns the intrinsically covert aspects of the self: images, feelings, ambitions, and other aspects of the private self. These the child learns not to disclose because the typical reactions of peers and unsympathetic adults are laughter, teasing, or caricature. Older children and adolescents are painfully inhibited about expressing affection ("crushes") because of a past history of intense embarrassment when such sentiments are disclosed. The problem is more severe in young men, who are teased unmercifully for expressing such "soft" sentiments as fear (cowardice), sympathy (crying is for sissies), or deep affection (for girls only).

In brief, children are socialized in roughly this sequence: for self-control, modesty, manners, and two kinds of privacy. One of the prime means of socialization is through teasing, laughter, and ridicule, which cause intense embarrassment. Subsequently, socialized adults react to their mistakes in these areas of social behavior with embarrassment.

This socialization approach accounts for three of the four immediate causes of embarrassment: impropriety, social incompetence, and breaches of privacy. But why does conspicuousness cause embarrassment? The answer may be found in the way children are treated by their parents, teachers, and friends. When are children most conspicuous?

They are singled out for attention mainly when they have violated some social taboo: immodesty, lack of manners, clumsiness, or a breach of privacy. The actions of peers and adults cause the children to become embarrassed. Thus during childhood a tight link is forged between conspicuousness and embarrassment. When a child is singled out, he or she is usually made to feel embarrassment. After hundreds of repetitions, conspicuousness becomes so closely associated with embarrassment that close scrutiny by others can cause embarrassment.

It must be added, however, that conspicuousness is probably one of the weaker causes of embarrassment; the other causes are stronger and more frequent. Furthermore, a minority of adults do not suffer embarrassment when they receive excessive attention. Exhibitionists not only experience no negative affect but they welcome the additional attention. When someone's behavior is designed to induce a "look at me" response, this attention is rarely painful. Such people were presumably socialized with a minimum of ridicule and teasing, together with strong rewards for good looks, performing talent, or both.

If this socialization approach is correct, there should be societies with entirely different socialization practices, which produce people who are rarely embarrassed. If recent reports are true, modern China is such a society. Children are not teased, laughed at, or ridiculed. Observers have commented on the absence of blushing among young Chinese, who evidently have not been laughed at for social mistakes. They may show strong shame reactions, but that is another matter. In brief, it may well be socialization practices that lead to the embarrassment so typical of our society. Change the way children are socialized, and embarrassment would be sharply reduced.

THE PUBLIC SELF

All normal children learn the instrumental responses needed to cope with the environment, the social skills needed to get along with others, and a code of morality that serves to minimize conflicts within society. Such learning, one aspect of socialization, does not require that children become aware of themselves as social objects, but public self-consciousness aids and hastens socialization. For present purposes, we need to consider only two aspects of the process of socialization: instrumental conditioning and learning social perspectives.

Instrumental conditioning

One of the tasks of childhood is to learn which behaviors are approved and which are disapproved. Much of this learning is accomplished through reward and punishment. Children are rewarded for being neat and clean, for being polite, for sharing possessions, and in general, for mature social behavior. And children are punished for being dirty and messy, for being impolite, for being selfish, and in general, for immature, self-centered behavior. By differentially praising or scolding children, parents and teachers help the children to modify their social behavior. Though not the only kind of learning involved, such instrumental conditioning is a crucial part of the process whereby children accommodate to those around them.

One end-point of such learning is a primitive public–private dichotomy. On the one hand, there are responses that children learn to make only when alone: scratching private body parts, picking the nose, masturbating, and so on. When these responses occur in the presence of others, the behavior is usually scolded. On the other hand, there are responses children are expected to make in public: sharing candy, saying "Please" and "Thank you," and so on. Thus, children learn that they can get away with certain behavior only when they are unobserved, and in public they are expected to display "company manners" and some degree of maturity.

If this primitive private–public distinction were all there were to public self-consciousness, we would not need the concept. Social animals easily learn their places in a dominance hierarchy: what they do when a dominant animal is present and what they can do when a dominant animal is absent. And human infants learn what they can get away with long before they have a cognitive self. Put another way, instrumental conditioning is an important part of socialization, but in itself it does not lead to public self-consciousness.

Social perspective-taking

To be aware of yourself as a social object requires that you assume the perspective of other people. You must observe yourself as others do. This is the meaning of such ideas as the *mirror-image self*, the *generalized other*, and the *imaginary audience*.[15]

How do children learn social perspective-taking? There is no good answer to this question; one can only speculate. Perhaps the basic process is an advanced form of imitation learning. Primitive imitation does not suffice. Many animals can imitate the behavior of others and so can infants only a few days old. But such imitation involves only the overt responses of the animal or person serving as a model.

Advanced imitation requires that the learner do cognitively what the model is doing, which is taking a particular perspective. Other people observe children; the children can imitate this observing behavior. But to be able to assume another's perspective, children must have developed cognitive abilities well beyond the sensorimotor period of infancy.[16] Children can assume spatial perspectives different from their own—what a scene looks like from the other side of the table, for instance—by the fourth year of life. But the ability to assume another's social perspective seems to be delayed until the fifth year of life.

A reasonable test of social perspective-taking is whether a child knows that other people have different preferences —in receiving gifts, for example—from the child's own preferences. The issue here is not whether the child has already learned the specific preferences of his mother, father, or friends, but whether he knows about the appropriateness of gifts for those around him. Children were shown each of the following: silk stockings, necktie, toy truck, doll, and adult book.[17] They were asked which they would choose as a gift for father, mother, teacher, brother, sister, and self. Three-year-olds tended to select the same gifts for others as for themselves. Some four-year-olds chose appropriate gifts for others, and half of the five-year-olds did. All of the six-year-olds chose appropriate gifts. Thus, sometime between four and six years of age, children have learned enough about the social perspective of others to select gifts different from their own preference and in line with the expected preferences of these others.

Any child who knows others' preferences so well should also be able to view himself from others' perspectives. This public self-awareness involves a shift from one's own perspective to that of another. The initial immature, self-bound perspective must give way, at least temporarily, to the mature, social perspective of others. Young children cannot make this shift. They are locked into their own egocentric view, a phenomenon Piaget calls *centering*. He calls the ability to switch to an alternative focus *decentering* or *decentration*. Children younger than four years can take another's spatial perspective, but at about five years they can take another's social perspective.[18]

Once a child develops public self-consciousness, the contingencies of instrumental conditioning take on an added dimension. Now social rewards and punishments not only affect the child's behavior, but also signal whether he is perceiving himself as others see him. Rewarded social behavior implies that he is "reading" his own behavior correctly—that is, in line with others' perspectives. Punished social behavior reveals a discrepancy between his own and others' perspectives. Thus punishment, especially scolding and ridicule, can make older children aware of themselves as social objects.

When embarrassment first appears

Mark Twain once said, "Man is the only animal that blushes, or needs to." True, embarrassment appears to be limited to our species and present in all normal older children and adults. But why is there no blushing in newborn children and infants? Why are the silliness and experienced embarrassment delayed for a few years?

To answer these questions, we must first determine why children become embarrassed. If you do something foolish or socially incorrect in public, why should you react with embarrassment? It must be because you have become acutely aware of yourself as a social object and recognize that others will view you as clumsy or foolish. If you were incapable of seeing yourself as a social object—if you could not take the perspective of another—there would be no reason to be embarrassed. A child without any public self-consciousness has nothing to be embarrassed about. My hypothesis, then, is that children cannot become embarrassed until they have developed a social self—that is, until they have developed at least some degree of public self-consciousness. On this basis, embarrassment is a marker that signals the presence of a social self. Any child who blushes or shows other signs of embarrassment must be given credit for an advanced, cognitive self.

There are no published data on the development of embarrassment. The response is infrequent, we are not sure how to induce it in young children, and attempts to do so would raise ethical questions. For these reasons two colleagues and I decided to ask parents about their children's embarrassment.[19] Though such a survey yields only second-hand data from untrained observers, such data provide at least a first approximation of when embarrassment first occurs and its frequency across age groups.

We sent a questionnaire to the parents of children in half a dozen elementary schools, kindergartens, and preschool nurseries.[20] The questionnaire inquired about blushing or other signs of embarrassment during the past six months.[21] We also asked what was the cause of the embarrassment.

The causes of embarrassment all fell within the categories discussed in Chapter 8: conspicuousness, social mistakes, lack of bodily modesty, clumsiness, being teased, and being held up to public scorn or ridicule. There were no gender differences in causes, and the only age trend we could discern was an increase over age in the frequency of "leakage" (disclosure or being teased about liking a member of the opposite sex).

We deliberately avoided defining embarrassment so that parents would not feel constricted by another's definition. As expected, the absence of defining criteria forced us to screen the parents' replies to ensure that embarrassment really did occur. If blushing was reported, embarrassment obviously occurred.[22] If no blushing occurred, we examined the reports. If the parents reported silliness, funny smile, a nervous laugh, or hands covering the mouth, we agreed that embarrassment had occurred. Some parents, however, reported as evidence of embarrassment that their children cried, ran away, hid behind a parent, or became angry. In these cases, we judged that embarrassment had not occurred. Such rescoring was necessary if we were to avoid confusing embarrassment with anger, distress, or shyness.[23]

Almost all the questionnaires were filled out by mothers, who tend to have more contact with their children than fathers. Amount of contact with mothers is undoubtedly greater in preschool children, who spend virtually all their time at home or nearby. Such contact must obviously diminish once children attend school. For this reason, embarrassment may be underreported in school-age children.

The developmental data are shown in Table 13.1. Gender differences were trivial and inconsistent. Embarrassment was reported in roughly a fifth of the three-year-olds, and in a tenth of the four-year-olds.[24] Half the five-year-olds, and the majority of children six years and above, showed embarrassment. Blushing was reported in roughly half of the

TABLE 13.1

Development of embarrassment (parents' reports)

Age	Ratio Emb/Total	Percent
3	3/14	21
4	2/20	10
5	15/30	50
6	28/39	72
7	35/49	71
8	34/50	68
9	30/50	60
10	24/32	75
11	13/21	62
12	13/18	72

embarrassed children, a percentage that was fairly constant throughout childhood.

These data can be interpreted as meaning that a social self has been achieved by three-year old children. So long as some children in the age range—in this instance 22% of the three-year olds—show embarrassment, that is when the social self first develops. This interpretation places considerable reliance on the small sample of three-year-old children. If we combine the three- and four-year-olds to achieve a larger sample, the ratio is 5 embarrassed out of 34, or roughly 15%. This is barely more than one child in seven. Furthermore, this interpretation rests on the ability of mothers of very young children to distinguish between the blush of embarrassment and the flush of anger. Of course, it is entirely possible that these few embarrassed children are socially precocious and have developed a social self a year or two before most children. Such precocity would be analogous to children who walk early or talk long before other children start. The developmental norms for walking and talking, however, are based on objective data with large samples of children. Our data on embarrassment are based on the reports of parents and a small sample of children.

In light of these possible errors by the parents of young children and the small sample size, I suggest a more conservative interpretation of the data. Embarrassment is reported in half the five-year-old children; after that, in most children. The percentage for five-year-olds represents a big jump over that for preschool children. I believe that this sudden increase is the best indicator of when embarrassment develops in children. Using this indicator, we are reasonably sure that at five years of age there is a social self; beyond that age, we can be almost certain.

This interpretation has the advantage of being consistent with other, relevant data. Recall the research on social perspective-taking, in which children chose gifts for family members.[25] Almost no three-year-olds and only a few four-year-olds chose appropriate gifts, but half the five-year-olds and all the six-year-olds chose appropriate gifts. I interpret the embarrassment data as showing similar age trends. In both social perspective-taking and embarrassment, the large jump in frequency occurs from the preschool age group to the five-year-olds. There is also evidence that at roughly five years of age children for the first time are able to use both inner speech and the more cognitive kinds of learning in mastering the environment.[26]

In summary, there appear to be three reasons for interpreting the embarrassment data as indicating that the social self (public self-consciousness) is present in five-year-olds but not before.[27] First, it appears to be more difficult for parents to distinguish embarrassment from shyness or distress in preschool children.[28] Second, there is a marked jump in frequency of embarrassment from the low levels of three- and four-year-olds to the 50% level of five-year-olds. Third, the appearance of a social self at five years of age coincides with related developments in social perspective-taking and cognitive learning. As these reasons indicate, my conclusion must be regarded as tentative.

TABLE 13.2

Early versus late social reactions

	Early sensory self: before five years	Late, cognitive self: after five years
Negative inputs from others	Threat of punishment leads to cringing, pseudoshame	Exposure of wrongdoing leads to shame
	Stranger, intrusiveness leads to wariness, early shyness	Novel context or social role leads to advanced shyness
	Teasing leads to anger or tears	Ridicule, teasing leads to embarrassment
Positive inputs from others	Excessive attention from others leads to exhibitionism	Praise for role enactment leads to self-presentation

Early and late social reactions

At the beginning of this chapter, I distinguished between early and late shyness and then separated early pseudo-shame from later, true shame. I suggested that embarrassment may not occur until roughly five years of age. And in Chapter 1 I distinguished between a primitive, sensory self and an advanced, cognitive self.

These developmental hypotheses have been assembled into a schema, which is shown in Table 13.2. Presumably, awareness of oneself as a social object changes the way children react to negative inputs from others. Infants and younger children have only a primitive, sensory self. They react to being caught at mischief by shrinking, cringing, and in general, by trying to escape an oncoming punishment. Strangers, especially those who advance too quickly or come too close, cause fright or wariness (early shyness). And children react to teasing with outbursts of temper or tears of distress.

Older children, having an advanced, cognitive self, are aware of themselves as social objects. When wrongdoing is revealed, they are ashamed. When they enter new places (school, others' homes) or try new social roles, they are tentative, inhibited, and uncomfortable in their awareness of how they are seen (advanced shyness). And they react to teasing or ridicule with blushing or other signs of embarrassment.

The presence of public self-consciousness also determines how children react to positive inputs from others. If attention is regularly lavished on very young children, they may become exhibitionists. Some children (and even some adults) prance, cavort, laugh and talk too loud, interrupt, and even annoy others to get their attention. Exhibitionists will try almost any response so long as it pays off with the desired reward: getting other people to look. Exhibitionists like being laughed at no more than anyone else, but they gladly pay the price because they occupy center stage. No advanced sense of self is involved. All that is needed is instrumental conditioning: learning which responses tend to get the attention of others.

Now consider self-presenation. Self-presenters tend to play roles, each role specific to a particular situation. Knowing what is expected or desired, they arrange their social selves to conform. Such conformity requires not only the ability to read social cues (or know generalized expectations) but also the ability to monitor and alter one's own style of behavior. Self-monitoring requires an advanced, cognitive self, including public self-consciousness. It occurs only in older children and is absent in infants. In contrast, exhibitionism occurs in infants and even in higher animals, for it requires nothing more than a primitive, sensory self.

The modern beauty contest nicely demonstrates the distinction between self-presentation and exhibitionism. Highly attractive women are already the center of attention long before they enter a beauty contest. Their everyday primping and attention to dress may be regarded as a mild form of exhibitionism. But to win or even do well in a beauty contest, they must conform to a rigid set of expectations. They must have excellent posture, reasonably clear diction, and a regal but friendly bearing. They must smile at everyone. When asked a serious question, they must appear to give it thought, even though they have already rehearsed the answer. It helps if their stated ambitions are altruistic. In brief, they must present themselves in a certain light if they are to win. Seen in this perspective, the beauty contest is merely an exaggeration of certain vocations (lawyer, banker, politician) in that people must monitor their social selves and alter their styles to suit known requirements.

Self-presentation represents the positive side of public self-awareness: using knowledge about one's social self as a basis for monitoring or altering social behavior, depending on the expectations of others. Successful salesmen, politicians, and hosts are keenly aware of how they come across to others, and they are careful to enact the expected roles that pay off in sales, elections, or popularity.

The negative side of public self-consciousness is, of course, social anxiety. If others' scrutiny has in the past been accompanied by ridicule, scorn, criticism, or rejection, one's own self-scrutiny is likely to cause embarrassment, shame, shyness, or audience anxiety. We tend to socialize our children mainly through punishment and correction of behavior. Given this negative slant, we must expect that most public self-awareness leads to social anxiety rather than self-presentation.

ADOLESCENCE

Self-consciousness is probably at a peak during adolescence. The years between 12 and 18 are marked by a heightened preoccupation with one's own body, impulses, ambitions, and social roles. Children who were not especially shy before puberty suddenly become tense and anxious in social situations. They tend to believe that they are the center of attention, that when they walk down the street, all eyes are on them. There are often intense fears of exposure and of "leakage" of thoughts, feelings, and impulses too embarrassing or shameful to be revealed. In brief, adolescence is the peak period of private and public self-consciousness and of social anxiety. Why? I suggest two main reasons: novelty and impulses.

Novelty

Puberty is marked by rapid bodily growth and the sudden development of secondary sex characteristics. Girls mature first, and some of them tower over not only other female classmates, but males as well. Girls' hips spread and become rounder, their breasts thrust out, and of course their menses begin. Many girls start eating too much and become chubby; others may develop acne. Many boys also develop skin disorders at puberty. Their growth spurt is more rapid than that of girls; as a result, many boys suffer from being too thin or excessively clumsy. And, while their voices are dropping to an adult pitch, many boys become embarrassed by sudden boyish breaks in their new-found bass voices.

These pubescent changes in the body tend to elevate both private and public self-consciousness. The body of a young adolescent feels different. The changes in bodily hair, in chest and hips, in muscle and bone all direct attention to oneself. At this time adolescents, confronted with changes in something as basic as body image, are driven to wonder about their own identity: Who am I? What am I becoming? And the rapid bodily changes are observed by others. The most benign comments merely refer to the fact of rapid change. Less benign comments refer to the girls' breasts (or lack of breasts), hips, or weight, or to the boys' awkwardness, excessive height (or small size), variations in voice, and so on. In brief, the rapid bodily changes of puberty focus attention on the self and foster embarrassment and shyness.

After the onset of puberty, bodily changes continue to

occur, but at a slower rate. Adolescents slowly habituate to both the changes and the slowly continuing changes. But there is a new source of novelty: social roles. As adolescents assume adult bodily proportions, they are expected to start adopting more mature roles. The role expectations are mixed and often conflicting: one set from parents and teachers, one set from peers, and still another set of role expectations from movies, television, magazines, and perhaps even books. In the face of conflicting role expectations, many adolescents are indecisive and tentative in attempting to play new roles. Worse still, they suffer from lack of knowledge about how to play the roles and skill in doing so. Consider, for instance, a 15-year-old boy on his first date. His head may be filled with images of John Travolta or Richard Dreyfuss (substitute any current media hero) and ideas of how any "real man" acts with a lady, but he has neither the experience nor the skill to cope with the first date. What do you say to the girl's father? How late can you stay out? How far can you go sexually? Will she like you? It is a rare adolescent who has not suffered acute self-consciousness, shyness, and even embarrassment on a first date. And dating is only one of a number of first experiences with social situations. There may be new schoolmates, fraternities, sororities, clubs, teams, class presentations, and so on. In each instance the adolescent must deal with the arousal of a new situation and try to cope with initially inadequate social skills. No one should be surprised, then, if there is considerable shyness, a tendency to blush, and an intense fear of standing up in front of an audience. And when an adolescent is caught in what he or she has been taught is immoral behavior or in a failure to achieve agreed-on goals, the outcome is usually feelings of remorse and shame.

Impulses

Some children have sexual and romantic impulses before puberty, but for most children such motives and ideas really begin at puberty or shortly thereafter. Adolescence is a time of intense romantic "crushes" directed toward television and movie stars, teachers, coaches, and peers. A girl may turn crimson when a certain male teacher talks to her; a boy may blush furiously when he is teased for liking a girl.

Several urges intensify, and for some adolescents masturbation is shameful. Others are disturbed that their peers or parents will discover the frequency or intensity of their sexual urges. Adolescent males become easily aroused, and the problem of how to hide the bulge in one's pants is a frequent preoccupation. Some girls must surely wonder why their male classmates refuse to stand up or hold their notebooks in strange positions. Thus, sexual and romantic impulses are the source of both social anxiety (discovery, "leakage") and private self-consciousness (increased awareness of moods and affects).

CONCLUDING COMMENTS

I have reviewed the developmental course of private self-consciousness, public self-consciousness, and the social anxieties, suggesting links with some cognitive and social aspects of development. Now I shall comment about how cycles during development can enhance individual differences in self-consciousness and social anxiety.

Let us start with an only child who is introverted, has vivid imagery, and is somewhat isolated from other children.[29] Such a child is likely to conjure up an imaginary companion and then substitute fantasies for actual social relationships with other children. Real social contacts— with school classmates, for example—are likely to be less rewarding and more unpleasant than the child's fantasies that involve the imaginary companion. It comes as no surprise that wish-fulfilling fantasies are usually more enjoyable than the positive-and-negative mixture of real-life events. As the years pass, such a child tends to continue exploring the developing aspects of the self: moods, emotions, ambitions, motives, and beliefs. In brief, unless events of childhood strongly oppose the child's initial thrust toward private self-consciousness, this trait will become a stronger personality disposition.

Now consider an extraverted child of little imagination, who is surrounded by brothers and sisters and other playmates. Lacking imagination, he or she finds few rewards for introspecting. Having abundant playmates and a strong tendency to focus attention outward, this child should rarely examine his moods, emotions, ambitions or motives.

These two hypothetical examples are extreme cases. Though most of us fall between these extremes, there are people at either end of the private self-consciousness dimension. There are college students who score so low on the Private Self-Consciousness scale that we can only wonder why they never examine their psychological "insides." At the other extreme, a woman who read the items on the Private Self-Consciousness scale said that the items were too weak. These individual differences in private self-consciousness are hidden from view. Unless you tell others, how can they know whether you self-reflect or not? Unaware of how much we differ from each other, people at either extreme find it hard to believe that there are others opposite to them. Those who often reflect about themselves cannot understand why someone would ignore such a rich psychological domain as oneself. And those who rarely or never reflect about themselves cannot imagine how anyone could be so self-absorbed with something as drab as oneself when there is an exciting world out there. It is almost as though there were two different species of people, each apparently speaking the same language but not really communicating.

Now consider a child who is relatively unsociable and high in emotionality.[30] Needing others less, this child spends more time alone and so may fail to develop the social skills that help us deal with others. Being more emotional, this child tends to become more upset in the face of novelty of context and of role. As a result, he or she tends to be more aroused and scared with strangers or casual acquaintances. Social contexts are escaped from early or avoided if possible. Such escape and avoidance prevent habituation from occurring and social skills from developing. So the cycle continues, and the child increases in social anxiety or at least maintains a high level.

At the opposite end, consider a child who is highly sociable and does not become distressed easily. The strong need to be with others makes this child tolerate the negatives of social contacts. Being low in emotionality, this child does not become especially upset because of novelty of place or of role; and habituation occurs faster when arousal is lower. Better motivated at the start and sticking with social contacts even when they have aversive components, this child is more likely to develop the necessary social skills. Those skills, in turn, make social contacts more pleasant and rewarding. So the cycle of less negative, more positive, less arousal, and better social skills continues and produces an adult low in social anxiety.

Extreme differences in social anxiety, unlike those in private self-consciousness, are easily observed. Shy people, for example, are easily contrasted with unshy people, and we rarely mistake one for the other. Nevertheless, each extreme finds it hard to understand the other. Unshy peple wonder what the trouble is: why don't these shy people just walk right in and enjoy meeting new people or renewing contacts with casual acquaintances? And shy people can only admire the social ease of their opposite numbers, surprised that people can be so relaxed and free of tension in dealing with strangers or people they hardly know.

These comments point to one obvious conclusion that emerges from this book: we differ markedly from one another in both kinds of self-consciousness and in the various social anxieties. Some of these individual differences can easily be observed; others are hidden. But unless we make a strong effort to understand how greatly others' perspectives can differ from our own and how different they are in these personality traits, we will fail to enjoy diversity in others. Worse still, we will fail to deal appropriately with others who might need our sympathy and help.

NOTES

1. Jung (1933)
2. Turner, Scheier, Carver, and Ickes (1978)
3. Singer and Streiner (1966)
4. Sroufe (1977)
5. Sroufe (1977, p. 735)
6. Buss and Plomin (1975)
7. Buss and Plomin (1975, Chapter 4)
8. Freedman (1971)
9. Buss and Plomin (1975, Chapter 5)
10. Bronson and Pankey (1977, p. 1181)
11. Bronson and Pankey (1977, p. 1182)
12. Gottman (1977, p. 513)
13. This section is an abbreviated version of material that appears in Buss (1978, Chapter 23). This reference also contains a contrasting developmental scheme for producing guilt.
14. The distinction between a primitive, sensory self and an advanced, cognitive self was discussed in Chapter 1.
15. See Chapter 6, sociological approaches, for a discussion of these concepts.
16. Piaget (1962). Children must have some degree of what Piaget calls *representative intelligence*, especially that aspect involving freeing oneself from a single, egocentric perspective.
17. Flavell (1968, pp. 164–166)
18. Flavell (1968)
19. Buss, Iscoe, and Buss (in press)
20. The schools, both private and public, included students of varying ethnic and racial backgrounds. Parents were sent a questionnarie asking about embarrassment in their school-age child and any other child in the age range of from 1 to 13.

Slightly more than one questionnaire in four was returned, which is all that can be expected from such mailings.

21. We used the six month interval on the assumption that longer periods would introduce too much error because of variations in parents' memory.

22. There were a few exceptions. One parent reported blushing in a 3-month old infant; another, in a year-old infant. There were so few children at these ages, however, that we omitted them from our tabulations and so avoided dealing with our doubts about the veridicality of such reports.

23. We assumed that it was better to stick to the unequivocal definition used in this book and rescore the parents' responses than to accept the parents' responses uncritically and run the risk of offering misleading data. Whether we were correct will be decided by subsequent research by other investigators.

24. The drop in four-year-olds is probably spurious, due to the small size of the sample. In a large sample, four-year-olds would surely show at least as high a frequency of embarrassment as three-year-olds.

25. Flavell (1968)

26. White (1965)

27. This interpretation is normative. There may be rare, precocious children who have developed a social self earlier.

28. This issue will be resolved when we use trained researchers to observe the occurrence of embarrassment in preschool children.

29. The reasons for social isolation—illness, bigotry, or a remote home—are less important here than the fact of isolation.

30. Having discussed this combination of personality traits earlier, I shall be brief here.

REFERENCES

Amsterdam, B. Mirror self-image reactions before the age of two. *Developmental Psychology* 5 (1972): 297–305.

Apsler, R. Effects of embarrassment on behavior toward others. *Journal of Personality and Social Psychology* 32 (1975): 145–153.

Argyle, M. *Social Interaction.* New York: Atherton, 1969.

Argyle, M., & Williams, M. Observer or observed? A reversible perspective in person perception. *Sociometry* 32 (1969): 396–412.

Bassett, R., Behnke, R. R., Carlile, L. W., and Rogers, J. The effects of positive and negative audience on the autonomic arousal of student speakers. *Southern Speech Communications Journal* 38 (1973): 255–261.

Behnke, R. R., and Carlile, L. W. Heart rate as an index of speech anxiety. *Speech Monographs* 38 (1971): 65–69.

Berscheid, E., and Walster, E. H. *Interpersonal Attraction.* Reading, Mass.: Addison-Wesley, 1969.

Bertenthal, B. I., and Fischer, K. W. Development of self-recognition in the infant. *Developmental Psychology* 14 (1978): 44–50.

Briggs, S., Cheek, J., and Buss, A. H. Components of the Self-Monitoring Scale. Unpublished manuscript, University of Texas, 1979.

Bronson, G. W., and Pankey, W. B. On the distinction between fear and wariness. *Child Development* 48 (1977): 1167–1183.

Brown, B. R., and Garland, H. The effects of incompetency, audience and acquaintanceship, and anticipated evaluative feedback on face-saving behavior. *Journal of Experimental Social Psychology* 7 (1971): 490–502.

Bruskin Associates. What are Americans afraid of? *The Bruskin Report* no. 53, 1973.

Buck, R., and Parke, R. D. Behavioral and physiological response to the presence of a friendly or neutral person in two types of stressful situations. *Journal of Personality and Social Psychology* 24 (1972): 143–153.

Buck, R., Parke, R., and Buck, M. Differences in the cardiac response to the environment in two types of stressful situations. *Psychonomic Science* 18 (1970): 95–96.

Buss, A. H. *The Psychology of Aggression.* New York: Wiley, 1961.

Buss, A. H. The effect of harm on subsequent aggression. *Journal of Experimental Research in Personality* 1 (1966): 249–255.

Buss, A. H. *Psychology: Behavior in Perspective.* New York: Wiley, 1978.

Buss, A. H., and Durkee, A. An inventory for assessing different kinds of hostility. *Journal of Consulting Psychology* 21 (1957): 343–349.

Buss, A. H., Iscoe, I., and Buss, E. H. Developmental survey of embarrassment. *Journal of Psychology* (in press).

Buss, A. H., and Plomin, R. *A Temperament Theory of Personality Development.* New York: Wiley, 1975.

Buss, D. M., and Scheier, M. F. Self-consciousness, self-awareness, and self-attribution. *Journal of Research in Personality* 10 (1976): 463–468.

Buss, L. Does overpraise cause embarrassment? Unpublished research, University of Texas, 1978.

Carpenter, J. C., and Freese, J. J. Three aspects of self-disclosure as they relate to quality of adjustment. *Journal of Personality Assessment* 43 (1979): 78–85.

Carver, C. S. Physical aggression as a function of objective self-awareness and attitudes toward punishment. *Journal of Experimental Social Psychology* 11 (1975): 510–519.

Carver, C. S. Self-awareness, perception of threat, and the expression of reactance through attitude change. *Journal of Personality* 45 (1977): 501–512.

Carver, C. S. A cybernetic model of self-attention processes. *Journal of Personality and Social Psychology* (in press).

Carver, C. S., Blaney, P. H., and Scheier, M. F. Focus of attention, chronic expectancy, and responses to a feared stimulus. *Journal of Personality and Social Psychology* 37 (1979): 1186–1195.

Carver, C. S. and Scheier, M. F. Self-consciousness and reactance. *Journal of Research in Personality* (in press).

Cheek, J. Shyness and sociability, Unpublished Master's thesis, University of Texas, 1979.

Cheek, J., and Buss, A. H. Scales of shyness, sociability, and self-esteem and correlations among them. Unpublished research, University of Texas, 1979.

Clary, E., Tesser, A., and Downing, L. Influence of a salient schema on thought-induced cognitive change. *Personality and Social Psychology Bulletin* 4 (1978): 39–43.

Coopersmith, S. *The Antecedents of Self-Esteem.* San Francisco: W. H. Freeman and Company, 1967.

Cooley, C. H. *Human Nature and the Social Order.* New York: Charles Scribner's Sons, 1902.

Cozby, P. C. Self-disclosure: A literature review. *Psychological Bulletin* 79 (1973): 73–91.

Cunningham, M. R. Personality and the structure of nonverbal communication of emotion. *Journal of Personality* 45 (1977): 564–589.

Daly, J. A. and McCroskey, J. C. Occupational choice and desirability as a function of communication apprehension. *Journal of Counseling Psychology* 22 (1975): 309–313.

Daly, S. Behavioral correlates of social anxiety. *British Journal of Social and Clinical Psychology* 17 (1978): 117–120.

Darwin, C. R. *The Expression of Emotions in Man and Animals.* New York: Appleton, 1873, (Philosophical Library, 1955).

Davis, D., and Brock, T. C. Use of first person pronouns as a function of increased objective self-awareness and prior feedback. *Journal of Experimental Social Psychology* 11 (1975): 381–388.

Diener, E., and Srull, T. K. Self-awareness, psychological perspective, and self-reinforcement. *Journal of Personality and Social Psychology* 37 (1979): 413–423.

Diener, E., and Wallbom, M. Effects of self-awareness in antinormative behavior. *Journal of Research in Personality* 10 (1976): 107–111.

Dixon, J. J., deMonchaux, C., and Sandler, J. Patterns of anxiety: An analysis of social anxieties. *British Journal of Medical Psychology* 30 (1957): 102–112.

Duval, S. Conformity on a visual task as a function of personal novelty on attitudinal dimensions and being reminded of the object status of self. *Journal of Experimental Social Psychology* 12 (1976): 87–98.

Duval, S., and Wicklund, R. A. *A Theory of Objective Self-Awareness.* New York: Academic Press, 1972.

Duval, S. and Wicklund, R. A. Effects of objective self-awareness on attribution of causality. *Journal of Experimental Social Psychology* 9 (1973): 17–31.

Epstein, S., Rosenthal, S., and Szphiler, J. The influence of attention upon anticipating arousal, habituation, and reactivity to a noxious stimulus. *Journal of Research in Personality* 12 (1978): 30–40.

Erickson, E. H. *Childhood and Society* 2d ed. New York: Norton, 1963.

Fenigstein, A. Self-consciousness, self-attention, and social interaction. *Journal of Personality and Social Psychology* 37 (1979): 75–86.

Fenigstein, A., Scheier, M. F., and Buss, A. H. Public and private self-consciousness: Assessment and theory. *Journal of Consulting and Clinical Psychology* 43 (1975): 522–527.

Fisher, S. *Body Experience in Fantasy and Behavior.* New York: Appleton-Century-Crofts, 1970.

Fisher, S. *Body Consciousness.* New York: Jason Aronson, 1974.

Flavell, J. *The Development of Role-Taking and Communications Skills in Children.* New York: Wiley, 1968.

Freedman, D. G. An evolutionary approach to research on the life cycle. *Human Development* 14 (1971): 97–99.

Froming, W. J., and Carver, C. S. Divergent influences of private and public self-consciousness in a compliance paradigm. Unpublished research, University of Florida, 1979.

Gallup, G. G., Jr. Self-recognition in primates: A comparative approach to the bidirectional properties of consciousness. *American Psychologist* 32 (1977): 329–338. (a)

Gallup, G. G., Jr. Absence of self-recognition in a monkey (*Macaca fascicularis*) following prolonged exposure to a mirror. *Developmental Psychobiology* 10 (1977): 281–284. (b)

Geller, D. M., Goodstein, G., Silver, M., and Steinberg, W. C. On being ignored: The effects of the violation of implicit rules of social interaction. *Sociometry* 37 (1974): 541–556.

Gibbons, F. X. Sexual standards and reactions to pornography: enhancing behavioral consistency through self-focused attention. *Journal of Personality and Social Psychology* 36 (1978): 976–987.

Gibbons, F. X., Scheier, M. F., Carver, C. S., and Hormuth, S. E. Self-focused attention, suggestibility and the placebo effect. *Journal of Experimental Social Psychology* (in press).

Goffman, E. Embarrassment and social organization. *American Journal of Sociology* 62 (1956): 264–274.

Goffman, E. *The Presentation of Self in Everyday Life.* Edinburgh, Scotland: University of Edinburgh Press, 1956.

Goffman, E. *Interaction Ritual.* New York: Doubleday, 1967.

Goleman, G. *The Varieties of Meditative Experience.* New York: Dutton, 1977.

Gottman, J. A. Toward a definition of social isolation in children. *Child Development* 48 (1977): 513–517.

Hall, E. T. *The Hidden Dimension.* New York: Doubleday, 1966.

Hamilton, P. R. The effect of risk proneness on small group situations, communication apprehension, and self-disclosure. Unpublished master's thesis, Illinois State University, 1972.

Hendrick, C., and Brown, S. R. Introversion, extraversion, and interpersonal attractiveness. *Journal of Personality and Social Psychology* 20 (1971): 31–36.

Ho, D. Y. On the concept of face. *American Journal of Sociology,* 81 (1976): 867–884.

Holzman, P. S., and Rousey, C. The voice as a percept. *Journal of Personality and Social Psychology* 4 (1966): 79–86.

Ickes, J., Wicklund, A., and Ferris, C. B. Objective self-awareness and self esteem. *Journal of Experimental Social Psychology* 9 (1973): 202–219.

Jaynes, J. *The Origins of Consciousness in the Breakdown of the Bicameral Mind.* Boston: Houghton Mifflin, 1976.

Jourard, S. M. An exploratory study of body accessibility. *British Journal of Social and Clinical Psychology* 5 (1966): 221–231.

Jourard, S. *Self-Disclosure.* New York: Wiley-Interscience, 1971.

Jung, C. G. *Psychological Types.* New York: Harcourt, 1933.

Kleck, R. E., Vaughn, R. C., Cartwright-Smith, J., Vaughn, K. B., Colby, C. Z., and Lanzetta, J. T. Effects of being observed on expressive, subjective, and physiological responses to painful stimuli. *Journal of Personality and Social Psychology* 43 (1976): 1211–1218.

Lerner, M. J., and Simmons, C. H. Observer's reaction to the "innocent victim": compassion or rejection. *Journal of Personality and Social Psychology* 4 (1966): 203–210.

Levin, J., Baldwin, A. L., Gallwey, M, and Paivio, A. Audience stress, personality, and speech. *Journal of Abnormal and Social Psychology* 61 (1960): 469–473.

Liebling, B. A. Effects of video-induced self-awareness on causal attributions and task performance. *Dissertation Abstracts* 35 (1975): No. 9, 4710-B.

Lykken, D. T., Tellegen, A., and Katzenmeyer, C. Manual for the activity preference questionnaire (APQ). *Reports from the Research Lab of the Dept. of Psychiatry,* University of Minnesota, 1973.

Lynd, H. M. *On Shame and the Search for Identity.* New York: Harcourt, 1958.

McCroskey, J. C. Measures of communication bound anxiety. *Speech Monographs* 21 (1970): 255–264.

McCroskey, J. C. Oral communication apprehension: A summary of recent theory and research. *Human Communication Research* 4 (1977): 78–96.

McCroskey, J. C., and Anderson, J. F. The relationship between communication apprehension and academic achievement among college students. *Human Communication Research* 3 (1976): 73–81.

McCroskey, J. C., and Leppard, T. The effects of communication apprehension on nonverbal behavior. Paper presented at Eastern Communication Association convention, New York, 1975.

Mandler, G., Mandler, J. M., and Uviller, E. T. Autonomic feedback: The perception of autonomic activity. *Journal of Abnormal and Social Psychology* 56 (1958): 367–373.

Markus, H. Self-schemata and processing information about the self. *Journal of Personality and Social Psychology* 35 (1977): 63–78.

Mead, G. H. *Mind, Self and Society.* Chicago: University of Chicago Press, 1934.

Mettee, D. R., Fisher, S., and Taylor, S. E. The effect of being shunned upon the desire to affiliate. *Psychonomic Science* 23 (1971): 429–431.

Miller, L., Murphy, R., and Buss, A. H. Private and public body awareness. Unpublished research, University of Texas, 1979.

Modigliani, A. Embarrassment and embarrassability. *Sociometry* 31 (1968): 313–326.

Modigliani, A. Embarrassment, facework, and eye contact: Testing a theory of embarrassment. *Journal of Personality and Social Psychology* 17 (1971): 15–24.

Moreno, J. L. *Psychodrama.* Beacon, New York: Beacon House Press, 1946.

Mulac, A., and Sherman, A. R. Behavioral assessment of speech anxiety. *Quarterly Journal of Speech* 60 (1974): 134–143.

Nichols, K. A. Severe social anxiety. *British Journal of Medical Psychology* 47 (1974): 301–306.

Paivio, A., Baldwin, A. L., and Berger, S. Measurement of children's sensitivity to audiences. *Child Development* 32 (1961): 721–730.

Paul, G. L. *Insight vs. Desensitization in Psychotherapy.* Stanford: Stanford University Press, 1966.

Phillips, G. M., and Metzger, N. J. The reticent syndrome: Some theoretical considerations about etiology and treatment. *Speech Monographs* 40 (1973): 220–230.

Piaget, J. *Play, Dreams, and Imitation in Childhood.* New York: Norton, 1962.

Piers, G., and Singer, M. D. *Shame and guilt.* Springfield, Illinois: Thomas, 1953.

Pilkonis, P. A. Shyness: Public behavior and private experience. Unpublished doctoral dissertation, Stanford University, 1976.

Pilkonis, P. A. Shyness, public and private, and its relationship to other measures of social behavior. *Journal of Personality* 45 (1977): 585–595. (a)

Pilkonis, P. A. The behavioral consequences of shyness. *Journal of Personality* 45 (1977): 596–611. (b)

Porter, D. T. Self-report scales of communication apprehension and autonomic arousal (heart rate): A test of construct validity. *Speech Monographs* 41 (1974): 267–276.

Pryor, J. B., Gibbons, F. X., Wicklund, R. A., Fazio, R. H., and Hood, R. Self-focused attention and self-report validity. *Journal of Personality* 45 (1977): 513–527.

Sadler, O., and Tesser, A. Some effects of salience and time upon interpersonal hostility and attraction during social isolation. *Sociometry* 36 (1973): 99–112.

Sandler, J., deMonchaux, C., and Dixon, J. J. Patterns of anxiety: The correlates of social anxieties. *British Journal of Medical Psychology* 31 (1958): 24–31.

Sattler, J. A. A theoretical development and clinical investigation of embarrassment. *Genetic Psychology Monographs* 71 (1965): 19–59.

Schachter, S., and Singer, J. E. Cognitive, social, and physiological determinants of emotional state. *Psychological Review* 69 (1962): 379–399.

Scheier, M. F. Self-awareness, self-consciousness, and angry aggression. *Journal of Personality* 44 (1976): 627–644.

Scheier, M. F. The effects of public and private self-consciousness on attitude–behavior consistency. Unpublished research, Carnegie-Mellon University, 1978.

Scheier, M. F., Buss, A. H., and Buss, D. M. Self-consciousness, self-report of aggressiveness, and aggression. *Journal of Research in Personality* 12 (1978): 133–140.

Scheier, M. F., and Carver, C. S. Self-focused attention and the experience of emotion: Attraction, repulsion, elation, and depression. *Journal of Personality and Social Psychology* 35 (1977): 625–636.

Scheier, M. F., Carver, C. S., and Gibbons, F. X. Self-focused attention and reactions to fear: When standards and affect collide. *Journal of Personality and Social Psychology*, in press.

Scheier, M. F., Carver, C. S., Schulz, R., Wishnick, G. I., Glass, D. C., and Katz, I. Sympathy, self-consciousness, and reactions to the stigmatized. *Journal of Applied Social Psychology* 8 (1978): 270–282.

Scheier, M. F., Fenigstein, A., and Buss, A. H. Self-awareness and physical aggression. *Journal of Experimental Social Psychology* 10 (1974): 264–273.

Schulman, A. H., and Kaplowitz, C. Mirror-image response during the first two years of life. *Developmental Psychobiology* 10 (1977): 133–142.

Singer, J. L., and Streiner, B. Imaginative content in the dream and fantasy play of blind and sighted children. *Perceptual and Motor Skills* 22 (1966): 475–482.

Snyder, M. Self-monitoring of expressive behavior. *Journal of Personality and Social Psychology* 30 (1974): 526–537.

Snyder, M. Self-monitoring processes. In *Advances in Experimental Social Psychology*, edited by L. Berkowitz, vol. 12. New York: Academic Press, in press. (a)

Snyder, M. Cognitive behavioral and interpersonal consequences of self-monitoring. In *Advances in the Study of Communication and Affect*, edited by P. Pliner, D. R. Blankstein, I. M. Speigel, T. Alloway, and L. Krames. vol. 5. New York: Plenum, in press. (b)

Sroufe, L. A. Wariness of strangers and the study of infant development. *Child Development* 48 (1977): 731–746.

Tesser, A., and Conlee, M. C. Some effects of time and thought on attitude polarization. *Journal of Personality and Social Psychology* 31 (1975): 262–270.

Tesser, A., and Cowan, C. L. Some attitudinal and cognitive consequences of thought. *Journal of Research in Personality* 11 (1977): 216–226.

Tesser, A., and Danheiser, P. Anticipated relationship, salience of partner and attitude change. *Personality and Social Psychology Bulletin* 4 (1978): 35–38.

Tompkins, S. S. *Affect, Imagery and Consciousness*, vol. 2, *The Negative Affects*. New York: Springer Publishing, 1963.

Turner, R. G. Private self-consciousness as a moderator of length of self-description. Unpublished research, Pepperdine University, 1977.

Turner, R. G. Consistency, self-consciousness and the predictive validity of typical and maximal personality measures. *Journal of Research in Personality* 12 (1978): 117–132.

Turner, R. G., and Peterson, M. Public and private self-consciousness and emotional expressivity. *Journal of Consulting and Clinical Psychology* 45 (1977): 490–491.

Turner, R. G., Scheier, M. F., Carver, C. S., and Ickes, W. Correlates of self-consciousness. *Journal of Personality Assessment* 42 (1978): 285–289.

Turner, R. N. The real self: From institution to impulse. *American Journal of Sociology* 81 (1976): 989–1016.

Watson, D., and Friend, R. Measurement of social-evaluative anxiety. *Journal of Consulting and Clinical Psychology* 33 (1969): 448–451.

Webster's New International Dictionary. Unabridged. Springfield, Mass.: Merriam, 1960.

Weinberg, M. S. Embarrassment: Its variable and invariable aspects. *Social Forces* 46 (1968): 382–388.

Weiner, A. N. Machiavellianism as a predictor of group interaction and cohesion. Unpublished master's thesis, West Virginia University, 1973.

White, S. H. Evidence for a hierarchical arrangement of learning processes. In *Advances in Child Behavior and Development*, edited by L. P. Lipsitt and C. C. Spiker, vol. 2. New York: Academic Press, 1965.

Wicklund, R. A. Objective self-awareness. In *Advances in Experimental Social Psychology*, edited by L. Berkowitz, vol. 8. New York: Academic Press, 1975.

Wicklund, R. A. Group contact and self-focused attention. In *Psychology of Group Influence*, edited by P. B. Paulus. Hillsdale, N.J.: Erlbaum, 1979.

Wylie, R. *The Self-Concept.* rev. ed. Lincoln: University of Nebraska Press, 1974.

Zimbardo, P. G. *Shyness.* Reading, Mass.: Addison-Wesley, 1977.

APPENDIX

Items and factor loadings of the self-consciousness scale

	Private self-consciousness	Factors[a] Public self-consciousness	Social anxiety
Private self-consciousness			
I'm always trying to figure myself out. (1)	.65		
Generally, I'm not very aware of myself. (3)[b]	–.48		
I reflect about myself a lot. (5)	.73		
I'm often the subject of my own fantasies. (7)	.45		
I never scrutinize myself. (9)[b]	–.51		
I'm generally attentive to my inner feelings. (13)	.66		
I'm constantly examining my motives. (15)	.62		
I sometimes have the feeling that I'm off somewhere watching myself. (18)	.43		
I'm alert to changes in my mood. (20)	.55		
I'm aware of the way my mind works when I work through a problem. (22)	.46		

Public self-consciousness

Item	Public self-consciousness	Social anxiety
I'm concerned about my style of doing things. (2)	.47	
I'm concerned about the way I present myself. (6)	.65	
I'm self-conscious about the way I look. (11)	.61	
I usually worry about making a good impression. (14)	.72	
One of the last things I do before I leave my house is look in the mirror. (17)	.51	
I'm concerned about what other people think of me. (19)	.73	
I'm usually aware of my appearance. (21)	.60	

Social anxiety

Item	Public self-consciousness	Social anxiety
It takes me time to overcome my shyness in new situations. (4)		.76
I have trouble working when someone is watching me. (8)	.26	.45
I get embarrassed very easily. (10)		.70
I don't find it hard to talk to strangers. (12)[b]		−.66
I feel anxious when I speak in front of a group. (16)	.21	.46
Large groups make me nervous. (23)		.69

Note: The numbers in parentheses indicate the sequence of items on the scale.
[a] Only factor loadings greater than .20 are listed.
[b] Item was reversed for scoring.

INDEX